Social Democracy Inside Out

Social Democracy Inside Out

Partisanship and Labor Market Policy in Industrialized Democracies

David Rueda

OXFORD
UNIVERSITY PRESS

OXFORD
UNIVERSITY PRESS

Great Clarendon Street, Oxford OX2 6DP

Oxford University Press is a department of the University of Oxford.
It furthers the University's objective of excellence in research, scholarship,
and education by publishing worldwide in

Oxford New York

Auckland Cape Town Dar es Salaam Hong Kong Karachi
Kuala Lumpur Madrid Melbourne Mexico City Nairobi
New Delhi Shanghai Taipei Toronto

With offices in

Argentina Austria Brazil Chile Czech Republic France Greece
Guatemala Hungary Italy Japan Poland Portugal Singapore
South Korea Switzerland Thailand Turkey Ukraine Vietnam

Oxford is a registered trademark of Oxford University Press
in the UK and in certain other countries

Published in the United States
by Oxford University Press Inc., New York

British Library Cataloguing in Publication Data

Data available

Library of Congress Cataloging in Publication Data

Rueda, David.
  Social democracy inside out : partisanship and labor market policy in
industrialized democracies / David Rueda.
      p.   cm.
  Includes bibliographical references and index.
  ISBN–13: 978–0–19–923405–9 (alk. paper)
  ISBN–13: 978–0–19–921635–2 (alk.paper)
  1. Labor market.   2. Labor policy.   3. Economic policy—Political aspects.
  4. OECD countries—Economic policy.   5. Socialism.   I. Title.
  HD5713.R84 2007
  331.1—dc22   2007020336

Typeset by SPI Publisher Services, Pondicherry, India
Printed in Great Britain
on acid-free paper by
Biddles Ltd., King's Lynn, Norfolk

ISBN 978–0–19–921635–2
ISBN 978–0–19–923405–9 (Pbk.)

1 3 5 7 9 10 8 6 4 2

To Heidi

Contents

List of Figures

List of Tables

Abbreviations

ALMPs	Active Labor Market Policies
CCOO	*Comisiones Obreras*
CDA	*Christen Democratisch Appèl*
CEOE	*Confederación Española de Organizaciones Empresariales*
CNV	*Christian-National Union Confederation*
D66	*Democraten 66*
FNV	*Confederation of Dutch Trade Unions*
INEM	*Instituto Nacional de Empleo*
MSC	Manpower Services Commission
PLMPs	Passive Labor Market Policies
PP	*Partido Popular*
PSOE	*Partido Socialista Obrero Español*
PvdA	*Partij van de Arbeid*
TUC	Trade Union Congress
UCD	*Unión de Centro Democrático*
UGT	*Unión General de Trabajadores*
VVD	*Volkspartij voor Vrijheid en Democratie*

1

Introduction

Comparative political economists often assume that the preferences of parties are exogenous and stable and that they are mediated by institutional configurations that produce differentiated political and economic outcomes. Yet it would be difficult to argue that the challenges facing social democratic parties have not fundamentally changed in the last thirty years. As Moene and Wallerstein, among others, have noted the golden age of social democracy in Western Europe ended in the mid-1970s 'with the first serious slump of the post-war period' (1999: 231). Up to that point, a strategy based on reducing the inequality and insecurity of the most vulnerable sectors of the labor market while more generally promoting growth and employment had been very successful. As argued by Esping-Andersen, '(i)n the era of the "Keynesian consensus" there was no perceived trade-off between social security and economic growth, between equality and efficiency' (1996: 3).

The ideas in this book originally emerged as the response to two related questions. Why is it that, when looking at some policies, the Left has become so similar to the Right? And why do we observe since the 1970s so many successful social democratic governments that are unconcerned about high levels of unemployment? Regarding the first question, a number of observers have asserted that a progressive decline in the political distinctiveness of social democracy has occurred since the first oil shock (see e.g. Piven 1992; Kitschelt 1994; Pontusson 1995). Regarding the second, any cursory examination of the partisan nature of governments and unemployment rates since 1970 will reveal the lack of a strong relationship. In this book, I propose that the answer to these questions lies in the differences between insiders and outsiders in industrialized democracies.

1

1.1. The Argument

The traditional conception of social democratic policymaking rests on the assumption that labor is affected disproportionately by unemployment. But in the following pages I will argue that labor is divided into two segments: those with secure employment (insiders) and those without (outsiders). Since the early 1970s, insiders have become insulated from unemployment. Not only do they enjoy high levels of protection, they also benefit from the fact that outsiders act as a buffer bearing the brunt of fluctuations in the business cycle. In response to the increasingly significant differences between insiders and outsiders, social democratic governments have transformed their policy goals.

The starting point for my analysis is that the interests of insiders and outsiders are fundamentally different and, in some circumstances, contradictory. Insiders care about their own job security much more than about the unemployment of outsiders. Outsiders, on the other hand, care about unemployment and job precariousness much more than about the employment protection of insiders. While dividing labor into insiders and outsiders could be considered to have some precedents in both the economics and political science literatures, trying to integrate this division into a coherent conception of partisanship and exploring its possible effects on policy represents a new endeavor.

I contend that social democratic parties have strong incentives to consider insiders their core constituency. The book focuses on three policy areas: employment protection (representing the main concern of insiders), and active and passive labor market policies (the main concern of outsiders). I argue that insiders benefit from higher levels of employment protection legislation while, inasmuch as lower insider job protection facilitates hiring, outsiders are not. Higher levels of active and passive labor market policies, however, benefit outsiders but not insiders. Labor market policy does not benefit insiders whose vulnerability to unemployment is low; they mean higher taxes and promote low-wage competition. Therefore, the implication of my insider–outsider model is that social democratic government is associated with higher levels of employment protection legislation but not with labor market policy.

Two additional factors are relevant to my general argument: the level of unemployment vulnerability and the role of corporatism. It is clear that insider–outsider differences promote the consideration of particularistic goals (more specifically the goals of insiders regardless of the consequences for outsiders) by social democrats. However, there are factors that make the interests of insiders more similar to those of outsiders. These factors can reduce insider–outsider differences and weaken their influence on social democratic governments. I argue that increasing levels of unemployment vulnerability will have this effect. Regarding corporatism, my analysis will show that it can either mitigate or magnify the effects of insider–outsider differences on policymakers.

This book's arguments represent an attempt to address three issues central to social democracy. The first one has to do with the transformation in party strategies resulting from new voter demands in industrialized democracies. While the relevance of other factors (like lower economic growth, demographic, or production changes, the emergence of post-Fordism, increasing internationalization, or competition from industrializing countries) has been recognized for some time, my analysis will make clear the significance of insider–outsider preferences as a determinant of government policy. The second is related to the very nature of social democracy. Our assumptions about the strategies of leftist parties have not changed substantially since the golden age of social democracy (when equality, social protection, and economic growth were perceived as compatible). My analysis questions these assumptions and provides a fuller understanding of the limitations and opportunities faced by social democrats in the post-oil crises era. The final issue concerns what the goals of social democracy should be. This book will demonstrate that, in the presence of conflict between different groups within labor, social democratic governments often do not promote the interests of the weakest members of society. At a time when Left parties in most industrialized democracies struggle to maintain their electoral support in the face of significant challenges, the future of truly egalitarian social democracy depends on the sort of critical analysis presented in this book.

The evidence I present contests some of the most influential interpretations of the political economy of advanced democracies. In a fundamental way, it contradicts some of the general conclusions of the traditional partisanship arguments maintaining that social democratic governments will at all times promote the interests of labor—including the unemployed and precariously employed (Hibbs 1977; Alt 1985; Garrett and Lange 1991). By emphasizing the role of outsiders and their abandonment by social democracy, my arguments also introduce some reservations about the influential 'varieties of capitalism' approach and its emphasis on high skilled insiders in coordinated market economies (Hall and Soskice 2001; Thelen 2001). Focusing on the three policies emphasized in the book, the following chapters call into question the conventional wisdom, and much of the existing literature, regarding the influence of partisanship on active policies (Janoski 1990, 1994; Boix 1998a; Swank and Martin 2001). My insider–outsider partisanship model also represents a challenge to the 'political class struggle' or 'power resources' approach to the relationship between parties and social policy (Cameron 1978; Stephens 1979; Korpi 1983; Alvarez, Garrett, and Lange 1991; Huber and Stephens 2001).

1.2. Policy, Preferences, Social Democracy, and Corporatism

I explain in detail in the ensuing chapters the insider–outsider model and its implications to our understanding of social democracy. At this stage, however, I will mention some of the elements that distinguish this book's analysis from many others in the comparative political economy literature.

The first has to do with the goals of the analysis. This book aims to explain the wide diversity in labor market policy in industrialized democracies since the 1970s. It is common for comparative political economists to produce arguments about the relationship between governments and economic outcomes (whether it is unemployment, growth, inequality, etc.). Governments, however, cannot transform the economy directly. They must rely on the design and implementation of policy to accomplish any degree of change. If we are interested in an accurate assessment of the relationship between partisanship and economic outcomes, therefore, it is imperative that we emphasize the effects of partisanship on policy.

Second, a wide division exists between work on comparative political economy (which pays little attention to individual preferences and often focuses on institutional factors) and on comparative political behavior and public opinion (which often ignores macro level variables, focusing instead on individual interests). This book attempts to bridge these two literatures. Comparative political economy analyses focusing on policy outcomes often put individual preferences into the category of untested assumptions. This book's arguments are fundamentally concerned with the relationship between government partisanship and labor market policy but I will explore in some detail the accuracy of the model's individual assumptions.

Third, the politics of labor market policy are fundamentally influenced by questions about political agency and institutional constraints. A large and influential literature in comparative politics has emphasized partisan differences as a determinant of political and economic outcomes (Hibbs

1977, 1987; Alt 1985 are commonly cited examples). According to this framework, political agency is important—different parties can and do promote distinct economic outcomes (in terms of equality, unemployment, inflation, etc.). Other authors, however, have emphasized the role of institutions as a mediating force. Institutions, they argue, shape the ability of political actors to affect the economy (see e.g. Steinmo, Thelen, and Longstreth 1992). I will argue that the effects of government partisanship on policy are indeed contingent on institutions. I emphasize that partisan differences do affect the policies that governments are likely to promote (although in ways that are very different to those predicted by the traditional partisanship approach). But I argue that these partisan differences will be influential only when some institutions are in place.

I would like to clarify, finally, what I mean by social democracy. The comparative political economy literature is not unanimous in the way social democracy is defined. The literature is divided into two approaches. The first considers social democracy a political economy regime, inclusive not only of left-wing parties in office but also of highly coordinated and centralized labor market and wage setting institutions.[1] In this book I adopt a more restrictive view. In line with a number of previous contributions, I define social democracy exclusively in terms of government partisanship.[2] Social democracy is therefore equivalent to Left government throughout this book. Since I am interested in how the changing characteristics of corporatism constrain the actions of social democratic government (as emphasized in the previous paragraph), this is a necessary distinction.[3]

1.3. Evidence Used and Plan for the Book

The book is divided into two halves. In the first three chapters, I present the main model and some systematic quantitative evidence to support it. I first explore some survey data to address whether the model's assumptions about individuals are indeed accurate. I then provide a quantitative analysis of OECD-wide data aimed to test the connection between partisanship

[1] See e.g. Stephens (1979); Korpi (1983); Katzenstein (1985); Garrett (1998); Wilensky (2002).

[2] Corporatism is then defined exclusively in terms of the organization of economic institutions. See details in Chapter 2.

[3] Other authors who share this approach are, for example, Hibbs (1977), Alt (1985), Alvarez, Garrett, and Lange (1991), Hicks and Kenworthy (1998), Iversen (1998), and Rueda and Pontusson (2000).

and policy. The second half of the book engages in a more detailed study of the relationship between insider–outsider politics and policy with reference to three cases: Spain, the UK, and the Netherlands.

The analysis therefore combines quantitative and qualitative data as well as different kinds of evidence (macrodata; surveys; party, union, and employer documents; newspaper information; scholarly analyses; interviews; etc.). This design accomplishes two goals. First, by combining the two methods, I attempt to bring together the benefits (and avoid the pitfalls) of quantitative and qualitative methodologies (King, Keohane, and Verba 1994). The quantitative analyses of survey and OECD-wide data will provide the analysis with clear tests of the theoretical claims and contribute to the robustness of the derived empirical generalizations—the generally acknowledged benefits of large-N studies (Lijphart 1971; King, Keohane, and Verba 1994). Through the detailed country studies, the recognized advantages of case studies (high degree of causal complexity and theoretical sophistication, theory corroboration, depth of knowledge, and extensive dialogue between data and theory) will also be a feature of my analysis (see Eckstein 1975; Amenta 1991; Bradshaw and Wallace 1991). The second goal is the use of different methodologies and different kinds of evidence to achieve a degree of 'triangulation' (Jick 1979; Tarrow 1995). My use of different methodologies and data facilitates conclusions that the employment of one methodology (or one kind of evidence) could not achieve.

Why Spain, the Netherlands, and the UK? These three country cases were selected because they represent a great degree of variation in our explanatory variables. In other words, if there is something to the insider–outsider arguments proposed in this book, we would expect it to explain the high variation of policy observed in these three countries. I have emphasized three explanatory factors: the main effects of government partisanship, and the mediating effects of employment protection, and corporatism.

Although the quantitative analyses I present in Chapters 2 and 3 are powerful evidence supporting the insider–outsider partisanship model, the case studies help us trace processes and identify the reasons for particular event dynamics (Tarrow 1995). They clarify the influence of electoral considerations (affecting insiders, outsiders, and upscale groups) on the policy choices of social democratic and conservative parties in three detailed country cases. They allow us to examine political (as well as policy) developments as they evolved after 1970 and to trace the causal processes affecting the outcomes of interest.

   In terms of government partisanship, Spain is an ideal case to look into the appropriateness of the insider–outsider model to the understanding of social democratic government (fourteen years of continued PSOE rule), the Netherlands offers a great variation of governing coalitions, and the UK is an optimal example of what a conservative party can do if given a considerable amount of time in government (eighteen years). Regarding employment protection, the chapters below will show that in Spain and the Netherlands, levels have remained steadily high in the face of important challenges. In the UK, on the other hand, the protection enjoyed by insiders has been drastically reduced in the 1980s and 1990s. As for corporatism levels, the countries represent an intermediate case (Spain), a coordinated one (the Netherlands), and a low corporatism economy (the UK). While tripartite institutions are not that common (or influential) in Spain and the UK (during the period under study), the political economy of the Netherlands has been profoundly affected by an ideology of social partnership, the informal coordination of objectives, and the actions of centralized interest groups (see, among many others, Lehmbruch 1979; Hemerijck and Van Kersbergen 1997; Visser and Hemerijck 1997). In the Netherlands centralization and coordination of wage bargaining is high, union density is relatively high (compared to the other cases), and unions tend to cooperate with each other. Spain is characterized by low union density, an intermediately coordinated bargaining system and competing unions. And the UK represents a case of very low centralization and increasingly weak unions.

   Variation in other factors also makes these cases attractive. Because of its very high unemployment rate and an increasingly large precarious employment sector since 1980, Spain is a country where the existence as well as the effects of an insider–outsider conflict are most obvious. As in Spain, in the Netherlands flexibility in the labor market has taken the form of increasing numbers of nonstandard contracts (especially part-time) since the late 1970s. However, unlike Spanish rates (which proved to be very persistent), Dutch unemployment has successfully declined since the 1980s (adding to the variation and complexity of the cases). In the UK, on the other hand, the high unemployment levels of the 1980s were met with a decrease in insider protection.

   The plan for the book is as follows. Chapter 2 ('Governments and Policy: The Insider–Outsider Partisanship Model') will present the main model regarding the effects of insider–outsider differences on policy and introduce the factors mitigating or magnifying these effects. Chapter 3 ('The Preferences of Insiders and Outsiders: Testing the Model's Assumptions about Individual Interests') introduces some survey data and tests assumptions about individual preferences using a number of logit random intercept multilevel maximum likelihood models. Chapter 4 ('The Relationship Between Partisan Government and Policy: An Analysis of OECD Data') explores the theorized relationship between government partisanship and policy outcomes (mediated by unemployment vulnerability and corporatism) by estimating error correction models using OECD-wide macrodata. Chapter 5 ('Partisan Government and Employment Protection') explores the relationship between government partisanship and employment protection in Spain, the Netherlands, and the UK since 1970. Chapter 6 ('Unemployment Vulnerability and Active Labor Market Policies') analyzes how the interaction between government partisanship and unemployment vulnerability affect the politics of active labor market policies (ALMPs) in the three country cases. Similarly, Chapter 7 ('Partisanship, Institutions and Social Policy') studies how the interaction between government partisanship and corporatism affects social policy in Spain, the Netherlands, and the UK. Chapter 8 ('Insiders, Outsiders, Partisanship and Policy: Concluding Remarks'), finally, brings the themes in the book together and provides some final thoughts.

1.4. Acknowledgements

This book has been a long time in the making and I have accumulated quite a few intellectual debts on the way. In its initial life as a Ph.D. dissertation, the main arguments in this book were greatly influenced by the members of my committee. Jonas Pontusson, Peter Katzenstein, Sidney Tarrow, and Walter Mebane provided me with innumerable valuable comments and more help than I had a right to expect. I also thank the many people who helped me during my field research at the Juan March Institute in Madrid, the Amsterdam School for Social Research (University of Amsterdam), and the London School of Economics. I especially want to thank José María Maravall, Andrew Richards, and Martha Peach at the Juan March Institute, Jelle Visser at the Amsterdam School for Social Research, and William Wallace at the LSE. Generous financial support for my research at that time was provided by the Social Science Research Council and the American Council of Learned Societies, the Fondazione Luigi Einaudi, and the Andrew W. Mellon Foundation.

I worked on different versions of this manuscript while at the Political Science Department at Binghamton University (SUNY) and the

Department of Politics and International Relations at Oxford University. My colleagues in these two places were extremely generous with advice, criticism, and encouragement. I want to thank, in particular, Chris Anderson, Tom Brunell, Dave Clark, Will Heller, Michael McDonald, and Katri Sieberg (at Binghamton) and Nigel Bowles, Giovanni Capoccia, Dan Kelemen, Des King, and Johannes Lindvall (at Oxford).

Different parts of this book were presented at the 2003 Annual Meeting of the Midwest Political Science Association, the 2002 Annual Meeting of the American Political Science Association, the 2002 Annual Meeting of the MPSA, and the 2000 International Conference of Europeanists. I have also presented portions of my research at the *Challenges to the Welfare State Conference* (Minda de Gunzburg Center for European Studies at Harvard University, 2006), the *Comparative Political Economy Workshop* (Cornell University, 2002), the *Workshop on the Comparative Political Economy of Inequality in OECD Countries* (Cornell University, 2002), the *Conference on the Political Economy of Developed and Less Developed Countries* (Yale University, 2001), and at talks at the University of Rochester, Binghamton University-SUNY, the Institute for European Studies at Cornell University, Washington University in Saint Louis, and Oxford University. I thank the participants in these presentations (too many to name) who provided me with helpful feedback.

The arguments in this book have been greatly influences by other people's responses (and my rethinking of many of the issues they brought up) to a number of articles I have published. This is particularly true in the case of two articles related to my insider–outsider model ('Insider–Outsider Politics in Industrialized Democracies: The Challenge to Social Democratic Parties' published in the *American Political Science Review* in 2005, and 'Social Democracy and Active Labor Market Policies: Insiders, Outsiders, and the Politics of Employment Promotion' published in the *British Journal of Political Science* in 2006).

For very beneficial comments and suggestions, I thank (in addition to those above) Roger Barker, Pablo Beramendi, Nancy Bermeo, Valerie Bunce, Raj Chari, Rachel Cremona, Thomas R. Cusack, Joseph Foudy, Geoffrey Garrett, Peter Hall, Kerstin Hamann, Anton Hemerijck, Torben Iversen, Lane Kenworthy, Herbert Kitschelt, Anirudh Krishna, Hyeok Yong Kwon, Andrew Martin, Cathie Jo Martin, Rafael Morillas, Peter Lange, Luis Ortiz, Bo Rothstein, Ronald Rogowski, Sebastián Royo, Wiemer Salverda, Herman Schwartz, Martin Seeleib-Kaiser, Lee Sigelman, David Soskice, John Stephens, Duane Swank, Yulia Tverdova, Marc Van der Meer, Jelle Visser, Christopher Way, Michael Wallerstein, Albert Weale,

Bruce Western, and Mark Wickham-Jones. At Oxford University Press, I am especially indebted to Dominic Byatt for helping me improve this manuscript.

I owe my greatest debt to three colleagues linked to the three institutions where I have developed as a scholar. First, I am especially grateful to Jonas Pontusson (chair of my dissertation committee at Cornell, mentor, coauthor, and friend) whose generosity and guidance were crucial at every stage of this project. I am also deeply indebted to Chris Anderson (a colleague while I was at Binghamton, now at Cornell) whose friendship and advice have supported me at every critical juncture. Last, but not least, I am profoundly grateful to my friend and colleague at Oxford, Des King, for reading the whole manuscript and helping me in countless ways with the book and with life.

I would have never entered the academic world without the encouragement of my family. My parents, Paco and Elena, infused me with their passion for all things political. My academic interests have been influenced by innumerable animated conversations around the table with them and my brother, Jesus. I look forward to many more. Finally, this book would have not been possible without the love and support of my wife (and editor *extraordinaire*), Heidi. Her help, sense of humor, advice, and intellectual inspiration make it all worthwhile. This book is dedicated to her.

2

Governments and Policy: The Insider–Outsider Partisanship Model

In the literature on the comparative political economy of advanced democracies, there has been a widespread theoretical consensus about the goals different political parties pursue when in power. In principle, social democratic governments are assumed to defend the interests of labor and conservative ones those of what some authors[1] have defined as the 'upscale groups'. Yet, since the early 1970s, many analysts have observed the coexistence of high levels of unemployment and social democratic government as well as a decrease in the distinctiveness of some of the policies traditionally associated with different political parties.

The analysis in this chapter focuses on the transformations in party strategies that result from new voter demands and political–economic conditions. It attempts to put together two important but often unrelated literatures: one focusing on electoral competition and the other on comparative political economy institutions. Herbert Kitschelt has accurately pointed out that the study of social democratic party strategies requires a 'bridge across the familiar divide between students of comparative political economy and parties and elections' (1999: 318). The model I present in the following pages attempts to do exactly that.

I argue that identifying social democratic governments with low unemployment and conservative ones with low inflation is not productive. This identification is based on the assumption that labor is disproportionately affected by unemployment. For reasons that will become clear in the following pages, I maintain that this assumption is inaccurate. The main thrust of this chapter's analysis is that labor is divided into those with secure employment (insiders) and those without (outsiders) and that the

---

[1] See e.g. Keech (1995: 70).

electoral goals of social democratic parties are sometimes best served by pursuing policies that benefit insiders while ignoring the interests of outsiders. |

Are there circumstances that make it easier for governments to promote policies that benefit outsiders? It is clear that insider–outsider differences promote the consideration of particularistic goals (more specifically the goals of insiders regardless of the consequences for outsiders) by social democrats. In the presence of insider–outsider conflict, social democratic governments will promote insider policies regardless of the consequences for outsiders. There are, however, some factors that can make the interests of insiders more similar to those of outsiders. These factors can reduce insider–outsider differences and weaken their influence on social democratic governments. Below, I will focus on the effects of two factors: employment protection and corporatism. I will show that integrating employment protection into the insider–outsider model means recognizing that insiders can become more like outsiders. In the initial model presented in this chapter, employment protection is identified as the characteristic distinguishing insiders from outsiders. It is because insiders are not as vulnerable to unemployment as outsiders that their policy objectives differ. As employment protection decreases, the distinction between insiders and outsiders weakens and so does its influence on social democracy. I will also show that corporatism has more ambiguous effects. On the one hand, corporatist arrangements represent protection and privilege for insiders. On the other, they prevent free riding and particularistic interests. After presenting the main model, its justification and implications, the rest of this chapter will analyze in more detail the effects of these two institutional factors.

2.1. The Insider–Outsider Partisanship Model

Like much of the literature that explores the relationship between partisan government and policy, I understand political parties to have electoral objectives as well as commitments to ideology and historically meaningful groups of voters. The existence of stable ideological and historical connections between parties and some social groups 'not only creates easily identifiable choices for citizens, it also makes it easier for parties to seek out their probable supporters and mobilize them at election time' (Powell 1982: 116). Ideology and history, however, are not enough. Elections need to be won and they inevitably revolve around issues, like employment protection or labor market policy, that give political meaning to partisan attachments and social divisions (Dalton 2002: 195). With Garrett and Lange/ I assume that 'while all governments would prefer, ceteris paribus, to pursue their partisan preferences, they will only do so if this does not prejudice their prospects for reelection' (1991: 543)./

The model presented in this chapter implies that party behavior is influenced by both vote-seeking and policy-seeking motivations. These two goals are not necessarily contradictory (see, e.g. Luebbert 1986) and, often, they are complementary. As Strom has pointed out, arguments in favor of the policy orientation of parties typically assume 'that parties also pursue office at least instrumentally, as elective office is taken to be a precondition for policy influence' (1990: 567).[2] Policy is then considered an instrument that molds public support and helps construct the electoral coalitions on which political parties depend (Przeworski and Sprague 1986: 125–6). Policy proposals 'impose costs on politicians, in the form of either bargaining costs to create a supporting coalition or the opportunity cost of foregoing alternative policies' (Alt 1985: 1,020)./

Unlike most of the comparative political economy literature, however, I do not conceptualize labor as a homogeneous political actor. I share an interest in disaggregating labor with some recent works on the determinants of party strategies and individual policy preferences.[3] My analysis is based on two propositions: first, that labor is divided into insiders and outsiders; and second, that the interests of insiders and outsiders are fundamentally different. I concur with the traditional partisanship approach in recognizing that parties tend to care about stable core constituencies and partisan preferences but I consider insiders (not labor as a whole) to be the core constituency of social democracy.

Two analytical frameworks directly influence the model that I propose. There is first the work of authors such as Piore (1969), Doeringer and Piore (1971), and Gordon (1972) on dual labor markets. Paying a great deal of attention to workers' attitudes and motivations (as well as their conceptualization of work), the dual labor market literature emphasized the differences between a primary labor market composed of better and more stable jobs and a secondary one characterized by precarious employment. Some of this literature's insights, in particular Berger and Piore's understanding (1980) of the emergence of the secondary sector as the

---

[2] For a unifying argument specifying the conditions under which different models of party behavior apply, see Strom (1990).

[3] See e.g. Kitschelt (1994), Iversen and Soskice (2001), and Estevez-Abe, Iversen, and Soskice (2001).

result of an upsurge in labor militancy, are very valuable. But the most important concepts in the approach became vague and confusing and, by the late 1970s, Piore acknowledged that market dualism had lost most of its analytical power (Berger and Piore 1980: 15).

Then there is an economic insider–outsider approach that emerged as a response to the difficulties encountered by the natural rate framework to satisfactorily explain the high European unemployment levels of the 1980s. A neoclassical interpretation of unemployment is characterized by an emphasis on the difference between the supply and the demand for labor. When the supply of labor exceeds its demand, unemployment results. In a Keynesian understanding, real factors determine a long-run equilibrium level of output and employment but wages and prices are considered to be sticky and outcomes diverge from their equilibrium values. As a consequence of price stickiness, changes in aggregate demand are considered to substantially affect the short-run level of employment (Summers 1988). Authors like Blanchard and Summers (1986), Lindbeck and Snower (1988, 1990), Lindbeck (1993), and Saint-Paul (1997, 2000) abandoned the natural rate of unemployment assumptions and developed a framework based on the differences between the employed and the unemployed. Their insider–outsider model rests on the assumption that unions primarily act in the interest of a group of insiders who are protected by labor turnover costs and more likely to secure wage gains for themselves than allow employment increases for the unemployed outsiders (Holmlund 1991: 10–11). These authors argued, therefore, that unemployment would not have a tendency to return to a natural level (an equilibrium rate defined in terms of supply-side variables) and that unemployment rates would reflect a high degree of hysteresis (see e.g. Nickell and Wadhwani 1990). Empirical analyses testing some of the theoretical claims of the model, however, have not provided unambiguous support (see Holmlund 1991 for a review).

The model that I propose takes these approaches as inspiration but significantly transforms some of their insights.[4] As mentioned above, I divide labor into insiders and outsiders. Insiders are defined as those workers with highly protected jobs. Factors like the nature of employment protection legislation, a company's firing and job search costs, insiders' production process skills and attained levels of company investment,

---

[4] In addition to the dual labor market and the economic insider–outsider literature, the arguments in this book have also been influenced by a number of other works. My analysis of the relationship between labor and social democracy is related to points made by Swenson (1989), Pontusson (1992), King (1995), and Western (1997), among others.

and the behavior of unions contribute to the level of protection that characterizes 'insiderness'. Insiders are sufficiently protected by the level of security in their jobs not to feel significantly threatened by increases in unemployment. Outsiders, on the other hand, are either unemployed or hold jobs characterized by low levels of protection and employment rights, lower salaries, and precarious levels of benefits and social security regulations. I consider the unemployed, the involuntary fixed-term employed and the involuntary part-time employed to be outsiders.

Given the importance of secure employment to the definition of insiders, including the unemployed within the category of outsiders is not controversial. The classification of fixed-term and part-time employment is perhaps not as straightforward. There are two aspects to employed 'outsiderness'. The first has to do with the precarious nature of employment. Fixed-term and part-time jobs are not simply insider contracts with flexibility added. They are in fact characterized by low wages, protection, and rights (see e.g. OECD 1998). The second has to do with the involuntary nature of outsider employment. Most outsiders would like to have access to insider jobs. This is particularly the case when looking at fixed-term employment (many workers holding fixed-term contracts in the OECD do so involuntarily). But it is also a defining factor of part-time employment. A large proportion of part-time outsiders would prefer to work full time (this is particularly the case with male outsiders, see OECD 1999).[5]

The interests of these two groups are fundamentally different and, in some circumstances, contradictory. Insiders care about their own job security much more than about the unemployment of outsiders. Outsiders, on the other hand, care about their unemployment and job precariousness much more than about the employment protection of insiders. These differences in the interests of insiders and outsiders will have dramatic consequences for the strategies of parties and the policies they are likely to pursue. The goals of both groups can be represented as two policy dimensions: employment protection and labor market policy. The first dimension captures pro-insider policy. As such, insiders strongly favor it (employment protection insulates insiders from unemployment) while outsiders do not (lowering the levels of employment protection will facilitate their exit from unemployment and precarious employment).

---

[5] It is often argued that some part-time workers, in particular women, do so voluntarily but, as Maier points out, the fact that many working women do not want to work full time does not imply that they prefer part-time jobs with precarious levels of protection and benefits (1994: 180). See also Asplund and Persson (2000) for an analysis of the over-representation of women in low-pay employment.

The second dimension captures pro-outsider policy. Outsiders are most vulnerable to unemployment and therefore most supportive of labor market policies directed to promote employment (or to compensate for joblessness). Insiders enjoy a high degree of job protection and are less vulnerable to unemployment. They would therefore be less likely to support labor market policy (since they are financed by taxes paid for by insiders[6] and can promote low-wage competition by outsiders successfully entering the market).[7]

While dividing labor into insiders and outsiders has some precedents in both the economics and political science literature, trying to integrate this division into a coherent conception of partisanship and exploring its effects on policy represents a new endeavor. Other factors have received a remarkable amount of attention in the explanations of the political and economic changes experienced in the industrialized democracies since the 1970s (lower economic growth, demographic or production changes, the emergence of post-Fordism, increasing internationalization, and competition from industrializing countries are but a few). My contribution to the comparative political economy literature is to emphasize the significance of insider–outsider politics as a determinant of social democratic policy.

In this book's stylized framework, political parties are considered to have a core constituency and a more general target they wish to attract to obtain a winning and stable electoral coalition. Because of the division of labor into insiders and outsiders, social democratic governments face an important choice. In the words of Esping-Andersen, they

are caught in a severe tension between preserving loyalty to traditional working-class causes and defending the position of the new strata of social losers. Such tensions are only aggravated by the fact that the conventional worker enjoys a menu of privileges and securities that, on one hand, are erstwhile labor movement achievements and, on the other hand, are obstacles to the social integration of the new 'outsiders'.   (Esping-Andersen 1999: 310)

It is my contention that (because, among other things, outsiders tend to be less politically active and electorally relevant as well as economically dependent on insiders)[8] social democratic parties will generally have

---

[6] On this point, Lindert (2004) and Cusack and Beramendi (2006) have shown that taxes to support the welfare state are paid disproportionally by one class (labor).

[7] See Saint Paul (1998) and Calmfors (1994). I provide a more extensive explanation of the preferences implied in my insider–outsider model, as well as a set of empirical tests, in Chapter 3.

[8] As argued by Esping-Andersen, the crystallization of outsiders into a coherent and influential electoral constituency is complicated. 'It is difficult to imagine', he observes, 'an

strong incentives to consider insiders their core constituency. In this model, therefore, the main policy objective of social democracy will be the continuation or increase of insider job security. The second implication of my insider–outsider argument, moreover, is that social democratic governments will not have an incentive to promote labor market policy (although it benefits outsiders, it is not favored by insiders).

Dividing labor into insiders and outsiders also has implications for the strategies of conservative governments. Like many other authors, I consider conservative parties to depend on a core constituency that consists of upscale groups (employers, the upper middle class, and the business and financial community). Paradoxically, the insider–outsider model implies that, in some cases, conservative governments may be able to pursue policies that are more attractive to outsiders than those promoted by social democrats. Having the upscale groups as their core constituency makes it difficult for conservative parties to promote the interests of insiders. But ignoring insiders allows conservatives to engage in some policies unavailable to social democrats. As mentioned above, outsiders favor lower levels of insider job protection legislation. By reducing insider job protection, conservative parties may attract some outsiders while reinforcing the support of their core constituency (upscale groups advantaged by flexible hiring and firing practices). While lower employment protection is favored by both outsiders and members of the upscale groups, this is not the case for labor market policies. Higher levels of labor market policies represent higher taxes and an intrusive role for government in the economy. Because of this, upscale groups (and therefore conservative governments) are not interested in the promotion of labor market policies.

2.2. Why Does the Traditional Approach to Partisanship Need to Be Changed? The Emergence of Insiders and Outsiders

There are two traditional theoretical approaches to the analysis of partisan effects on policy. The first can be categorized as the party differences school. Its authors—Hibbs (1977, 1987) and Alt (1985) being the most cited examples—believe that social democratic parties will tend to promote the interests of labor while conservative parties will attempt to satisfy the demands of upscale groups. The best way to explain the assumptions that have directed much of the research of the party

alliance of housewives, early retirees, excluded youth, and a variety of groups with a more or less irregular connection to the labor market' (1999: 304–5).

differences school is to summarize Hibbs's initial argument. Alt provides a brief statement that is worth quoting:

Hibbs (1977) argues that the impact of unemployment varies across social classes (...). Blue-collar workers are more likely to become unemployed when unemployment rises and thus *ceteris paribus* more likely to favor government intervention to reduce unemployment and to support parties that promise to do so. Left-wing parties (...) organize platforms to elicit this class-based support and reward their supporters by reducing unemployment while in office. (Alt 1985: 1,017)

The right-wing constituency is then assumed to be most affected by inflation. Conservative governments, therefore, are expected to elicit the support of these groups and to reward them by reducing inflation.

I would argue that this argument lies at the heart of most comparative political economy analyses exploring the effects of partisan government on policy. The examples are legion but I will just mention that these initial partisan assumptions have been taken as the starting point of an influential literature on the welfare state (see e.g. Korpi 1978; Stephens 1979; Korpi 1983; Esping-Andersen 1985, 1990; Pierson 1994; Huber and Stephens 2001) and on the effects of social democracy (Alvarez, Garrett, and Lange 1991; Boix 1998*a*; Garrett 1998; Hall and Franzese 1998; Swank 2002, among others).

The second approach to the partisan determinants of policy can be categorized as the electoral cycle school. Its authors argue that there is a relationship between macroeconomic policymaking and electoral cycles. The idea that incumbents have an interest in stimulating the economy right before elections regardless of the long-term economic consequences of such economic policy maneuvering has been put forward by Nordhaus (1975) and Tufte (1978), among others. Williams summarizes the starting point of this school as follows:

the 'political business cycle proposes that politicians find their self-interest best served by manipulating the economy in a way that maximizes votes. Longer-term policy concerns, such as price stability, are mortgaged in order to ensure that the public is satisfied with short-term macroeconomic performance when an election occurs'. (Williams 1990: 767)

These two alternative approaches to the influence of politics on policy need not be contradictory. As Williams has argued, there is not an inescapable discrepancy between a partisan model of policy and an electoral one (1990: 768). In fact, they can be complementary. It is not unreasonable to accept that different parties have distinct macroeconomic

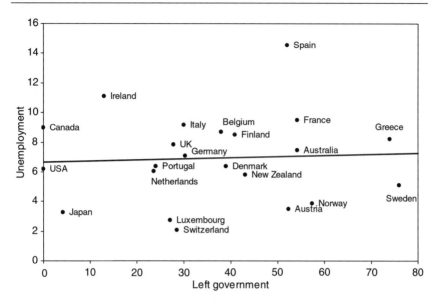

Figure 2.1. Left government and unemployment, 1980–2003

strategies designed to attract different electoral groups and that, at the same time, there may be electoral temptations to develop short-term policies that please a chosen electoral core.[9] This discussion is relevant to this chapter's discussion because my model is essentially a transformation of the partisan differences approach. Like the authors mentioned above, I consider parties to have distinct interests as well as policy goals fundamentally related to those of their core constituencies. My insider–outsider analysis departs from this framework in its consideration of the core constituencies social democratic parties aim to attract.

Why is it necessary then to transform the initial assumptions of the traditional partisanship approach? The original impetus for the arguments developed in this book emerged as a consequence of an empirical puzzle. The traditional view of partisan differences rests on the assumption that labor is disproportionally affected by unemployment and that social democratic governments will therefore promote policies that promote higher employment. There is, however, very little evidence to indicate that this is the case.

Figure 2.1 presents the relationship between social democracy and unemployment. The figure plots social democracy (measured here as the

---

[9] Alesina, Roubini, and Cohen (1997) is a good example of this approach.

percentage of cabinet seats held by Left parties)[10] against unemployment rates.[11] The figures represent averages for the 1980–2003 period. The almost completely flat trendline makes clear that the influence of government partisanship on unemployment has been terribly weak over this period. There is no clear pattern: countries with widely divergent partisanship averages (like Canada, Italy, Belgium, France, and Greece) exhibit similar unemployment rates while countries with very similar partisanship averages (like Spain, France, Australia, and Norway) have widely divergent unemployment rates. The association between social democracy and low unemployment proposed by the traditional partisanship approach does not seem to hold.

Why is this the case? The insider–outsider partisanship model explained above is an important part of the answer to this question. According to the traditional partisanship approach, workers feel threatened by unemployment. They vote for social democratic parties because they believe these parties will promote policies that decrease unemployment when they are in power. Disaggregating labor into insiders and outsiders corrects a critical weakness in this approach. It is misleading to categorize all labor as vulnerable to unemployment. High levels of employment protection effectively guard a group within labor (the insiders) against unemployment. Social democratic governments become more tolerant to unemployment in a way that is directly related to the emergence of 'insiderness'. In the insider–outsider model, the acceptance of higher levels of unemployment by social democracy in Figure 2.1 results from the decreasing vulnerability of insiders.

Two parallel historical processes can be identified as significant in the emergence of insiders and outsiders. First, starting in the late 1960s, firms accepted highly restrictive tenure and severance pay arrangements—see Blanchard et al. (1986) and Bentolila and Bertola (1990). It could be argued that, in many respects, the creation of a significant degree of 'insiderness' starts at this point in most OECD countries. Most employment protection legislation was enacted during the late 1960s and in many cases it was strengthened during the early 1970s. Commenting on the initial wave of legislation in the late 1960s, Blanchard et al. (1986) argue that this process was influenced by a pattern of stability and growth which allowed firms to consider employment protection as relatively costless. Excessive hiring was judged an error that could be easily corrected in,

[10] See Armingeon et al. (2005).
[11] The unemployment rate is measured according to the Eurostat definition. See European Commission (2006).

at most, a few months. Bentolila and Bertola point out that the post-Oil Shock crises contributed to a further reinforcement of legislation in France and the UK, among other countries, around 1975 (1990: 394). Most analysts also agree that these later developments were influenced, to a considerable degree, by social unrest and the actions of unions. It is in any case clear that during the period of interest to this book's analysis, a considerable proportion of labor became significantly insulated from unemployment by restrictive legislation that did not exist before.

The second factor affecting the vulnerability of some members of labor to unemployment was that, as 'insiderness' increased, so did 'outsiderness'. The emergence of outsiders as a significant segment of the labor market was a complex process with several causes. The increase in unemployment experienced by many OECD countries during the post-Oil Shock crises is very significant. But, simultaneously, in a number of countries labor supply shocks caused by larger numbers of women entering the labor force applied further pressure on the labor market. A number of authors have argued that since the mid-1970s there has also been a production change in certain sectors of the economy caused by 'firms using "working time" variations as an instrument of gaining flexibility and higher productivity' (Maier 1994: 151). As Dore explains, until the 1970s, 'growing oligopoly' had 'made it possible for more and more managers to "afford the luxury of a contented and loyal workforce"' but the 'intensification of international competition' and the 'change in the nature of work' altered this (1994: 21–2). The need for flexibility to achieve international competitiveness, however, did not result in the lowering of employment protection in most OECD countries. Rather, the flexibilization of labor market legislation that took place in the 1980s affected in most cases entry into (not exit from) the labor market (see e.g. Bentolila and Bertola 1990). One of the consequences of this process was a dramatic increase in part-time work and temporary contracts to the point that, Maier argues, 'whole sectors of national economies have reorganized their employment/working-time patterns around various forms of part-time work' (1994: 152). As mentioned above, however, the great majority of part-time work and temporary contracts pay poorly, are concentrated in low-skilled activities, and offer a precarious level of benefits, social security regulations, and employment rights.[12] Moreover, the precariously employed and the unemployed are the main, if not only, group to suffer

---

[12] See e.g. Maier (1994) for an analysis of part-time legislation and Mosley (1994) for a description of temporary employment in Europe. See also the contributions in Gregory, Salverda, and Bazen (2000).

the consequences of economic fluctuations (being hired in good times and fired in downturns).[13]

To assume that unemployment disproportionately harms labor as a whole is, therefore, clearly misleading when analyzing OECD countries from the early 1970s. When we divide labor into insiders and outsiders, it is reasonable to assume instead that insiders do not feel particularly concerned about unemployment. Outsiders are the main victims of increasing levels of unemployment and precarious employment. Since insiders do not feel threatened by unemployment to the same degree that they did in the pre-1970s period, social democratic parties do not need to organize political platforms that focus on the problem of unemployment and they do not have to reward their insider supporters with policies designed to reduce unemployment. Unless social democratic parties make outsiders, in addition to insiders, their core constituency, the traditional partisan framework is of very limited use.

2.3. Partisanship and Policy

While the previous sections have been pretty explicit about the preferences of insiders, outsiders, and upscale groups, it is important to turn to the theoretical justification for the connection between parties and policies in a little more detail.

2.3.1. *Employment Protection*

Within the context of this book's partisanship model, it is clear that lowering employment protection directly attacks the interests of insiders. Because the immediate result of decreasing protection legislation is that firing insiders becomes easier, and since insiders care about their employment stability most of all, it is reasonable to assume that any proposal for such change would produce the strongest insider opposition.[14] For

[13] Immigration also plays an important role in buffering insiders. In fact, it could easily be argued that immigrants are the ultimate outsiders. Immigrant labor is not emphasized in this book, but see King and Rueda (2006) for a more detailed analysis of this issue taking the insider–outsider model as its starting point.

[14] In this section I concentrate my analysis on what we could call labor market exit flexibility. Increasing labor market entry flexibility (particularly if high labor market exit costs remain untouched) may be beneficial to insiders. This may have been the case in some European countries (like Spain, Italy, Portugal, France, Germany, and the Netherlands) where fixed-term contracts and temporary work (overwhelmingly directed to women and young people) have been increasingly common since the early 1980s (see Maier 1994; Mosley 1994).

outsiders, on the other hand, it is easy to believe that high levels of insider protection impede employment growth. The reasons why employment protection may negatively affect employment can be summarized briefly. Employment protection, it is feared, limits 'the flexibility required for firms and national economies to prosper' (OECD 1999: 49). This limitation mainly results from the increase in labor costs that employment protection implies. In the words of the OECD, employment protection 'is, in effect, a tax on work-force adjustments' (1999: 68). As such it may inhibit firms from shedding labor in economic downturns but also from hiring in periods characterized by good performance.[15]

My partisanship hypotheses derive directly from this analysis. Social democratic governments that give preference to the interests of insiders over those of outsiders will clearly support greater levels of employment protection. Conservative parties, on the other hand, have important reasons to promote lower levels of employment protection. First, inasmuch as employers and managers are a very influential portion of the upscale groups, the lowering of employment protection will be positively received by the conservative party's core constituency. But a lowering of employment protection will also be perceived by some outsiders as helping their chances for employment and will therefore represent a widening of the conservative electoral appeal. The insider–outsider model consequently implies the existence of marked partisan differences regarding employment protection.

2.3.2. Labor Market Policy

There are two kinds of labor market policies that are relevant to the insider–outsider partisanship model: passive labor market policies (PLMPs) provide unemployment compensation whereas active labor market policies (ALMPs) are aimed at reducing unemployment by shaping the supply, demand, and mobility of labor.

---

[15] Although a relative consensus exists regarding the theorized effects of employment protection, the empirical evidence has not been conclusive. Most authors attempting to assess these effects have concluded that employment protection influences employment dynamics more significantly than the average level of employment (see Bentolila and Bertola 1990; Bertola 1990, 1992; Booth 1997). Lazear (1990), however, finds support for the argument linking severance pay and unemployment (Lazear's findings have been questioned by Addison and Grosso (1998) and Addison and Teixeira (1999)). More recently, Risager and Sørensen (1999) have shown that in an open economy, where unions do not reduce their wage demands and the domestic industry bears the cost of employment legislation, firing costs may result in higher long-term unemployment.

As an important element of the welfare state, PLMPs have received quite a lot of attention in the comparative political economy literature. Regarding these policies, my insider–outsider partisanship model represents a challenge to the 'political class struggle' or 'power resources' approach to the relationship between parties and policy. This framework emphasizes the role played by two main actors: the working-class and socialist parties (especially when in power). The strength of social democratic parties and the power of working-class mobilization are understood to be the main influences affecting the evolution of the welfare state. Several authors can be identified as strong proponents of this approach[16] but perhaps the clearest description of the core of this argument is provided by Shalev. He notes,

> The essential argument of this perspective on the welfare state, is that the growth of reformist labor unions and parties which reflect the class divisions of capitalist society, and in particular the ascension of labor parties to executive power, have been the preeminent forces in the initiation and development of public policies for furthering justice and equality between the classes.

> (Shalev 1983: 317)

More recently, the influence of international forces has been integrated into these analyses. The conventional wisdom about this topic has been that increasing international openness results in a blurring of partisan differences caused by the inability of social democratic parties to produce policies that do not conform to market forces (see e.g. Scharpf 1991; Scharpf and Schmidt 2000). Some authors have argued, however, that international forces do not affect some partisan differences (like Boix 1998a; Garrett and Lange 1991) or that they actually have strengthened the influence of partisanship on policy because of some groups' need for compensation (Garrett 1998).

It is clear that my insider–outsider partisanship model does not share the optimism of the power resources approach regarding the interests of labor. Like Esping-Andersen (1990), I believe it is problematic to assume that there is a linear relationship between social democracy and the development of welfare policies. The solution for Esping-Andersen is to integrate a class-coalition logic into the theory of welfare development.[17]

---

[16] For example, Cameron (1978), Stephens (1979), Korpi (1983), and Alvarez, Garrett, and Lange (1991). More recently, Huber and Stephens (2001) support, but also amend, this power resource approach to the welfare state.

[17] For Esping-Andersen, the existence of alliances with farmers and white-collar workers is a very significant factor in determining welfare policy.

In my model, it is the insider–outsider distinction which helps us understand the policy effects of partisan differences. I argue that, to the degree
that they are protected from unemployment, insiders have little incentive to support PLMPs. The insider–outsider model therefore challenges
the power resources framework by exploring the possibility that social
democrats will be less interested in PLMPs than we have traditionally
expected.

The traditional partisanship literature has paid much less attention to
ALMPs. In many respects, however, ALMP levels are an optimal measure
for testing the accuracy of the insider–outsider model. First, they are, in
Janoski's words, 'preponderantly discretionary' and can 'be either a major
recipient of fiscal resources (. . .) or relatively ignored by politicians and
budget makers' (1994: 54). Second, the unambiguous objective of ALMPs
is to benefit outsiders. Unlike other policies whose goals may be difficult
to distinguish in insider–outsider terms, ALMPs are designed to produce
stable employment for those who do not possess it. Finally, the economics
literature provides some evidence that higher levels of ALMP do promote
lower levels of unemployment indeed.[18] But the existence of scholarly
analyses demonstrating the beneficial effects of ALMPs is not as relevant
as the general acceptance of ALMP as a tool against unemployment by
policymakers. And this acceptance has been quite general. Transferring
public resources into ALMPs has been an objective repeatedly endorsed
by OECD Labor Ministers in recent years. As Martin points out, it has also
become part of the EU's official strategy to decrease unemployment since
the Essen Summit in December 1994 (1998: 12).

The growing interest in ALMPs as a way to combat increasing levels
of unemployment and precarious employment is understandable. Calmfors (1994) relates it both to the disillusionment produced by demand
management policies which are now perceived as measures that can
increase inflation while not affecting unemployment and to the belief
that other supply-side structural reforms may work too slowly or be too
difficult to implement. In spite of both the recent popularity and the
perceived importance of ALMPs, however, the relationship between these
policies and government partisanship has not received enough attention
in political science. The economics literature has been largely concerned
about the economic effects of ALMPs and has generally ignored the role of
government partisanship. We know comparatively little about the politics

---

[18] See Jackman, Pissarides, and Savouri (1990), OECD (1993), OECD (1994), and Martin
(1998).

that determine ALMPs (unlike other government policies such as demand management or the welfare state).[19]

This is all the more surprising when we consider that ALMPs are recognized as one of the policy options still open to social democrats in the era of internationalization. Increasingly international capital is identified as the main limitation facing social democratic governments since the early 1970s. Highly mobile capital, it is argued, powerfully constrains the ability of social democratic governments to promote policies that are significantly different from those implemented by conservative ones. In an open economy, however, some options are still open to social democratic governments. ALMP belongs within the group of supply-side policies that can be used by partisan governments to promote employment, growth, and equality in an environment characterized by increasing levels of internationalization (see Garrett and Lange 1991; Boix 1998a). In spite of their modest presence in national budgets, ALMP levels have become one of the clearest signals of a government's political choices in industrialized democracies greatly influenced by international forces (including European integration).[20]

In the framework proposed in this book, outsiders are the unambiguous beneficiaries of ALMPs while insider interests may actually be hurt by the policies' effects on taxes and labor market competition.[21] As mentioned above, the immediate effect of an increase in the level of ALMPs is a higher tax burden for insiders. In the long run, insider taxes may decrease if ALMPs are successful at bringing new workers into employment but at least in the short run, insiders bear the brunt of the policies' costs. Additionally, ALMPs will, if successful, promote the entry into employment of individuals who can underbid insiders' wage demands. From an insider perspective, dedicating public resources to ALMPs may in fact result in low-wage competition. When insiders feel protected enough not to significantly fear unemployment, lack of support for these policies may result from what Saint-Paul has called insiders' 'interest in being sheltered from competition' (1998: 162).

As was the case with PLMPs, there is then a convincing logic for social democratic governments not to favor ALMPs if their objective is to satisfy the interests of insiders. The insiders' lack of concern for unemployment

[19] Notable exceptions are Janoski (1990, 1994), Garrett and Lange (1991), Boix (1998), Swank and Martin (2001), and Rueda (2005, 2006).

[20] For a more detailed analysis of the choices available to (and the constraints faced by) partisan governments in the open economy, see Scharpf and Schmidt (2000).

[21] These observations about the effects of ALMPs follow Calmfors (1994) and Saint-Paul (1998).

as well as their perception of the costs of ALMPs contribute to this outcome. Conservative governments, on the other hand, are also expected to be uninterested in pursuing ALMPs. This is because upscale groups do not favor them (since they represent higher taxes and an increase in the government's participation in the economy) and because conservative parties consider the reduction of employment protection a more attractive way to appeal to outsiders.

2.4. Factors that Mitigate Insider–Outsider Differences: Unemployment Vulnerability and Corporatism

This book's partisanship model is based on a fundamental difference in insiders' and outsiders' vulnerability to unemployment. Since the early 1970s, two factors had effectively insulated insiders from the threat of unemployment: the establishment of restrictive severance legislation and the emergence of 'outsiderness'. To the extent that insiders are protected from unemployment, their interests will be significantly different from those of outsiders. The potential benefits for insiders of policies to promote employment, for example, are small while the actual costs (in terms of taxes and low-wage competition) are high.

Factors that increase the insiders' vulnerability to unemployment, however, will align their interests with those of outsiders. The analysis developed in the following pages will focus on two aspects of the labor market: the levels of employment protection and the presence of corporatist arrangements.

2.4.1. *Employment Protection Legislation*

The reasons why we need to consider the level of employment protection as a factor that can make insiders more like outsiders are very straightforward. Employment protection legislation affects 'the rules governing unfair dismissal, lay-offs for economic reasons, severance payments, minimum notice periods, administrative authorization for dismissals, and prior discussion with labor representatives' (OECD 1994: 69). As was explained in great detail above, it is clear that decreasing levels of employment protection directly increase the vulnerability of insiders to unemployment. If firing insiders becomes easier, it is reasonable to assume that the interests of insiders and those of outsiders will become more similar. The benefits of policies directed to promote employment will then become more attractive to insiders as they themselves become more likely to need them. The insider–outsider model therefore implies that decreasing levels of employment protection should be associated with increasing levels of pro-outsider policy when social democratic governments are in power. As insiders become more vulnerable to unemployment, they will pressure social democratic parties to promote labor market policies.

The arguments in previous sections make clear that employment security is a fundamental part of the definition of 'insiderness'. It is therefore necessary to understand employment protection not only as a defining characteristic of insiders, but also as a policy outcome that they pressure social democratic governments to promote. The relationship between insider–outsider differences and employment protection can be best understood as a reinforcing loop playing itself out in industrialized democracies since the early 1970s. Once employment protection exists, it divides insiders and outsiders. Insiders then use their influence to make social democratic governments increase or maintain high levels of employment protection. The degree of their success in securing high levels of employment protection, finally, feeds back into the existence of insider–outsider differences and their subsequent influence on partisanship.

2.4.2. The Role of Corporatism

Like social democratic parties, unions face a host of choices that range from pro-insider (maximizing the job security levels of insiders while not pressuring governing parties to promote employment) to pro-outsider (pressuring governing parties to minimize unemployment while sacrificing job security). In a more significant way than social democratic parties (since upscale groups are of no importance to unions that depend primarily on insiders), they have strong incentives to defend the interests of insiders. The decision of a union will be influenced by consideration of two goals: fulfilling the aspirations of existing members and increasing the number of members. Since insiders tend to be both more unionized and a more influential constituency than outsiders, the first goal is a strong reason for unions to side with insiders. The second contributes to making the interests of outsiders a relative objective of a union's strategies but it is a weaker goal with a more uncertain payoff. After all, nonunionized insiders (or, in contexts of competitive labor representation, insiders affiliated to other unions) are a more attractive target for unions trying to expand membership. It is also questionable whether outsiders who benefit from union strategies will become members. It is likely that as soon as outsiders become insiders they will be satisfied with particularistic union policies. As insiders, even those who were recently outsiders will be more likely to support unions that deliver on their promises about job security.

Both because of their direct involvement in industrial relations (negotiations covering work regulations and wages being the most clear examples) and because of their capacity to influence political parties, the behavior of unions is a relevant factor in a government's policy orientation. I expect social democratic governments to be more likely to produce pro-insider policies when they are subjected to pro-insider pressure from unions. I logically also expect social democratic governments to be more likely to produce pro-outsider policies when unions exert pro-outsider pressure. The dependence of social democrats on insider support would imply that the influence of unions would be greater when social democratic parties are in power, but there is no reason to assume that unions will not significantly affect the strategies of conservative governments to some degree. Strongly pro-insider unions may limit the ability of conservative governments to develop their preferred anti-insider measures. It is my contention that the existence of corporatist arrangements will affect whether unions make insider goals their main priority and, in turn, the impact of union strategies on governments.

The influence of institutions on political processes has been emphasized by a great number of scholars.[22] Regarding labor market policy, I argue that the effects of insider–outsider divisions on parties and the effects of government partisanship on policy are contingent on institutions. I focus on a set of interrelated labor market institutions that have been grouped often under the name of corporatism. The effects of corporatism on labor market policy can be interpreted in two very different ways: there is an economic insider–outsider approach that emphasizes corporatism as a representation of the privileges of insiders, and an Olsonian one that emphasizes the effects of institutional encompassment in promoting common goals.

2.4.2.1. THE ECONOMIC INSIDER–OUTSIDER APPROACH TO CORPORATISM

Most mainstream economists regard trade unions as rent-seeking labor market cartels. The economic insider–outsider model shares this starting

---

[22] See Steinmo, Thelen, and Longstreth (1992), Pontusson (1992), and Hall and Taylor (1996) for an analysis.

point and goes on to argue that unions have no incentives to take into consideration anyone's interests but those of their employed members, the insiders. In this framework, corporatism is simply the reflection of insider power. Corporatism would then represent a variety of coordinated capitalism in which interest organizations, especially those representing insiders, play an important role in political processes and labor market outcomes. It may be the case that in the golden age of social democracy, before insider–outsider divisions become significant, a central feature of corporatism was its nonexclusive and egalitarian nature (see e.g. Pekkarinen, Pohjola, and Rowthorn 1992: 3). As outsiders become more numerous, however, corporatist arrangements serve to protect insiders, rather than facilitate the integration of outsiders.

It is not complicated to see that there is a relationship between the economic interpretation of corporatism and the arguments about unemployment vulnerability explained above. If corporatism is understood as an extension of insider privileges, its effects are in fact very similar to those of higher employment protection levels. When corporatist arrangements protect insiders and are not extended to outsiders, they insulate insiders against unemployment and make the consideration of outsider interests by social democratic parties extremely difficult.

This interpretation of the influence of corporatism seems to be supported by, for example, Kunkel and Pontusson (1998) and Notermans (2000). Although Kunkel and Pontusson's argument distinguishes between Swedish and Austrian varieties of corporatism, they argue that corporatism in Austria has reinforced the dominant position of male industrial workers within the union movement and constrained the ability of Austrian unions to mobilize new categories of wage earners. Notermans's analysis of social democratic economic policy since 1918, on the other hand, makes clear that a regime that required workers to abstain from fully exploiting their market strength (i.e. corporatism) was very difficult to sustain in unfavorable economic circumstances. Notermans argues this to be the case starting as early as the 1960s and even in countries like Sweden (the paragon of social democracy).[23] In line with this argument, the analysis in Mares (2006) can also be interpreted as supportive of an economic insider–outsider approach to corporatism. Before the end of the golden age of social democracy, corporatism was based on a deal between unions and governments whereby governments provided an

---

[23] See Notermans (2000: ch. 5). For a different but related argument about the failure of corporatism as an explanation of national responses to the 1974–85 unemployment crisis, see Therborn (1988).

ever-increasing welfare state and unions committed to wage moderation (see Cameron 1984; Crouch 1994; Beramendi and Rueda 2007). According to Mares, different political circumstances since the 1970s (welfare state maturation, the changing composition of social policy, increasing taxes) have made corporatism unsuccessful in promoting wage moderation and employment.

2.4.2.2. THE OLSONIAN APPROACH TO CORPORATISM

Is it the case that after the 1970s corporatism only promotes the interests of insiders? Proponents of the Olsonian interpretation of corporatism would disagree. Mancur Olson (1982) argued that institutions for collective action that are encompassing in relation to firm or industry have a strong incentive to contribute to the prosperity and expansion of the host firm or industry. Aware of the possibility of an emergence of monopoly power and its consequences over inefficiency, Olson believed that sufficiently encompassing organizations would 'internalize much of the cost of inefficient policies and accordingly have an incentive to redistribute income to themselves with the least possible social cost, and to give some weight to economic growth and to the interests of society as a whole' (1982: 90). Following a similar logic, Calmfors and Driffill (1988) considered the macroeconomic effects of three levels of wage bargaining by unions and employers. They argued that good economic performance would result if wage bargaining took place either at the company or at the national level. In the first case, the actions of unions would not be powerful enough to distort efficient market outcomes. In the second, unions would be encompassing enough to act in favor of the interests of society as a whole. Poor economic performance would be associated with wage bargaining at the industry level because wage bargaining would be powerful enough to affect the market equilibrium outcome while insufficiently encompassing to take society's interests into consideration. This argument's implications for the evolution of unemployment have subsequently been emphasized by Rowthorn (1992) and Pohjola (1992). Extending the previous framework, Rowthorn contends that there is, particularly in the early 1980s, a U-shaped relationship between the centralization of wage bargaining (i.e. centralized unions and employer associations) and employment.

In analyzing the effects of labor market organization over macroeconomic outcomes, other authors have suggested that the level of wage bargaining centralization is not as important as 'the degree to which bargaining is coordinated across the economy' (Hall 1994: 4). Soskice (1990),

Golden (1993), Hall (1994), and Hall and Franzese (1998) have argued that the degree of wage coordination is more relevant to macroeconomic outcomes than the level of wage bargaining. In this view, increasing levels of union concentration (a small number of unions that do not compete) are associated with better employment outcomes. The concentration logic stresses collective action by considering that fewer actors reduce coordination problems and that unions which do not compete 'have fewer incentives to engage in wage militancy' (Golden 1993: 441). Although this approach emphasizes a different factor, the analysis is compatible with the centralization argument and the conclusions are similar (the main difference being the suggestion by the concentration framework that a linear relationship may be more accurate than a U-shaped one).

The behavior of unions and their influence over policymaking is also affected by the degree of union density. The encompassing nature of unions significantly depends on whether union members are a high or a low proportion of the labor force. Once the effects of the centralization/coordination of wage bargaining have been taken into consideration, unions that represent a larger proportion of the labor force are more likely to favor pro-employment policies. Following the Olsonian framework outlined above, unions that have a larger constituency should be more aware of, and concerned about, the consequences of their actions over the economy as a whole and more able to internalize the costs of nonparticularistic strategies.

Teulings and Hartog provide a good explanation of the encompassment logic contained in the union density and centralization/coordination arguments I have presented. They point out that '(w)ith sufficiently high membership and sufficient spread across firms, the union can withstand pressures from its members to let idiosyncratic shocks [like particularistic demands by insiders] be the dominant factor in its wage demands' (1998: 279). They have to play a strategy of being both *representative* and *reasonable*. A centralized union with a high number of members

will care less about its membership, as firms have little incentive to get rid of the union. Instead, it will invest in being an encompassing union that is able to negotiate a large number of contracts and is not sensitive to the pressure of small groups within its membership. As soon as any small group had an overwhelming influence on the policy of the union, this would make the union *unreasonable*, and firms would no longer be prepared to accept the union as a party to which the power to renegotiate can be delegated safely. As the union has not invested in a large membership in a few firms, it will have difficulty in countering this attack. There are therefore considerable incentives to maintaining the reputation of being *reasonable.* Clearly, a union must always be *representative* because otherwise the workers will not be prepared to delegate renegotiation power to it.

(Teulings and Hartog 1998: 279)

Following a similar logic, an employer association faced with an encompassing union will also have strong incentives to be both representative and reasonable.

The centralization/coordination of wage bargaining and the level of union density, however, are not the only factors that can affect the influence of insider–outsider differences on social democracy. Many comparative analyses in political economy distinguish among clusters of countries that share a number of relevant characteristics—Katzenstein (1985), Hall (1986), Esping-Andersen (1990), Soskice (1990), and Hall and Soskice (2001) being some notable examples. Most authors would agree that these clusters represent institutional configurations that cannot easily be reduced to the values of a couple of labor market variables. I will emphasize the difference between corporatist and noncorporatist countries. Like Katzenstein (1985), I understand that the most important distinguishing feature of corporatism is the formation of government policy through bargaining among centralized interest groups and the ideology of social partnership.[24] Corporatism encompasses the labor market factors that I have mentioned above (centralization/coordination of wage bargaining and union density). But it is more than that. In Katzenstein's words, three traits define corporatism:

an ideology of social partnership expressed at the national level; a relatively centralized and concentrated system of interest groups; and voluntary and informal coordination of conflicting objectives through continuous political bargaining between interest groups, state bureaucracies and political parties.

(Katzenstein 1985: 32)

As argued by Rueda and Pontusson (2000), a fourth trait could be added: a high degree of institutionalization of collective bargaining and coordination of wage formation.[25]

---

[24] Corporatism has been defined in many ways. As Therborn notes, corporatism 'has become a bit like God. Many people believe it is an important phenomenon, crucially affecting social life. But nobody really knows what it looks like, so disagreement persists, apparently forever, about what it is and about what it does' (1992: 24).

[25] This factor may appear to be too closely related to the centralization of wage bargaining and union density. Rueda and Pontusson (2000) argue convincingly that the institutionalization of collective bargaining is conceptually different from the other two variables (whether, practically, they coincide or not in some countries). While union density and centralization represent the two most important characteristics of the formal organization of the wage

The reasons why, in the Olsonian approach, corporatism should affect the policy outcomes that I am interested in analyzing are pretty straightforward. Corporatist arrangements are considered to facilitate the consideration of general goals by actors that may be tempted not to act solidaristically. The expectation therefore is that corporatism would promote pro-outsider policies through two channels. First, they promote solidaristic preferences for individuals and, second, they promote solidaristic behavior by the social partners. Corporatism would facilitate the consideration of general goals through, for example, the existence of tripartite institutions. The Olsonian view would imply that when matters of general economic or political interest are debated in fora characterized by an ongoing dialogue among relatively cooperative social partners, the possible future costs of particularistic behavior become clearer and more widely known. This affects the individuals (insiders would become more likely to understand the negative implications of demanding high employment protection at all costs) and the social partners (unions would become more likely to understand the negative implications of acquiescing to the particularistic demands of insiders).

The Olsonian analysis predicts then that encompassing corporatist arrangements will limit the power of insiders. There is some evidence in favor of this argument (see Holmlund and Zetterberg 1991; Teulings and Hartog 1998). It is, however, not uncontroversial. Going back to their emphasis on representativeness and reasonableness, Teulings and Hartog recognize that

(i)n practice, unions can get into very difficult situations as their *representativeness* sometimes requires them to stand for the demands of insider groups, although that goes against their peace duty [the peace clause that obligates unions to not get involved in any actions undermining collective agreements] and against the reputation of *reasonableness*.　　　　　(Teulings and Hartog 1998: 285)

They show that this has been the case, for example, in the Netherlands with particularly influential workers, like those in domestic transport and computer services.

We have now a clear set of hypotheses about the preferences of insiders, outsiders, and upscale groups. We also have an equally clear set

bargaining process, the institutionalization of collective bargaining is meant to capture the influence of collectively bargained conditions over the circumstances of workers across the entire economy. In other words, the level of collective bargaining institutionalization (most easily represented by the percentage of the labor force covered by collective bargaining agreements) indicates the extent to which nonunion workers are affected by the employment terms achieved by unions through collective bargaining.

of hypotheses about the influence of these preferences on parties and, in turn, on the relationship between parties and policy. Finally, I have analyzed two intervening variables expected to potentially transform the effects of government partisanship on policy: employment protection and corporatism. The rest of the book is dedicated to testing these claims.

3

The Preferences of Insiders and Outsiders: Testing the Model's Assumptions about Individual Interests

The theoretical model presented in Chapter 2 is fundamentally concerned about the relationship between government partisanship and policy but it relies quite heavily on a number of assumptions about the preferences held by different individuals. For the insider–outsider partisanship model to make sense, it must be the case that insiders support employment protection more strongly than outsiders or members of the upscale groups and that outsiders support labor market policies more than insiders and upscale groups. These are the fundamental assumptions on which this book's model is built. It is common for the comparative political economy literature focusing on macro level variables to put individual preferences into the category of untested assumptions. A strong divide exists between work on comparative political economy (which pays little attention to individual preferences and often focuses on institutional factors) and on comparative political behavior and public opinion (which often ignores macro level variables and often focuses on individual interests). As I mentioned in the Introduction, this book attempts to bridge these two literatures. While Chapter 4 will address the macro implications of the insider–outsider model, this one will take the testing of the individual level assumptions very seriously.

Having defined the ambitious goals for this chapter, I will reveal one of its weaknesses. The most important difficulty when trying to provide an initial test for the assumptions in this book's arguments involves finding surveys that allow insiders, outsiders, and upscale groups to be differentiated and that then ask questions related to their policy preferences. The importance of a fine-grained definition of labor market status and the need for questions related to labor market policy preferences limit the data I use to one Eurobarometer survey conducted in 1996. Unlike the macro level analysis to be presented in Chapter 4, this Eurobarometer survey does not provide data for a large number of industrialized democracies or for an extended period of time. It only provides a snapshot in time of a sample of European countries. This is a considerable limitation. However, it is one that must be accepted in order to develop an analysis that closely addresses the individual claims implied in the insider–outsider model.

This chapter's analysis has two main goals: to produce data that provide a more complete picture of the preferences of insiders, outsiders, and upscale groups and to test whether these preferences do indeed fit into the partisanship model proposed in this book. The chapter proceeds as follows. First, I will provide a brief explanation of the survey used in the analysis and of the way I have categorized insiders, outsiders, and upscale groups. The second section will offer a detailed explanation of the individual preferences implied in the insider–outsider model and an initial and descriptive assessment of their accuracy. The third section contains a systematic multilevel analysis of the individual preferences of insiders, outsiders, and upscale groups. A set of logit random intercept multilevel maximum likelihood models provide estimates for the effects of insider–outsider differences (controlling for a number of other individual characteristics). As will be clear from the analysis below, the results strongly support the claims on which this book's argument rest. The fourth section introduces the two macro factors which, in Chapter 2, were hypothesized to affect the differences between insiders and outsiders: job security and corporatism. I remind readers of the reasons why this should be the case and describe the variables used in the analysis. The final section presents multilevel maximum likelihood models estimating the effects of job security and corporatism. The results corroborate once more the model's claims. Lower levels of employment protection do indeed make insiders more like outsiders (i.e. more supportive of labor market policy). Finally, the results support an economic insider–outsider interpretation of the effects of corporatism on insider preferences.

3.1. Defining Insiders, Outsiders, and Upscale Groups

The data analyzed in this chapter come from a survey belonging to the Eurobarometer series. Starting in the early 1970s, the Eurobarometer surveys have been conducted regularly on behalf of the European Commission. They provide information on the political, social, and economic preferences of the European public and have been used by numerous political scientists in analyses of public opinion and political behavior. The Eurobarometer survey conducted from February to April of 1996 focused on a number of issues relevant to the arguments presented in this book. All data used in this chapter, therefore, refers to Eurobarometer 44.3OVR (Employment, Unemployment, and Gender Equality, February–April, 1996).

The sampling procedure in this survey can be summarized briefly. As suggested by its title, the survey in Eurobarometer 44.3OVR focused on employment issues. The data were obtained in two stages. The first consisted of multistage national probability samples while in the second the data were merged with an oversample. In the first stage, a set of primary sampling units from each of the administrative regions[1] in every country were selected. The choice of primary sampling units was determined with probabilities proportional to population size and it was stratified according to degree of urbanization. Clusters of addresses were then systematically selected using standard route procedures, beginning with an initial address selected at random. In each household, the respondent was also chosen by a random procedure. The second stage introduced an oversample of approximately 300 persons per country who were either full-time housewives/husbands or were unemployed (students and retirees excluded).[2] The universe for the survey included those persons of at least 15 years of age residing in the fifteen member nations of the European Union.[3]

The distinction among insiders, outsiders, and upscale groups follows from the theoretical claims presented in Chapter 2. My partisanship model relies on the disaggregation of labor into insiders and outsiders. I defined insiders as those workers with protected jobs and outsiders as those who are either unemployed or hold jobs characterized by low levels of protection and employment rights. For the analysis of the survey, I define those individuals employed full-time with a permanent job, or with part-time or fixed-term jobs who do not want a full-time or

---

[1] These are Eurostat regions.

[2] For details, see Reif and Melich (1993); Reif and Marlier (1996).

[3] In 1996, these were Austria, Belgium, Denmark, Finland, France, Germany, Greece, Ireland, Italy, Luxembourg, the Netherlands, Portugal, Spain, Sweden, and the UK. Please note that in this chapter's analysis, East and West Germany (which are separated in the Eurobarometer survey) were merged into Germany, and Great Britain and Northern Ireland were merged into the UK.

Table 3.1. Insiders, outsiders, and upscale group as percentage of sample

	Insiders	Outsiders	Upscale	Others
All countries	**21.59**	**40.68**	**8.49**	**29.24**

Notes: Data from Eurobarometer 44.3OVR (1996). 18,779 respondents from 13 countries.

permanent job, as insiders. This group includes manual workers (skilled and unskilled) and those in employed positions (whether working at a desk, traveling, in services, or employed professionals) with full-time and permanent contracts (defined as contracts for an unlimited period of time).[4] Outsiders are then defined as those who are unemployed, employed full-time in fixed-term and temporary jobs (unless they do not want a permanent job), or employed part-time (unless they do not want a full-time job). The upscale group category, finally, includes those not employed by someone else or who define themselves as managers. This group includes self-employed professionals (lawyers, architects, etc.), owners of shops, business proprietors, farmers, fishermen, and general and middle management.

Before providing evidence showing that the preferences on which my partisanship model rests are in fact reasonable, it is important to check that the survey used in this chapter's analysis provides enough of a sample for the different categories under consideration. Table 3.1 provides the numbers of insiders, outsiders, and upscale groups in the analysis to be developed in this chapter. There are 18,779 respondents from thirteen countries in total.[5] Of these, almost 22 percent are insiders, almost 41 percent are outsiders, and about 8 percent are members of the upscale groups. Two things should be noted. First, there are large numbers of insiders (4,054) and outsiders (7,639) in the sample.[6] The claims made about the differences in their preferences can therefore be investigated thoroughly. Even in the case of the upscale groups, the total number of respondents (1,595) is large enough to allow us to systematically test

---

[4] My conception of insiderness is clearly related to the level of protection enjoyed by workers. It is equally unambiguous from the definition above, moreover, that I do not consider the more general category of labor to consist of only manual workers. Like a number of authors (see e.g. Zweig 2000), I emphasize the lack of power over production (being an employee) rather than manual work as the defining characteristic of labor.

[5] Eurobarometer 44.3OVR contains data for 15 countries, but Greece and Luxembourg were excluded due to missing data.

[6] The number of outsiders is high due to the oversampling described above.

claims about their preferences. Second, considering the small number of upscale group members, it would be tempting to conclude that they are not a significant part of the electorate. It is important to remember, however, that the purpose of this chapter is to analyze the individual preferences on which this book's arguments depend, not to evaluate the relative weight of insiders, outsiders, and upscale groups in the market of potential voters. As indicated in Chapter 2, my insider–outsider partisanship model understands parties to have ideological and historical commitments in addition to electoral objectives.[7] Like the traditional partisanship school, then, I consider the connection between conservative parties and upscale groups not to be entirely dependent on the number of upscale individuals as a proportion of the total adult population.[8] The importance of the upscale groups is also related to their economic power, their influence on policymaking, etc.

3.2. Policy Preferences of Insiders, Outsiders, and Upscale Groups

The most critical test of my model's individual assumptions concerns the policy preferences of insiders, outsiders, and upscale groups. The implications of the insider–outsider model presented in Chapter 2 are summarized in Figure 3.1.

There are two dimensions represented in Figure 3.1: employment protection and labor market policy. I have placed the three groups on these dimensions according to the preferences specified in the model. On the first dimension, insiders are expected to be strongly in favor of employment protection while upscale groups and outsiders are expected to place themselves closer to the other side of the spectrum. Clearly, lowering employment protection legislation directly attacks the interests of insiders. The preferences of outsiders are justified by their belief that lower employment protection will facilitate their exit from unemployment and precarious employment. The upscale groups (especially employers and managers) benefit from the flexibility of lower levels of employment protection, and thus their placement at the left of the spectrum.

---

[7] See e.g. Powell (1982).

[8] It is also true that the importance of upscale groups in purely individual terms would be much greater if Table 3.1 contained figures for likely voters instead of all adults. The greater tendency to vote of upscale individuals (compared to both insiders and outsiders) would increase the proportion of this group within the total of likely voters.

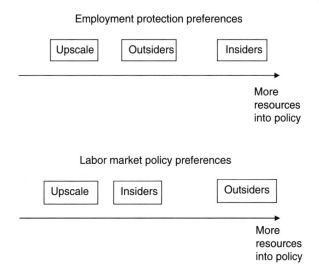

Figure 3.1. Theorized preferences

On the second dimension, insiders (who enjoy a high degree of job protection) are considered less affected by unemployment and less interested in dedicating more resources to labor market policies. Outsiders are most vulnerable to unemployment and therefore more concerned about labor market policies. As for the upscale groups' preferences, their position is justified by their desire to reduce the taxes that pay for these policies and a general inclination to limit the role of government in the economy.

There are reasons for insiders to favor higher levels of labor market policy. Insiders face some probability of losing their jobs (e.g. when companies become economically unviable) and labor market policies can reduce the intensity of job searches by outsiders and therefore reduce competition for wages. But the reasons for insiders to oppose labor market policies are more powerful. An increase in the levels of labor market policies, after all, represents a higher tax burden for insiders. Additionally, some of these policies may, if successful, promote the entry into employment of individuals who can underbid insiders' wage demands.[9] As Saint-Paul has argued, when insiders feel protected enough not to significantly fear unemployment, lack of support for labor market

---

[9] See Calmfors (1994); Saint-Paul (1998). For the relationship between the effects of different kinds of labor market policies, see Calmfors (1993). For an analysis showing that the effects of ALMPs on labor market competition may be dependent on whether they target particular individuals, see Calmfors and Lang (1995).

policies may result from the insiders' interest in being sheltered from low-wage competition (1998: 162).

The emergence of employment protection, on the one hand, and precarious employment, on the other, creates these insider–outsider differences. As was explained in more detail in Chapter 2, two processes started to develop in the 1970s. First, because of the growth and stability of the late 1960s as well as the social unrest and union activism that characterized the early 1970s, firms accepted highly restrictive tenure and severance pay arrangements (see Blanchard et al. 1986; Bentolila and Bertola 1990). As a consequence, a considerable proportion of labor became significantly more protected from unemployment. Second, as 'insiderness' emerged, the number of outsiders also grew. Increases in unemployment, larger numbers of women entering the labor force, and an intensification of international competition are all factors that contributed to an emerging emphasis on working time flexibility (see e.g. Dore 1994; Mosley and Kruppe 1996). One of the consequences of these developments is a dramatic increase of part-time work and temporary contracts. This shift away from traditional models of employment has dramatic consequences for the creation of insider–outsider differences.

Looking ahead to the analysis in Chapter 4, Figure 3.1 sharply illustrates the reasons why the insider–outsider model implies the absence of partisanship effects in one of the policy dimensions. The analysis in Chapter 2 suggested that insiders are the core constituency of social democratic parties while upscale groups are the core constituency of conservative parties. However, the figure shows that insiders and upscale groups have very similar preferences on the labor market policy dimension. They are both relatively uninterested in policies that promote employment. When analyzing the relationship between government partisanship and policy, no effect will be expected in this policy area. The figure illustrates with equal clarity the drastically different preferences of the two core constituency groups regarding employment protection. It is in this dimension that the behavior of social democratic parties (mainly caring about insiders) and that of conservative parties (mostly concerned about the interests of upscale groups) should be most different.

Returning now to the preferences of insiders, outsiders, and members of the upscale groups, the next step is to test whether the preferences presented in Figure 3.1 are in fact accurate. To do this, I turn to the Eurobarometer survey. To address the hypotheses, questions need to be found in the survey which sufficiently approximate individual preferences regarding employment protection and labor market policy. This is not completely straightforward, even when using a Eurobarometer that focused on employment issues.

To determine a respondent's opinion about employment protection, the first dimension in Figure 3.1, I use a question about job security. Respondents were asked the following question: 'For you personally, how important do you think each of the following is in choosing a job?' Respondents were then given several characteristics that they could rate from very important to not important at all. Responses that considered a secure job very important were given a 1 and those that did not were given a 0. This seems a reasonable way to capture a respondent's preferences regarding employment protection. Other questions could have been selected (e.g. about the security enjoyed by the respondent in his/her present job). But the alternatives are more difficult to apply to all groups in my analysis (the questions are not usually asked of those without employment). The question chosen is as meaningful when asked to an unemployed outsider as to an employed insider. In the sample used in my analysis, 58 percent of all respondents declared that job security was very important in choosing a job.

To capture preferences about labor market policy, two different questions are used, reflecting the two kinds of labor market policies that respondents can support. Labor market policies can be either active (aimed to promote employment directly) or passive (aimed to provide compensation when an individual no longer works).[10] Eurobarometer 44.3OVR provides a question that addresses ALMP concerns. Respondents were asked whether they would tend to agree or disagree with the following statement: 'I would be ready to pay more tax if I were sure that it would be devoted to creating new jobs.' Responses that tended to agree were given a 1 and those that did not were given a 0. This again seems a reasonable way to capture a respondent's preferences regarding labor market policies directed to promote employment. The respondents do not only express an abstract view on whether policies to promote employment are good or not but they have to declare an opinion about their willingness to pay taxes to support these policies. This reference to the costs of ALMPs is crucial to the test of the differences between insiders

---

[10] The analysis of macro policies in Chapter 4 contains a more detailed explanation of the distinction between active and passive labor market policies in the context of my insider–outsider model.

and outsiders. In the sample, 41 percent of all respondents tended to agree with the idea of paying more taxes to promote employment.[11]

I also use the Eurobarometer survey to explore individual preferences about PLMPs. The third question I analyze asks respondents whether they would tend to agree or disagree with the following statement: 'The welfare state costs too much to be maintained in its present form.' To capture support for PLMPs, those responses that tended to disagree with the statement were given a 1 and those that did not were given a 0. This question is not as closely related to the theoretical claims as the other two. Unfortunately, no other question in this Eurobarometer is better at addressing public opinion regarding social policy. Other questions are either too general or related to areas that are difficult to consider as passive labor market policy (PLMP). An analysis of the responses to this question will, nevertheless, provide some evidence in support of this book's insider–outsider hypotheses. As hypothesized in Figure 3.1, we would expect outsiders to be most clearly in disagreement with the statement that the welfare state costs too much. As the main potential beneficiaries of passive social policies, outsiders would be in favor of putting more resources into this policy. Insiders, on the other hand, are sufficiently protected from unemployment to feel that the welfare state may cost too much in its present form. Keeping in mind the limitations of the question, insiders are therefore expected to disagree with the statement less strongly than outsiders. In the sample, 30 percent of total respondents tended to disagree that the welfare state costs too much.

I have so far introduced the questions to be used in the analysis and provided some general figures about answers, in total percentages. By distinguishing among insiders, outsiders, and upscale groups, it is possible to test the claims in Figure 3.1 more directly. We turn to employment protection preferences first.

Figure 3.2 depicts the employment protection preferences of insiders, outsiders, and upscale groups. Each bar reflects the mean response for each group. As explained above, responses indicating that employment security was very important when choosing a job were given a 1. The most significant thing about Figure 3.2 is that the mean preferences of the three groups confirm the hypothesis in Figure 3.1. As expected, insiders were

---

[11] Elsewhere, I complement my analysis by also looking at a more abstract formulation (respondents were asked whether they would tend to agree or disagree with the following statement: 'The government should offer a guarantee of training, or a job, to all young people leaving school'). See Rueda (2005) for details.

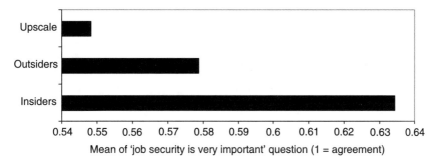

Figure 3.2. Employment protection preferences

most concerned about job security while outsiders and upscale groups were much less likely to consider job security very important. Almost 64 percent of insiders believed that employment protection was very important when choosing a job, while only 58 percent of outsiders and 55 percent of the upscale groups did so.

The numbers in Figures 3.2 are suggestive but an initial assessment of their statistical significance can help confirm their meaningfulness. I estimate Pearson chi-square statistics to test whether a significant relationship exists between being an insider, outsider, or upscale individual and holding the specific opinions about employment protection contained in the figure. The null hypothesis in this test is that there is no association. The results suggest (at better than a 99 percent level of confidence) that a relationship does exist between insider–outsider–upscale status and employment protection preferences.[12]

Turning now to the second dimension in my analysis, Figure 3.3 presents the mean responses of the three groups when asked about ALMP. In this case, respondents that tended to agree with paying more taxes if the money was devoted to promote employment were given a 1. As was the case with employment protection, the preferences for labor market policy reflected in Figure 3.3 confirm the hypothesis in Figure 3.1. As expected, outsiders were most willing to promote employment, even at the cost of taxes. Insiders, less likely to be vulnerable to unemployment themselves, were more reluctant to agree to pay higher taxes to create jobs. Members of the upscale groups, also as hypothesized in Figure 3.1, were the least supportive. The figure indicates that almost 45 percent

[12] The sections below will provide a more systematic test of the implications of the insider–outsider model to employment protection and labor market policy preferences.

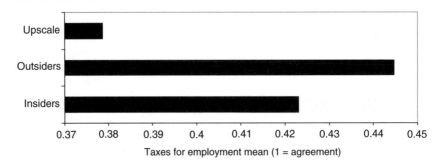

Figure 3.3. Active labor market policy preferences

of outsiders were in favor of employment promotion (even if it meant higher taxes) while only about 42 percent of insiders and 38 percent of the upscale groups had the same preferences.[13] Whether an individual is an insider, an outsider, or a member of the upscale groups does prove to be a statistically significant determinant of his/her attitude toward ALMP (a Pearson chi-square test shows that the association is significant at better than a 99 percent level of confidence).

The second dimension in Figure 3.1 is also explored by looking at preferences about PLMP. Figure 3.4 presents the mean responses of insiders, outsiders, and upscale groups when asked about whether the welfare state is too costly. As mentioned above, responses that tended to disagree were given a 1. In spite of the limitations of this question, Figure 3.4 shows a similar pattern to the one found in Figure 3.3. This confirms the expectations summarized in Figure 3.1. Outsiders were most supportive of the welfare state. Insiders and, especially, members of the upscale groups do not see themselves as potential beneficiaries of social policy and dislike paying the costs of a generous welfare state. As a consequence, their support is much more muted. While almost 32 percent of outsiders disagree that the welfares state is too costly, fewer than 31 percent of insiders and a much lower 25 percent of the upscale groups share this preference. A Pearson chi-square statistics shows (at better than a 99 percent level of confidence) that a relationship does exist between insider–outsider–upscale status and PLMP preferences.

The similarity in insiders' and outsiders' preferences with respect to PLMP shown in Figure 3.4 could introduce a degree of doubt in the

[13] As mentioned in footnote 11, in Rueda (2005) I test this same claim with a slightly different question. The pattern suggested in Figure 3.3 is confirmed by an analysis of the support for active labor market policy looking at responses for that question as well.

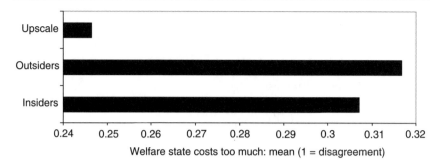

Figure 3.4. Passive labor market policy preferences

model's claims. However, it is important to remember that the question used for measuring these preferences is far from ideal. To support this initial analysis (a more systematic one follows this section), we can turn to the conclusions in Boeri, Börsch-Supan, and Tabellini (2001). They show that the preferences in my model are in fact reasonable. They find that the individuals I define as outsiders would be ready to accept higher costs (i.e. taxes) in return for more unemployment insurance. Insiders and upscale groups do not seem to share these preferences.

3.3. Multilevel Analysis of Preferences

Section 3.2 offers a meaningful initial take on the data supporting this book's arguments, but it is mostly descriptive. The frequency tables on which the analysis was based do not control for the influence of a number of possibly relevant factors. They illustrate in a powerful way that the model's assumptions are accurate but they should be complemented by more rigorous tests. This section represents an effort to produce such tests. Below, I present the results of regressions designed to examine whether the conclusions explained in previous paragraphs are reliable.

The nature of the dependent variables to be used in the analysis is dichotomous, or binary. The responses to the questions about employment protection and labor market policy preferences are either 0 or 1. It is well known that ordinary least squares (OLS) estimation is not appropriate when analyzing the determinants of binary responses (see e.g. Hosmer and Lemeshow 2000). Instead, I estimate a logistic model.

In a binary logistic model, we estimate the following equation:

$$P(Y \mid x) = \frac{e^{\beta_0 + \beta_1 x}}{1 + e^{\beta_0 + \beta_1 x}}$$

which can also be written as:

$$P(Y \mid x) = \frac{\exp(\beta_0 + \beta_1 x)}{1 + \exp(\beta_0 + \beta_1 x)}$$

where $P(Y \mid x)$ means the probability that the response is 1 and the x's are the explanatory variables.

The interpretation of the constant and coefficients in a logistic model is not as straightforward as in the OLS case. In the linear case, β_0 refers to the constant and β_1 to the slopes of the explanatory variables. In the logistic case, the coefficients represent the change in the logit for a change in one unit in the explanatory variables. A positive logit means the independent variable has the effect of increasing the odds that the dependent variable equals 1. A negative logit means the independent variable has the effect of decreasing the odds that the dependent variable equals the given value.

Thinking in terms of logits is not easy, so it is common to transform the coefficient into odds ratios [odds ratio = $\exp(\beta_1)$]. The odds ratio reflects the increase in the probability that Y equals 1 associated with a unit increase in X. Once the logit has been transformed into an odds ratio, it can be interpreted as a percent increase in the odds. The odds ratio is the probability of the event represented in the outcome variable divided by the probability of the nonevent. If the odds ratio estimate for an explanatory variable is 2, then, this would mean that an increase in one unit in the explanatory variable (e.g. being an insider) makes the probability of the event (e.g. having strong preferences for employment protection) twice as likely. Since odd ratios have a much more intuitive interpretation than coefficients, I report both in the analysis below. The significance tests of the coefficients are extended to the odds ratios and I report those as well.

The data used in the analysis have a multilevel structure (one level, the individual, is nested within the other, the country). Developing an analysis that ignores the multilevel nature of the data could create a number of statistical problems (clustering, nonconstant variance, underestimation of standard errors, etc.).[14] Like other recent analyses of similar data (see e.g. Rohrschneider 2002; Anderson and Tverdova 2003), I follow the

---

[14] For a more detailed analysis of these issues, see Zorn (2001).

recommendations for modeling multilevel data structures of Steenbergen and Jones (2002).

To test the claims summarized in Table 3.1, therefore, I run some logit random intercept multilevel maximum likelihood models. In these models, a subject-specific random intercept is included in the general equation as a predictor. Then maximum likelihood estimates are obtained for all parameters in the model.[15]

The analysis proceeds as follows. I estimate models for the determinants of preferences about employment protection and labor market policy. The dependent variables in each case are the questions already described in the section above. The explanatory variables are the insider, outsider, and upscale group dummy variables (this coding was also explained above) alongside some controls (age, gender, income, and education).

Although age, gender, income, and education are commonly used as control variables when exploring public opinion and political behavior, there are also substantive reasons why they should be included in this chapter's analysis. In industrialized democracies, new social risks have become increasingly important when analyzing preferences for employment protection and the welfare state. Although new social risks have become a prominent focus of the literature on the welfare state, a precise definition is not easily available (see e.g. Esping-Andersen 1999). Bonoli (2005) explains that current socioeconomic transformations have brought into existence postindustrial labor market and family structures which are generating new social risks. These new risks tend to concentrate among women, the young, and the low skilled. I attempt to control for the effect of these new social risks by including variables capturing age, gender, income, and education in the analysis. In the following pages, I will be paying special attention to gender. Female participation in the labor market has significantly increased in the last twenty years. In fact, employment growth in the OECD from 1983 to 1992 consisted almost exclusively of an increase in female employment participation (see Rubery et al. 1996; Daly 2000). Furthermore, women are disproportionately represented in precarious employment (whether it is fixed-term or involuntary part-time employment).[16] In the following pages, I try to distinguish

---

[15] For more details about maximum likelihood estimation of random intercept multilevel models, see Rabe-Hesketh, Skrondal, and Pickles (2005). For more details about estimating these models with Stata, as was done for the results below, see Rabe-Hesketh and Skrondal (2005).

[16] See Maier (1994) and the policy-specific chapters in this book.

between the effects of insider–outsider status and those of gender on policy preferences.

Table 3.2 presents the results of the analysis of employment protection preferences. As is the case with all the tables in this chapter, the first column depicts the estimates of the coefficients, their standard errors, and p values from z tests of significance. To make the interpretation of the results easier, the significance levels of the estimates are also indicated by asterisks in the usual manner (*** if p value < .01, ** if < .05, and * if < .1). The second column provides the odds ratios associated to the coefficients. Table 3.2 provides a substantial amount of support for the claims in the insider–outsider model. In Figure 3.1, I argued that insiders would be strongly in favor of employment protection while upscale groups and outsiders would not. Table 3.2 makes clear that this is the case. Only insider status is significantly associated with employment protection preferences (the relationship is significant at higher than a 99 percent confidence level). Neither outsider nor upscale group status, on the other hand, reaches statistical significance as a determinant of these preferences. Moreover, the second column in the table indicates that insider status is not only statistically significant but also has important effects. The odds ratio suggests that being an insider is associated with a 45 percent increase in the probability of considering employment security very important when choosing a job. It is clear, therefore, that lowering employment protection is perceived by insiders as a direct attack on their interests. Because they understand that lower employment protection will facilitate their exit from unemployment and precarious employment, outsiders, on the other hand, do not share these concerns. This lack of concern is also reflected in the preferences of the members of the upscale groups.

The table shows that several of the control variables are also significant. I will not dedicate much attention to the controls for age, income, and education. But I will mention that once we control for the effects of insider–outsider differences, gender is still a significant determinant of employment protection preferences. The gender variable is coded so that females get a 1 and males a 0. The odds ratio for gender in Table 3.2 suggests that the probability of considering employment security very important when choosing a job decreases by 11 percent if the respondent is a female. This effect is statistically significant at better than a 99 percent confidence level. This result is interesting and it seems to reflect a difference between females and insiders. Given the fact that females are

Table 3.2. The effects of insider, outsider, and upscale status on employment protection preferences

	Coefficients	Odds ratios
Constant	**.874*****	—
	(.089)	
	.000	
Outsider status	**.077**	**1.080**
	(.047)	
	.107	
Insider status	**.371*****	**1.449**
	(.049)	
	.000	
Upscale group status	**−.093**	**.911**
	(.061)	
	.133	
Age	**−.072*****	**.930**
	(.021)	
	.001	
Gender	**−.115*****	**.891**
	(.031)	
	.000	
Income	**−.021***	**.980**
	(.011)	
	.055	
Education	**−.136*****	**.873**
	(.019)	
	.000	
N		18,779
Number of countries		13

Notes: Employment protection preferences measured as agreement in 'job security is important' question.

All entries are from logit random intercept multilevel maximum likelihood estimation.

In the first column, numbers in bold are estimated coefficients; numbers in parentheses are standard errors; numbers in italics are p values from z tests.

The asterisks signify statistical significance in the usual manner (*** if p value < .01, ** if < .05, and * if < .1).

over represented in the sectors of the economy characterized by precarious employment, this may not be a surprising result.

The odds ratios reported in Table 3.2 are meaningful but a complementary explanation of the variables' effects can be provided. Using the coefficients in the table, we can calculate the probability that an individual with a particular set of values in all the independent variables would consider employment security very important when choosing a job. By looking at the probabilities associated with some combinations, it is possible to get a more intuitive impression of the effect of the explanatory variables.

We do this by calculating:

$$P(Y = 1) = 1/(1 + \exp(-X\beta))$$

In this case:

$$= 1/(1 + \exp(-(\beta_0 + \beta_1\text{outsider} + \beta_2\text{insider} + \beta_3\text{upscale} + \beta_4\text{age} + \beta_5\text{gender} + \beta_6\text{income} + \beta_7\text{education})))$$

The estimates for all βs are in the table, by providing the values of the explanatory variables we can calculate the probability associated to them. First I calculate the probability of considering employment security very important for a male insider. In this case, *insider* equals 1 and *outsider*, *upscale*, and *gender* equal 0. I also set the individual control variables (*age*, *income*, and *education*) to their most common values. For *age*, the most common response is 2 (26 to 44 years), for *income* 4 (the lowest quartile in the household income distribution), and for *education* 2 (the respondent was 16 to 19 years old when he/she finished full-time education). Replacing estimates and values, we obtain:

$$
\begin{aligned}
P(Y = 1) &= 1/(1 + \exp(-(.874 + (.077^*0) + (.371^*1) + (-.093^*0) + (-.072^*2) \\
&\quad + (-.115^*0) + (-.021^*4) + (-.136^*2)))) \\
&= 1/(1 + \exp(-(.874 + (.371^*1) + (-.072^*2) + (-.021^*4) \\
&\quad + (-.136^*2)))) \\
&= 1/(1 + \exp(-.745)) \\
&= .678
\end{aligned}
$$

This means that being a male insider is associated with a 68 percent probability of considering employment security very important when choosing a job.[17] We can do the same calculations to estimate the probability when a respondent is a female outsider. The probability this time is only 58 percent. The probability for a female member of the upscale groups is still lower, only 54 percent. Clearly, being an insider represents a substantive increase in one's preferences for employment protection.

Table 3.3 presents the results of the analysis of ALMP preferences. The estimates provide once again a substantial amount of support for the claims in the insider–outsider model. Going back to the explanation of Figure 3.1, I argued that outsiders are most vulnerable to unemployment and therefore most supportive of higher levels of active and passive labor market policies. I also argued that insiders face some probability of losing

[17] To put this figure in context, it is important to remember that 54 percent of the total sample considered employment security very important when choosing a job.

Table 3.3. The effects of insider, outsider, and upscale status on active labor market policy preferences

	Coefficients	Odds ratios
Constant	−**.671*** (.090) *.000*	—
Outsider status	**.206*** (.048) *.000*	**1.229**
Insider status	**.127** (.050) *.011*	**1.136**
Upscale group status	−**.068** (.064) *.289*	**.934**
Age	**.021** (.021) *.326*	**1.021**
Gender	−**.067** (.031) *.031*	**.935**
Income	−**.016** (.011) *.160*	**.985**
Education	**.108*** (.019) *.000*	**1.114**
N	18,779	
Number of countries	13	

Notes: Active labor market preferences measured as agreement in 'ready to pay more tax if devoted to creating new jobs' question.

All entries are from logit random intercept multilevel maximum likelihood estimation.

In the first column, numbers in bold are estimated coefficients; numbers in parentheses are standard errors; numbers in italics are p values from z tests.

The asterisks signify statistical significance in the usual manner (*** if p value < .01, ** if < .05, and * if < .1).

their jobs but they are much less vulnerable to unemployment than outsiders. As a consequence, their support of active and passive labor market policies was expected to be much more muted. Members of the upscale groups see these policies as expensive government intervention in the labor market and they were expected not to support them. The results in Table 3.3 support these hypotheses: being an outsider is significantly associated with higher active labor market preferences (the relationship is significant at higher than a 99 percent confidence level). The odds ratio indicates that the probability of agreeing to pay more tax to promote employment increases by 23 percent when the respondent is an outsider.

This is both a significant and a substantively important increase. Being an insider, on the other hand, is also statistically significant (at higher than a 95 percent confidence level) but less influential. The willingness to pay more tax to promote job creation only increases by 14 percent when the respondent is an insider. As hypothesized, insiders are not as concerned about labor market policy as outsiders. Also consistent with the claims in Figure 3.1, members of the upscale groups exhibit a lack of concern for ALMPs (being in this category is not significant in the analysis).

As for gender, it is again a significant determinant of individual preferences. The odds ratio for gender in Table 3.3 indicates that the probability of supporting ALMP decreases by 6 percent if the respondent is a female. This is not a very noticeable effect in substantive terms. But the sign of the change is, nevertheless, surprising. While the results in Table 3.2 placed the preferences of females closer to those of outsiders (they were less likely to support employment protection), those in Table 3.3 seem to distance them. Females do not share a concern for ALMPs with outsiders.

As was the case with the results in Table 3.2, the effects of the explanatory variables can be illustrated by calculating the probabilities associated to particular values. Using the estimates as described above, we can calculate the probability of supporting ALMP for a male outsider. As before, I set the individual control variables (*age*, *income*, and *education*) to their most common values. The calculations show that the probability of agreeing to pay more tax if it was devoted to create jobs is 43 percent when the respondent is a male outsider. Being a male insider reduces the probability of supporting ALMP to 41 percent (this was, in fact, the average response for the total sample) while being a male member of the upscale groups reduces it even further, to only 37 percent.

The results of the analysis of PLMP preferences are presented in Table 3.4. The expectations explained when considering ALMP apply here as well. And, as was the case with Table 3.3, the results provide considerable support for the model's hypotheses. Being an outsider is significantly associated with support for PLMP (the relationship is significant at higher than a 95 percent confidence level). The probability of disagreeing with the statement that the welfare state is too costly increases by 11 percent when the respondent is an outsider. Insider status, on the other hand, is not a significant determinant of passive labor market preferences. While the analysis of Table 3.3 showed that insiders are less supportive of ALMP, Table 3.4 indicates that being an insider is not significant at all when considering PLMP. The third category in the analysis, the upscale groups,

Table 3.4. The effects of insider, outsider, and upscale status on passive labor market policy preferences

	Coefficients	Odds ratios
Constant	−**.957***** (.098) *.000*	—
Outsider status	**.102**** (.051) *.047*	**1.107**
Insider status	**.054** (.051) *.298*	**1.055**
Upscale group status	−**.231***** (.070) *.001*	**.794**
Age	−**.023** (.023) *.303*	**.977**
Gender	−**.124***** (.033) *.000*	**.884**
Income	**.019*** (.011) *.091*	**1.019**
Education	**.083***** (.020) *.000*	**1.087**
N	18,779	
Number of countries	13	

Notes: Passive labor market preferences measured as disagreement in 'welfare state costs too much' question.

All entries are from logit random intercept multilevel maximum likelihood estimation.

In the first column, numbers in bold are estimated coefficients; numbers in parentheses are standard errors; numbers in italics are p values from z tests.

The asterisks signify statistical significance in the usual manner (*** if p value < .01, ** if < .05, and * if < .1).

is highly significant (at higher than a 99 percent confidence level). Being a member of the upscale group is associated with a substantial 21 percent decrease in the probability of supporting PLMP, which is consistent with the claims of the insider–outsider model.

The influence of gender on the likelihood of agreeing that the welfare state costs too much is very similar to the one discussed when looking at the previous table. Gender is a significant determinant of PLMP preferences. Being a female decreases the probability of supporting these policies by 12 percent. As was the case in Table 3.3, females do not seem to share the levels of support for labor market policies (whether active or passive) exhibited by outsiders.

I will once again illustrate the effects of the explanatory variables by calculating the probabilities associated to particular values. The estimates in Table 3.4 indicate that the probability of disagreeing that the welfare state costs too much is 34 percent when a respondent is a male outsider (as before, the control variables are set to their most common values). This number may seem low, but it must be put in context by remembering that 30 percent of the total sample disagreed with the statement in this question. Being a male insider reduces the probability of supporting PLMP to 33 percent (not a substantial change from the one associated with being an outsider) but being a male member of the upscale groups does promote a much greater reduction, to only 27 percent. It is possible that the limitations inherent to this question as a proxy for social policy preferences affect the lack of a greater difference between insiders and outsiders. But it is still the case that outsider status is a statistically significant determinant of PLMP (as shown in the table) while insider status is not.

3.4. Factors Mitigating Insider–Outsider Differences: The Effects of Employment Protection and Corporatism

In Chapter 2, I explained in some detail that there are factors that can affect the differences between insiders and outsiders. My argument focused on two main ones: employment protection and corporatism. The insider–outsider model is based on the existence of very different preferences for insiders and outsiders. All circumstances that make the interests of insiders more similar to those of outsiders will transform the strategies of social democratic parties. Insiders will remain the core constituency of social democratic parties, but the more insiders become like outsiders, the greater the incentives for Left parties to promote what I have defined as pro-outsider policies. Both employment protection levels and the existence of corporatist arrangements affect the existence of differences in the preferences of insiders and outsiders. They do so, however, quite differently. While employment protection is straightforwardly related to the unemployment vulnerability of insiders, corporatism has more ambiguous effects.

It is clear that decreasing levels of employment protection directly increase the vulnerability of insiders to unemployment. If firing insiders becomes easier, the interests of insiders and those of outsiders will become more similar. The benefits of policies directed to promote employment become more attractive to insiders as they themselves become more likely to need them. A hypothesis emerges directly from this: the insider–outsider model implies that decreasing levels of employment protection should be associated with increasing demands for labor market policy. In other words, as the insider loses his/her employment protection and becomes more vulnerable to unemployment, he/she is expected to get closer to the preferences we had defined for outsiders. Increasing the levels of labor market policy (whether active or passive) therefore becomes part of these insiders' goals.

I explained above that there are costs and benefits to labor market policies for insiders. The costs are related to taxation and competition. An increase in the levels of labor market policies represents a higher tax burden for insiders and it may also promote low-wage competition from new entrants into the market. The benefits, on the other hand, are related to the possibility that insiders may ever need these policies (either as compensation for losing a job or assistance to find a new one). To the degree that insiders face a low probability of losing their jobs, the costs of labor market policy greatly outweigh the benefits. As the probability of losing a job increases (as insiders become more like outsiders), the benefits of labor market policy become more meaningful.[18]

A number of different options exist for measuring the levels of employment protection in OECD countries. For the analysis in this chapter, I will use a variable provided in Baker et al. (2004). The data were created by joining together several series: an original one from Lazear (1990), an update using OECD data from Blanchard and Wolfers (2000), and a further update and interpolation from Nickell and Nunziata (2000). It is important to note that the OECD data, used from 1985 onward, is constructed on the basis of a more extensive collection of employment protection dimensions.[19] The variable ranges from 0 to 2, where higher values mean stricter employment protection.

---

[18] Elsewhere, I also look at increases in unemployment as having a potential effect on the vulnerability of insiders. One of the claims in Rueda (2006) is that as unemployment becomes unstable, insiders will increase their demands for employment promotion policies. This argument, and the analysis supporting it, complement the ones presented in this chapter.

[19] Lazear's index measures the severance pay and advance notice a blue-collar worker with ten years of service receives upon termination without cause. The OECD index is constructed by averaging the scores obtained by each country in three categories: 'procedural inconveniences which the employer faces when trying to dismiss employees; notice and severance pay provisions; and prevailing standards of and penalties for unfair dismissal' (OECD 1999: 54).

Table 3.5. Employment protection, 1996

Country	
Austria	1.30
Belgium	1.19
Denmark	0.74
Finland	1.08
France	1.50
Germany	1.41
Italy	1.41
Ireland	0.54
Netherlands	1.23
Portugal	1.91
Sweden	1.32
Spain	1.62
UK	0.35

Notes: Employment protection is measured as an index ranging from 0 to 2, higher values mean more employment protection.

Source: Baker et al. (2004).

Table 3.5 shows the employment protection levels of the 13 countries in this chapter's analysis. The figures show the great cross-national diversity in employment protection that exists in our sample. Liberal countries like the UK or Ireland exhibit a very low level of employment protection (0.35 and 0.54, respectively). On the other hand, the Mediterranean countries (Portugal, with 1.91, Spain, with 1.62, and France, with 1.50) are examples of very high levels. The insider–outsider model implies that these differences will have an effect on the preferences of insiders.

While it is certainly true that employment protection legislation is an important factor affecting the vulnerability of insiders, it is also possible to capture the individual aspects of job security. Political scientists have long been interested in the effects of individual employment insecurity on public opinion and political behavior (see e.g. Mughan and Lacy 2002).[20] This is particularly the case since job insecurity seems to have become a widespread feature of many industrialized democracies. A great deal of evidence suggests that employment-related worries have been on the rise in recent years (OECD 1997). The structural changes in favor of flexible and part-time employment mentioned in previous sections have contributed to these changes. The erosion of lifetime employment and the shift to more temporary contracts has promoted a sense of insecurity in many workers. Although job insecurity at the individual level is related

[20] For an analysis of the determinants of job insecurity, see Anderson and Pontusson (2007).

to the macro level measure of employment protection used above, it is clearly not the same thing. Employment protection legislation is an important contributing factor, but many other variables affect the levels of individual job insecurity. I therefore explore whether subjective feelings of individual job insecurity affect preferences for labor market policy.

The question I use asked employed respondents whether a number of statements about their current jobs were very true, quite true, a little, true, or not at all true. Those who believed the statement 'my job is secure' was not true at all were given a 1. It is important to note the differences between the question I used for the analysis of employment protection preferences and the one used here to measure insider vulnerability. Previously, I needed to analyze the differences among insiders, outsiders, and upscale groups regarding support for employment protection. So I used a question that asked respondents how important job security was to them when choosing a job. In this analysis, I am interested in the question of whether unemployment vulnerability makes insiders more like outsiders. I use a question posed only to those in employment that focuses on the job security they enjoy at present. I also code it differently, to capture their unemployment vulnerability (rather than the existence of employment protection). In the sample, 10 percent of insiders feel insecure about their jobs.

The second macro level factor in my analysis affecting the differences between insiders and outsiders is corporatism. Employment protection legislation has a straightforward effect on insider vulnerability to unemployment. Corporatism, on the other hand, has more ambiguous effects. As was suggested in Chapter 2, corporatism could be interpreted as a set of institutional arrangements that systematically protect the interests of insiders. The economic insider–outsider framework argues that unions, even in corporatist countries, have little incentive to consider the interests of outsiders. Is it the case that corporatism is designed to promote the interests of insiders only? An alternative interpretation of the effects of corporatism is possible. As Chapter 2 explained in more detail, what I call the Olsonian interpretation of corporatism emphasizes the effects of institutional encompassment. In this view, corporatism would be expected to translate into a decrease in the policy preference differences among insiders, outsiders, and upscale groups. If corporatism does indeed promote solidaristic preferences, we would expect insiders in highly corporatist systems to be more supportive of labor market policies (employment promotion being a solidaristic goal that would benefit labor as a whole, not only protected insiders). If the economic insider–outsider framework

Table 3.6. Corporatism, 1994

Country	
Austria	0.96
Belgium	0.66
Denmark	0.61
Finland	0.83
France	0.36
Germany	0.76
Italy	0.40
Ireland	0.11
Netherlands	0.53
Portugal	—
Sweden	0.78
Spain	—
UK	0.07

Notes: Corporatism is measured as an index ranging from 0 to 1.
Source: Hicks and Kenworthy (1998).

is more accurate, however, we would expect exactly the opposite effect.[21]

The measure for corporatism used in this chapter is provided by Hicks and Kenworthy (1998). It is an index that encapsulates a number of economic characteristics: the centralization and coordination of unions, business, and wage-setting; the cooperation between government and interest groups; the existence of tripartite organizations, the degree of cooperation among economic actors, etc. The variable ranges from 0 to 1, where higher values mean more corporatism.

Table 3.6 shows the corporatism index values for all countries in this chapter's analysis. Because of missing data, two countries are lost when the corporatism measure is introduced. Hicks and Kenworthy do not provide observations for either Portugal or Spain. The data are also provided only until 1994. Although the Eurobarometer survey was conducted in 1996, we have to make do with this, the latest observation available.[22] As was the case with employment protection, the table shows a great deal of cross-national variation. Unsurprisingly, liberal countries like the UK or Ireland exhibit a very low level of corporatism (0.07 and 0.11, respectively) while the Northern European countries have very high levels. Austria (0.96) is the most corporatist country but Finland (0.83), Sweden

[21] For a theoretical attempt to integrate these two views, see Teulings (1997). For an empirical analysis of the two alternative frameworks, see Kittel (2000).
[22] Since the index of corporatism is relatively stable through time, using the corporatism measure from 1994 does not seem too problematic.

60

(0.78), and Germany (0.76) are also good examples of strong corporatist arrangements.

3.5. Multilevel Analysis of the Effects of Job Security and Corporatism: What Happens When Insiders Become More Like Outsiders?

I test the claims about the effects of job security and corporatism by developing an analysis similar to that in the previous sections of this chapter (I estimate logit random intercept multilevel maximum likelihood models). As indicated by the title, the focus of this section is to explore whether insiders become more like outsiders when: (a) they suffer greater job insecurity and (b) they are influenced by corporatist arrangements. The insider–outsider model implies that, like outsiders, insiders will become more supportive of labor market policy as their job insecurity increases. The analysis will also allow us to assess whether the economic or the Olsonian interpretation of the effects of corporatism is correct. I estimate models for the determinants of preferences about active and passive labor market policy. As in previous analyses, the explanatory variables are the insider, outsider, and upscale status variables, alongside some controls (age, gender, income, and education). In this case, however, I add the variables capturing job insecurity and corporatism described in section 3.4 (two at the macro level, employment protection and corporatism, and one at the micro level, subjective job insecurity). Because my argument concerns the influence of the job insecurity and corporatism variables on insider preferences, I introduce an interaction term consisting of the multiplication of each of these variables and the insider status variable. I analyze first the influence of employment security and then of corporatism.

Table 3.7 presents the effects of job security on active and passive labor market policy preferences. The table follows the format of the previous analyses but includes estimates for two different models (one for active and one for passive labor market policy preferences). To test whether the preferences of insiders become more like those of outsiders when they are exposed to higher levels of unemployment vulnerability, I have introduced into the models a measure of individual job insecurity and another of macro level employment protection. To assess the effects of these two variables on insiders, I have also introduced interactions of the variables with the one capturing insider status. Given

Table 3.7. The effects of job security on active and passive labor market policy preferences

	Active labor market policy preferences		Passive labor market policy preferences	
	Coefficients	Odds ratios	Coefficients	Odds ratios
Constant	**−.278*** (.104) *.008*	—	**−.735*** (.109) *.000*	—
Outsider status	**.221*** (.049) *.000*	**1.248**	**.079** (.051) *.126*	**1.082**
Insider status	**−.039** (.114) *.733*	**.962**	**−.212*** (.122) *.083*	**.809**
Upscale group status	**−.051** (.065) *.429*	**.950**	**−.233*** (.071) *.001*	**.792**
Individual job insecurity	**−.087** (.092) *.345*	**.917**	**.018** (.098) *.850*	**1.019**
Insider status*individual job insecurity	**.198** (.143) *.165*	**1.219**	**−.044** (.151) *.769*	**.957**
Employment protection index	**−.202*** (.041) *.000*	**.817**	**−.250*** (.044) *.000*	**.779**
Insider status*employment protection index	**.154*** (.087) *.077*	**1.167**	**.220*** (.094) *.020*	**1.246**
Age	**.028** (.021) *.180*	**1.029**	**−.025** (.023) *.267*	**.975**
Gender	**−.067*** (.031) *.032*	**.935**	**−.123*** (.033) *.000*	**.884**
Income	**−.019*** (.011) *.088*	**.981**	**.013** (.012) *.263*	**1.013**
Education	**.110*** (.019) *.000*	**1.112**	**.083*** (.020) *.000*	**1.086**
N			18,779	
Number of countries			13	

Notes: Active labor market preferences measured as agreement in 'ready to pay more tax if devoted to creating new jobs' question. Passive labor market preferences measured as disagreement in 'welfare state costs too much' question.

All entries are from logit random intercept multilevel maximum likelihood estimation.

In the coefficient columns, numbers in bold are estimated coefficients; numbers in parentheses are standard errors; numbers in italics are p values from z tests.

The asterisks signify statistical significance in the usual manner (*** if p value < .01, ** if < .05, and * if < .1).

the focus of this part of the analysis (and the fact that the estimation of other variables is very similar to that reported in previous models), I will concentrate the following observations on the effects of these variables.

From Tables 3.3 and 3.4, we know what the differences between insiders and outsiders are regarding active and passive labor market policy. I showed that being an outsider was significantly associated with support for ALMP (the relationship was significant at higher than a 99 percent confidence level). Being an insider was also statistically significant (but only at higher than the 95 percent confidence level) but less influential in substantive terms. In Table 3.7 we can see how these estimates change when we take into account the influence of job security. When we introduce our measures of job security, insider status becomes insignificant in relation to ALMP preferences but significant in relation to passive ones. It is difficult to interpret these results without taking into consideration the combined effects of the interaction variables. The estimates for individual job insecurity, however, suggest that this is not an important factor determining insider preferences. Neither individual job insecurity nor its interaction with insider status are statistically significant as determinants of active and passive labor market policy preferences. It is perhaps surprising that subjective feelings about job security do not influence an insider's likelihood to support policies either promoting employment or compensating for job loss. The influence of the employment protection index, on the other hand, fully supports the expectations of the insider–outsider model. The results suggest that the direct effects of employment protection at the macro level are significant (at better than a 99 percent confidence level) and negative in both models. As hypothesized, the willingness to pay tax to support employment promotion and the likelihood to disagree that the welfare state is too costly decrease as the levels of employment protection increase. The interaction terms are also significant (only at better than the 90 percent level in ALMP analysis) but its effects are more complicated to assess by looking simply to the coefficient or odds ratio.

To get a better impression of the effects of job security (both at the individual and macro levels) on the likelihood of supporting active and passive labor market policy, I will calculate the probabilities associated to particular values of the explanatory variables.[23] More specifically, I am interested in the change in the probability of supporting labor market

---

[23] Probabilities are calculated as explained in previous sections.

policy for a male insider associated to changes in individual job insecurity and levels of macro level employment protection. In these calculations, *insider* equals 1 and *outsider*, *upscale*, and *gender* equal 0. As before, I set the individual control variables (*age*, *income*, and *education*) to their most common values. To capture change in the job security variables, I set *individual job insecurity* to either 0 or 1 and *employment protection index* to either the level in Denmark, 0.74 (as shown in Table 3.5, this is a moderately low level of employment protection in our sample), or that of Germany, 1.41 (a moderately high level of employment protection in the sample). The estimates in Table 3.7 indicate that with individual job insecurity and a low level of employment protection the probability for a male insider to agree to pay taxes for employment promotion is 49 percent. When a male insider does not exhibit individual job insecurity and experiences a high level of employment protection the probability goes down to 45 percent. The results also indicate that the probability of disagreeing that the welfare state is too costly is 30 percent for a male insider with individual job insecurity and a low level of employment protection but does not change when there is no individual insecurity and a high level of employment protection.

The results in Table 3.7, therefore, support this chapter's claims regarding ALMP very strongly. Without individual job insecurity and enjoying high levels of employment protection, a male insider has a 45 percent probability of supporting ALMPs. When a male insider experiences individual job insecurity and low levels of employment protection, the likelihood goes up to a much more substantive 49 percent.[24] This is exactly what the insider–outsider model would lead us to expect.[25] The results, however, do not support the expectations when looking at PLMP preferences. The probability of supporting PLMP does not change for a male insider whether the measures of job security are high or low. The lack of confirmation of this chapter's hypotheses in this case may have to do with the nature of the question itself (as mentioned above, it is not ideal as a proxy for PLMP preferences).

Finally, Table 3.8 presents the effects of corporatism on active and passive labor market policy preferences. The goal of the analysis this time is to test whether the effects of corporatism on insider preferences

[24] The results in Table 3.7 make clear that this increase is mostly the result of employment protection changes at the macro level, rather than the effects of individual job insecurity.

[25] Using a different estimation model, these results are confirmed in Rueda (2006). In that analysis, I estimate logit random intercept multilevel maximum likelihood Restricted Iterative Generalized Least Squares (RIGLS) models and confirm my results with parametric and nonparametric bootstrapping models.

Table 3.8. The effects of corporatism on active and passive labor market policy preferences

	Active labor market policy preferences		Passive labor market policy preferences	
	Coefficients	Odds ratios	Coefficients	Odds ratios
Constant	**−.832*****	—	**−.870*****	—
	(.103)		(.109)	
	.000		.000	
Outsider status	**.252*****	1.286	**.096***	1.101
	(.053)		(.054)	
	.000		.077	
Insider status	**−.073**	.930	**−.053**	.948
	(.095)		(.102)	
	.444		.601	
Upscale group status	**−.070**	.933	**−.269*****	.764
	(.071)		(.075)	
	.322		.000	
Corporatism	**−.660*****	.517	**−.179****	.836
	(.069)		(.079)	
	.000		.023	
Insider status*corporatism	**.424*****	1.527	**.134**	1.143
	(.143)		(.151)	
	.003		.376	
Age	**.059****	1.061	**−.020**	.981
	(.023)		(.024)	
	.011		.416	
Gender	**−.080****	.923	**−.119*****	.888
	(.034)		(.035)	
	.018		.001	
Income	**.002**	1.002	**.010**	1.010
	(.011)		(.012)	
	.890		.402	
Education	**.134*****	1.144	**.082*****	1.086
	(.021)		(.022)	
	.000		.000	
N		16,176		
Number of countries		11		

Notes: Active labor market preferences measured as agreement in 'ready to pay more tax if devoted to creating new jobs' question. Passive labor market preferences measured as disagreement in 'welfare state costs too much' question.

All entries are from logit random intercept multilevel maximum likelihood estimation.

In the coefficient columns, numbers in bold are estimated coefficients; numbers in parentheses are standard errors; numbers in italics are p values from z tests.

The asterisks signify statistical significance in the usual manner (*** if p value $< .01$, ** if $< .05$, and * if $< .1$).

Data from Portugal and Spain are missing.

are economic or Olsonian. Do insiders become more like outsiders when corporatism is high or not? To answer this question I have introduced the measure of corporatism described in section 3.4 into the analysis (both as a direct effect and as an interaction with insider status).

The reader has already been reminded of the results in Tables 3.3 and 3.4; Table 3.8 shows the estimates obtained when introducing corporatism into the analysis. Insider status becomes insignificant when looking at both active and passive labor market policy preferences. As above, to interpret these effects we must now take into consideration the combined effects of the interaction variables. The estimates for corporatism, however, suggest that this is an important factor determining insider preferences in both the active and the passive models. The results suggest that the direct effects of corporatism are significant and negative in both models. This means that the willingness to pay tax to support employment promotion and the likelihood to disagree that the welfare state is too costly decrease as the levels of corporatism increase (in support of the economic insider–outsider interpretation regarding the effects of corporatist arrangements). The interaction terms are also significant, but only in the model for ALMP preferences.

Once again I calculate the probabilities associated to particular values of the explanatory variables to acquire a better impression of the effects of corporatism. In this case, I am interested in the change in the probability of supporting labor market policy associated with different levels of corporatism. As before, I set the variables to represent a male insider (with the most common values of the control variables). I then set the corporatism variable to the levels in France, 0.36 (as shown in Table 3.6, this is a moderately low level of corporatism in our sample), and then Germany, 0.76 (a moderately high level of corporatism in the sample). The estimates in Table 3.8 indicate that with a low level of corporatism the probability for a male insider to agree to pay taxes for employment promotion is 35 percent while with a high level of corporatism it is only 33 percent. As was the case in the analysis of job security, corporatism does not make a difference regarding preferences for PLMP. The results indicate that the probability to disagree that the welfare state is too costly is 31 percent for a male insider whether the level of corporatism is high or low.

The results in Table 3.8 provide a limited amount of support for an economic approach to the effects of corporatism regarding active and passive labor market policy. When corporatism is low, the probability of supporting ALMPs for a male insider is higher than when corporatism is high. Admittedly, it is not a large effect. It is, nevertheless, an effect more consistent with the economic insider–outsider interpretation of corporatism than with an Olsonian one. It is clearly not the case that insiders become more like outsiders when corporatism is high. The results also support these expectations when looking at PLMP preferences. The probability of supporting PLMP does not change for a male insider whether the measures of job security are high or low. This is again more understandable in the economic framework than in an Olsonian one. I hasten to add, however, that the nature of the question is (as mentioned above) not a good proxy for PLMP preferences.

4

The Relationship between Partisan Government and Policy: An Analysis of OECD Data

Chapter 3 has shown that the preferences of the insider–outsider model are accurate. Insiders care more about the levels of employment protection that they enjoy than about labor market policies that will benefit outsiders. Outsiders, on the other hand, have strong preferences about labor market policy, but are not concerned about the employment security of insiders. The analysis of survey data also showed that when employment protection levels decline, insiders do become more likely to share the preferences of outsiders. Corporatism, finally, emerged as a factor that also affected insider–outsider differences. In agreement with the economic insider–outsider expectations, corporatism seemed to insulate insiders from unemployment and to make their preferences more different from those of outsiders.

Once we know what insiders and outsiders want, we need to explore what parties do. My insider–outsider partisanship model is based on a set of individual-level assumptions that has received a significant amount of support from the analysis in Chapter 3. But this is only the first step. The second step involves analyzing whether parties respond to the preferences of their core constituencies when they get to power. The arguments presented in Chapter 2 have straightforward implications for our understanding of the relationship between government partisanship and policy. For reasons that should now be apparent, the insider–outsider model predicts the following partisan differences regarding policy: (*a*) partisanship will significantly affect pro-insider policies, as I expect social democratic governments to be associated with higher levels of employment protection; and (*b*) partisanship will not significantly affect pro-outsider policies (given the preferences of their core constituencies, neither social democratic nor conservative governments have an incentive to promote labor market policy).

The previous chapters have made clear that in the presence of insider–outsider conflict, social democratic governments will promote insider policies regardless of the consequences for outsiders. I have also argued, however, that there are factors that make the interests of insiders more similar to those of outsiders. I have focused on the effects of employment protection and corporatism. Part of this chapter is therefore dedicated to testing whether the relationship between government partisanship and policy is affected by these factors. In the following pages I will first analyze the dependent variables and their relationship to this book's hypotheses. Then I will introduce the explanatory variables. Finally, I will briefly explore some methodological issues relevant to the statistical analysis, present the results, and relate them to the model developed in previous chapters.

4.1. The Dependent Variables

Three goals guide the choice of dependent variables in this chapter's analysis: that they help distinguish whether governments favor insiders or outsiders, provide evidence that tests my model against other theoretical alternatives, and, ultimately, contribute to an explanation of macroeconomic outcomes in OECD countries since the early 1970s. The previous chapters have shown what policy outcomes the insider–outsider model implies. I therefore use three policy measures to test the hypotheses: employment protection legislation represents pro-insider policy; and ALMPs and PLMPs represent pro-outsider measures. These are important policies that greatly affect a nation's political economy. They are the subject of continuous political attention by the public and impact the strategies of parties, whether in government or not. Levels of employment protection, ALMP, or the welfare state also deeply influence economic outcomes in industrialized democracies. As such, they have received a significant amount of attention from scholars in comparative politics. In the following pages I demonstrate that the model proposed in this book is a better explanation of these policy outcomes than the existing alternatives in the literature.

While the differences between insiders and outsiders have been emphasized in the preceding chapters, I must note that the existence of two distinct groups within labor only affects the strategies of partisan governments when there is a conflict between insiders and outsiders. The coincidence of insider and outsider goals is possible in some policy areas. One such policy is demand management (a traditional Keynesian macroeconomic strategy for social democrats). Demand management policies surely pose less of a conflict between insider and outsider preferences. There is, however, an important literature showing the difficulties social democratic governments face when trying to develop Keynesian policies after the early 1970s. The challenges posed by rational expectations (Alesina 1989) and increasing levels of internationalization (Alt 1985) are often identified as the reasons for the end of the golden age of social democracy. In Boix's words, '(m)anaging demand has become a rather inane issue' (1998*a*: 2).

Accepting the relevance of these challenges, however, still leaves some options open to social democratic governments. Employment protection and labor market policies can be used by partisan governments to promote employment, growth, and equality in an environment that impedes demand management. In a context characterized by openness and capital mobility, producing a satisfactory political explanation for these policies, therefore, becomes an even more important challenge.

4.1.1. *Employment Protection*

Employment protection legislation covers measures affecting dismissals, lay-offs, severance payments, notice periods, administrative authorization, and union consultation rights (OECD 1994). The model developed in Chapter 2 made clear that lowering employment protection directly attacks the interests of insiders. For outsiders, however, lower insider employment protection means a higher likelihood of exiting unemployment and precarious employment. For the members of the upscale groups, employment protection is a limitation to market forces and to their autonomy as employers. Because insiders and upscale groups have opposing interests (as shown in Chapter 3) and they are the core constituencies of social democratic and conservative governments, the insider–outsider model implies the existence of marked partisan differences regarding job protection.

As was the case for the multilevel analysis in Chapter 3, I use a variable provided in Baker et al. (2004). I remind readers that the data were created by joining together several series: an original one from Lazear (1990), an update using OECD data from Blanchard and Wolfers (2000), and a further update and interpolation from Nickell and Nunziata (2000).[1] Lazear's index measures the severance pay and advance notice a blue-collar worker with ten years of service receives upon termination without cause. Cause is illustratively explained by Lazear as generally meaning 'for reasons having to do with the worker's own shortcomings, and it must be extreme. A reading of the rules suggests that in most countries, dismissal with cause requires the kind of evidence necessary to with-draw an American academic's tenure' (1990: 708). The OECD index is constructed by averaging the scores obtained by each country in three categories: 'procedural inconveniences which the employer faces when trying to dismiss employees; notice and severance pay provisions; and prevailing standards of and penalties for unfair dismissal' (OECD 1999: 54). Conceptually, the overall strictness of protection against dismissal is an ideal dependent variable with which to test my hypothesis. This measure, however, suffers from the unfortunate practical limitation of being available only as a summary value for the 1980s and the 1990s. The transformations and updates from Blanchard and Wolfers (2000) and Nickell and Nunziata (2000) make the OECD index into a yearly variable which allows for a significant increase in the number of observations as well as in the complexity of the estimated models.[2]

Table 4.1 shows the employment protection levels for all the countries in this chapter's analysis from 1970 to 1995. As the table points out, the variable ranges from 0 to 2, where higher values mean stricter employ-ment protection. Table 4.1 makes clear two things: the great degree of cross-national variation in employment protection levels and the exist-ence of a diversity of temporal patterns throughout the 1970–95 period.

In terms of the variation across countries, there are three distinct groups in the sample. The first group, comprising mostly the liberal market economies, has the lowest levels of employment protection. The USA (0.1 throughout the period) is the country where the smallest amount of protection is provided. It is followed closely by Canada (0.3 throughout the period) and by the UK (which starts out with an index equal to 0.24 in 1970 and then experiences a relative increase to 0.35 for the rest of the period). Australia and Switzerland can also be included in this group, with still quite low employment protection (0.5 and 0.55, respectively) for the whole period under analysis. A second group with intermediate

---

[1] For an analysis of the close relationship between severance pay and overall employment protection, see OECD (1994).

[2] The OECD data, used from 1985 onward, is constructed on the basis of a more extensive collection of employment protection dimensions.

Table 4.1. Employment protection in industrialized democracies, 1970–95

Country	1970	1975	1980	1985	1990	1995
Australia	0.5	0.5	0.5	0.5	0.5	0.5
Austria	0.65	0.78	1.13	1.3	1.3	1.3
Belgium	1.37	1.55	1.55	1.55	1.41	1.19
Canada	0.3	0.3	0.3	0.3	0.3	0.3
Denmark	1.02	1.1	1.1	1.1	0.97	0.74
Finland	1.2	1.2	1.2	1.2	1.15	1.08
France	0.8	1.17	1.3	1.3	1.38	1.5
Germany	1.28	1.65	1.65	1.65	1.56	1.41
Italy	2	2	2	2	1.94	1.78
Japan	1.4	1.4	1.4	1.4	1.4	1.4
Netherlands	1.35	1.35	1.35	1.35	1.3	1.23
Norway	1.55	1.55	1.55	1.55	1.49	1.39
Sweden	0.36	1.32	1.8	1.8	1.62	1.32
Switzerland	0.55	0.55	0.55	0.55	0.55	0.55
UK	0.24	0.33	0.35	0.35	0.35	0.35
USA	0.1	0.1	0.1	0.1	0.1	0.1

Notes: Employment protection is measured as an index ranging from 0 to 2, higher values mean more employment protection.

Source: Baker et al. (2004).

levels of employment protection can be identified. It contains Austria, Denmark, Finland, France, and the Netherlands. In this group, Denmark has a relatively low level of employment protection throughout the period (around 1 or 1.1) while Finland (around 1.2), Austria (1.3 after 1980), and the Netherlands (around 1.35 for most of the period) have slightly higher levels. France has a highly variable level of employment protection (from 0.8 in 1970 to 1.3 in 1980 and 1.5 in 1995) and it moves from a moderately low index to quite a high one. The final group comprises those countries with the highest employment protection in our sample: Belgium, Germany, Italy, Japan, Norway, and Sweden. The averages for the period are around 1.5 for Belgium, Germany, and Norway. Japan's index is a little lower (1.4) and Italy's is much higher (this is the country with the highest level of employment protection, around 2 for most of the period). Sweden is a special case in this group. Although generally a country with high levels of employment protection, the variation through time is quite dramatic.

The levels of employment protection are very stable in some countries. The index does not vary in Australia, Canada, Japan, Switzerland, and the USA. There are, however, some considerable changes through time in most of the countries. Austria and the UK experience a pattern in which employment protection levels increase in the 1970s and then remain stable from 1980 until 1995. The pattern for Belgium, Denmark, Germany, and Sweden, on the other hand, is one in which protection increases in the 1970s, remains stable in the 1980s, and then decreases in the 1990s. In Finland, Italy, the Netherlands, and Norway, the index remains stable throughout the 1970s and 1980s and then declines in the 1990s. Finally, the table suggests that in France employment protection experiences a pretty stable increase throughout the period.

4.1.2. Labor Market Policies

The previous chapters have explained why labor market policies are considered to represent the interests of outsiders in this book's model. ALMPs are aimed at reducing unemployment by shaping the supply, demand, and mobility of labor while PLMPs provide unemployment compensation.

I argued in Chapter 2 that several factors make ALMPs an ideal policy for analyzing the insider–outsider partisanship model: they are unambiguously pro-outsider, since they are aimed at the creation of employment; they can reflect partisan differences in an unambiguous fashion, since they can receive a significant amount of resources or be mostly ignored by governments; and they are widely believed by policymakers to be an effective tool against unemployment.

Unlike the abundant literature on demand management or the welfare state, the politics that determine ALMPs have not received enough attention in the political science literature.[3] Theoretically, the starting point for most authors is to consider ALMPs one more measure that social democratic parties will employ to benefit labor.[4] But the empirical tests of whether this is in fact the case suffer from real limitations. Most analyses rely on a very limited number of observations—Boix's regressions, for example, range from 18 to 21 observations (1998a: 75–9) and Janoski's from 36 to 38 (1994: 70–8). This severely limits the possibility of systematically testing alternative hypotheses while simultaneously controlling for other relevant factors (these regressions typically have no more than three variables), which in turn introduces great caveats into the significance of the results. Others do not systematically assess the validity of their claims

---

[3] Notable exceptions are Janoski (1990, 1994), Garrett and Lange (1991), Boix (1998a), Swank and Martin (2001), Martin and Swank (2004), and Rueda (2005, 2006).

[4] This is the case in Janoski (1990, 1994), Garrett and Lange (1991), Boix (1998a), Swank and Martin (2001), and Martin and Swank (2004).

across countries and through time, which limits the generalizability of their conclusions.[5]

In this book's model, outsiders are considered the beneficiaries of ALMPs. As explained in more detail in previous chapters, insiders, on the other hand, pay the costs of these policies (through taxation) but do not benefit from them, since they are significantly protected from unemployment. In addition, ALMPs are designed to promote entry into the labor market of outsiders who will underbid insiders' wage demands. Since insiders are the core constituency of social democratic parties, my argument implies the absence of any government partisanship effects on ALMPs (neither social democrats nor conservatives have incentives to promote them).

ALMPs are generally defined as those labor market policies directed to training and rehabilitation; information, counseling, and financial support to find a job; and government job creation.[6] The OECD data used in the statistical analysis encompasses the following five areas: (*a*) public employment services and administration, (*b*) labor market training, (*c*) youth measures, (*d*) subsidized employment, and (*e*) measures for the disabled.[7] Table 4.2 shows the levels of ALMP (measured as a percentage of GDP) in the countries included in this chapter's analysis.

As was the case with Table 4.1, Table 4.2 reflects a high degree of cross-national and temporal variation in our sample. Examining the existing cross-national diversity in more detail, we can place countries into three general groups with low, intermediate, and high levels of ALMPs. The largest group is the one characterized by low levels of ALMPs. Australia, Austria, Canada, Italy, Japan, Switzerland, the UK, and the USA all belong to this group. All these countries dedicate less than 1 percent of GDP to ALMPs, some of them significantly less. Within this group, Australia, Austria, Italy, Japan, Switzerland, and the USA have an average from 1980 to 2000 that is significantly less than 0.5 percent of GDP dedicated to ALMPs. Canada and the UK are only slightly higher, with averages that do not reach 0.75 percent of GDP. The second group is a small one, with countries whose intermediate levels of ALMP hover around the 1 percent of GDP mark. Finland and Norway are in this group (in both countries, however, 1995 represents a spike in the pattern with higher levels than in the

---

[5] This applies to Janoski's country-specific treatment of the determinants of ALMPs (1990, 1994).

[6] See, among others, Wilensky and Turner (1987); Jackman, Pissarides, and Savouri (1990); Janoski (1990, 1994).

[7] See the OECD's *Employment Outlook* for details.

Table 4.2. Active labor market policy in industrialized democracies, 1980–2000

Country	1980	1985	1990	1995	2000
Australia	0	0.41	0.25	0.81	0.46
Austria	—	0.27	0.3	0.36	0.5
Belgium	—	1.31	1.21	1.37	1.31
Canada	0.29	0.65	0.53	0.57	0.41
Denmark	0.43	0.85	1.09	1.88	1.58
Finland	0.99	0.91	0.99	1.54	1
France	0	0.66	0.81	1.29	1.31
Germany	—	0.7	1.09	1.26	1.16
Italy	—	—	0.24	0.18	0.5
Japan	—	—	0.31	0.31	0.29
Netherlands	0.58	1.01	1.09	1.11	1.47
Norway	—	0.61	0.92	1.33	0.74
Sweden	1.21	2.12	1.67	2.23	1.31
Switzerland	0.07	0.19	0.23	0.49	0.37
UK	0.56	0.73	0.59	0.44	0.36
USA	0.16	0.12	0.22	0.2	0.15

Notes: ALMPs are measured as a percentage of GDP.

Source: Armingeon et al. (2005).

rest of the period). The high ALMP group comprises Belgium, Denmark, France, Germany, the Netherlands, and Sweden. Although there is a high degree of variation throughout the period for some of these countries, the averages for the members of this group tend to approach 1.2 percent of GDP (in some cases, the level is much higher). Two countries are unusual in this group: Sweden and France. Sweden is a case that is difficult to put together with any other because of its uncommonly high levels of ALMPs. ALMP consistently receives more resources in Sweden than anywhere else (in 1985 2.12 percent of GDP was dedicated to ALMPs while in 1995 it was 2.23 percent). France is unusual because of the increase experienced in the period under analysis. While in 1980 and 1985 only 0 percent and 0.66 percent of France's GDP was dedicated to ALMPs, by 2000 it had reached 1.31 percent.

Turning now to temporal variation within the countries in the sample, several interesting patterns emerge from the numbers in Table 4.2. Reflecting the increasing importance of these policies in industrialized democracies, a number of countries in the table have experienced a systematic rise in the resources dedicated to ALMPs. Austria, France, and the Netherlands are the best examples of this pattern. But Denmark, Germany, Norway, and Switzerland are also in this group (with increases up to 1995). The countries with either stable or no clear pattern in ALMPs are Australia, Belgium, Finland, Italy, Japan, Sweden, and the USA. No country experiences a systematic decrease, although the UK is the exception that comes closest (there is growth from 1980 to 1985, and steady decline since then).

The second and complementary side to the labor market analysis emphasized PLMPs as the goal of outsiders. PLMPs have received a remarkable amount of attention in the comparative political economy literature. My insider–outsider partisanship model goes against the grain of much of the traditional literature arguing for the association of social democracy and the welfare state. When analyzing the last thirty years, I do not share the assumptions of many political scientists exploring the political determinants of the welfare state. The implications of the insider–outsider partisanship model regarding PLMPs are not different from those relating to ALMPs. Outsiders are considered the main beneficiaries of PLMPs. Before the widespread adoption of employment protection in the early 1970s, the interests of insiders and outsiders regarding labor market policy were closely aligned. Insider vulnerability to unemployment was higher and social democratic governments could promote labor market policies that favored outsiders. The emergence of employment protection caused the interests of insiders and outsiders to diverge. As PLMPs increasingly became policies that insiders pay the costs of while outsiders receive the benefits from, social democratic governments become less likely to promote them and partisanship becomes insignificant.

The variable used to capture PLMPs in this chapter's analysis measures total public social expenditure as a percentage of GDP. The data come from the OECD, and the measure is described as follows: '(s)ocial expenditure is the provision by public (and private) institutions of benefits to, and financial contributions targeted at, households and individuals in order to provide support during circumstances which adversely affect their welfare' (OECD 2004). These figures for social expenditure mainly include social benefits for old age, survivors, incapacity, health, family support, ALMP, unemployment, and housing.[8] It is important to point out that this is a very encompassing measure of social policy. Rather than only looking at unemployment benefits, I capture a wide range of social policies provided to individuals when their employment income does not support them.[9] I would like to point out, however, that all the results to be analyzed in the sections below are confirmed when I use a more restrictive measure of PLMPs including only unemployment benefits.

---

[8] A few other minor policies fall under the OECD definition of social expenditure. See OECD (2004) for details.

[9] This includes ALMPs, although they are a small proportion of the total.

Table 4.3. Passive labor market policy in industrialized democracies, 1980–2000

Country	1980	1985	1990	1995	2000
Australia	11.32	13.48	14.22	17.83	18.56
Austria	22.46	24.1	24.1	26.64	26.02
Belgium	24.13	26.91	26.92	28.07	26.71
Canada	14.32	17.45	18.61	19.62	17.33
Denmark	29.06	27.87	29.32	32.4	28.89
Finland	18.53	23	24.75	31.1	24.5
France	21.14	26.62	26.61	29.24	28.34
Germany	22.98	23.62	22.8	27.46	27.17
Italy	18.42	21.27	23.26	23.02	24.07
Japan	10.19	11.03	11.2	13.5	16.13
Netherlands	26.95	27.32	27.65	25.58	21.77
Norway	17.91	19.1	24.68	25.98	23
Sweden	28.83	29.96	30.78	32.96	28.6
Switzerland	14.17	15.14	17.92	23.88	25.4
UK	17.93	21.1	19.55	23.01	21.69
USA	13.26	12.96	13.43	15.45	14.24

Notes: PLMPs are measured as a percentage of GDP.

Source: Armingeon et al. (2005).

Table 4.3 shows the levels of PLMP (measured as a percentage of GDP) in all countries. The high degree of cross-national variation in the table is best illustrated by dividing the countries into three groups, as I did when describing the levels of employment protection and ALMP. Australia, Canada, Japan, and the USA all belong to the group characterized by low levels of PLMP. All these countries dedicate less than 20 percent of GDP to social policy. Japan is the country with the lowest levels of PLMP in our sample (around 10 percent of GDP from 1980 to 1990 and around 15 percent in 1995 and 2000). Within this group, Canada dedicates the highest level of resources to social policy, with an average of around 17 percent of GDP for the entire period. The second group is characterized by intermediate levels of PLMPs. Austria, Italy, Norway, Switzerland, and the UK are in this group. The average levels of PLMPs in all these countries fluctuate around the low 20s as a percentage of GDP. Although Norway, Switzerland, and the UK start the period with low levels that are more similar to the previous group, they experience intermediate levels of PLMPs in more recent years. The high PLMP group comprises Belgium, Denmark, Finland, France, Germany, the Netherlands, and Sweden. Although there is a high degree of variation throughout the period for some of these countries, the averages for this group tend to fluctuate around the high 20s as a percentage of GDP. Sweden is the country with the highest levels of PLMPs (passing the 30 percent mark in 1990 and 1995), but countries like Denmark and Finland are not that far behind. It is also the case that France, Finland, and Germany start the period with much lower levels of PLMPs and only join this group in the more recent years.

In terms of temporal variation, several patterns are present in the data in Table 4.3. There is first a group of countries that experience relatively steady growth in social policy. Australia, Austria, Germany, Italy, the Netherlands, and Switzerland are all countries whose levels of PLMP increase more or less continuously throughout the period. Then there is a second group characterized by increases in the levels of social policy from 1980 to 1995, but decline in the year 2000. Belgium, Canada, Finland, France, the Netherlands, Norway, and Sweden all fit this pattern of growth and decline in the resources dedicated to PLMP. The only exception in this group is the Netherlands, since the decline started in 1995 rather than 2000 in this country. There is finally a group defined by the lack of a clear temporal pattern. The evolution of social policy in Denmark, the UK, and the USA throughout this period does not seem to follow a particular temporal design (with increases and decreases in several years of the series).

4.2. Explanatory Variables

The previous paragraphs have illustrated the high degree of cross-national and temporal variation that the dependent variables in this chapter's analysis display. It is my contention that the insider–outsider model will be a significant contribution to the explanation of all this variation. I emphasize the direct effects (or absence thereof) of government partisanship as a determinant of policy and the intermediating effects of employment protection and corporatism.

4.2.1. *Government Partisanship*

Very little needs to be said at this point about the theorized influence of government partisanship on employment protection and labor market policy. But some attention should be paid to the operationalization of partisanship.

The government partisanship measure used in my analysis attempts to capture the ideological position of governments in relation to a left-right continuum. Two variables are needed for the construction of this kind of measure: one that reflects the presence of parties in government and another that measures their ideological characteristics. There are, however, important questions surrounding the quantification of both these factors. There is first the issue of how to measure the influence of parties in government.[10] One option is to take into consideration the proportion of cabinet seats that all parties in government possess. But once a party is in government, the support it enjoys may be influenced not only by its position in the cabinet but also by the degree of support it has in parliament. Numerous authors have found evidence supporting that a government's behavior will be influenced by its share of seats in parliament (see e.g. Müller and Strøm 2000). As argued by Garrett, the balance of power in cabinet governments delineates the direct control of parties over policy while the balance of power in parliament captures the broader political constraints facing the government (1998: 59).

Regarding the second factor influencing government partisanship, the measurement of party ideological positions is not straightforward either. Assessments of left-right party positions are mainly based on two different measures: the analysis of expert opinions and of party manifestos. These two measures imply a different set of complications. Expert opinions are produced from surveys that are administered rarely and therefore do not reflect changes through time. In addition, questions may be interpreted differently in different national contexts (Gabel and Huber 2000). Data extracted from party manifestos, on the other hand, can be criticized for being a reflection of what parties say to win elections, and not necessarily of what they will do once they have won them. This is a particularly relevant problem for the analysis in this chapter. Social democratic parties, for example, may not wish to emphasize in their election manifestos their intentions not to increase ALMP levels to prevent critics from describing them as unconcerned about unemployment (even if this is what they will do to satisfy insiders).

No choice is therefore free of costs. I follow much of the comparative political economy literature and use a measure of the percentage of cabinet seats held by social democratic and other Left parties (see Armingeon et al. 2005).[11] This variable captures the influence of Left parties in power as a function of their presence in the cabinet. Not factoring in the degree of support enjoyed in parliament is not problematic since, as shown

---

[10] See Huber and Powell (1994) for a more detailed analysis of some of the options.

[11] Regarding partisan options to the Left of the social democrats, some communist parties are included in this measure. But the government participation of communist parties in the sample that I analyze is limited enough not to affect the conclusions made about the influence of partisanship over policy.

by Powell, governments tend to 'apportion their cabinet portfolios to parties in simple proportion to the relative percentage of seats held by each in the lower house of the legislature' (2000: 173, see also Laver and Schofield 1990). Ideology in this case is assigned in a simple fashion, a party is either considered to be Leftist or not.[12] In most cases, this is a straightforward endeavor (in the UK, for example, Labor is Leftist). In others, it is not so simple. In Belgium, for example, five parties are categorized as belonging to the Left: *Belgische Socialistische Partij* (BSP, Flemish), *Kommunistische Partij van Belgie* (KPB), *Parti Socialiste Belge* (PSB, Francophone), *Agalev*, and *Ecolo*. In two of our countries, moreover, no party is considered to be Leftist enough to fall into this category. Since neither the Liberal Party in Canada nor the Democratic Party in the USA are considered to belong to the Left, this variable is always 0 in these two countries.[13]

Elsewhere, I have used other variables to measure government partisan-ship. In Rueda (2005, 2006), government partisanship is captured by two different variables. The first is an index of the cabinet ideological center of gravity that uses expert opinions to measure ideology (see Cusack 1997 for details). The second one uses party manifestos to assess a party's left-right position. I will refer to these alternative results to confirm this chapter's findings.

Table 4.4 presents the levels of Left government in the countries (from 1970 to 2000) included in this analysis. As the table shows, the presence of social democratic government is highly variable depending on the country. Some countries are unmistakably characterized by very low levels of Left government. Of course the USA and Canada, since they are not considered to have a Left party, belong to this group. But so do Japan and Switzerland (in Japan the Left is a marginal portion of the cabinet only in 1995, while in Switzerland it constitutes only 29% of the cabinet throughout the entire period). There is then a group with intermediate levels of social democratic government (hovering around the 50% mark). Belgium and Finland belong to this group. A third group with generally high levels of Left government comprises Australia, Austria, and Sweden. Although there is some temporal fluctuation (especially in Austria, where Left government experiences a marked decline starting in 1990), in these three countries the social democratic presence in cabinets is higher than 80 percent for most of the period. There is finally a large group that

---

[12] The classification of parties is done following Schmidt (1996).
[13] See Armingeon et al. (2005) for details.

Table 4.4. Left government in industrialized democracies, 1970–2000

Country	1970	1975	1980	1985	1990	1995	2000
Australia	0	86.3	0	100	100	100	0
Austria	64.24	85.71	100	80	46.68	50	4.29
Belgium	40.74	0	43.43	0	47.37	53.33	53.33
Canada	0	0	0	0	0	0	0
Denmark	0	88.22	100	0	0	75	79.89
Finland	47.66	31.22	47.06	47.06	44.96	40.03	50
France	0	0	0	95.65	66.67	0	100
Germany	75	75	75.22	0	0	0	100
Italy	26.53	0	29.02	30	37.5	0	48.65
Japan	0	0	0	0	0	28.57	0
Netherlands	0	56.25	0	0	50	35.71	40
Norway	0	100	100	0	16.16	100	79.24
Sweden	100	100	0	100	100	100	100
Switzerland	28.57	28.57	28.57	28.57	28.57	28.57	28.57
UK	46.58	100	0	0	0	0	100
USA	0	0	0	0	0	0	0

Notes: Left government measured as percentage of Left parties in total cabinet posts, weighted by days.
Source: Armingeon et al. (2005).

displays too high a degree of variability to be easily classified. Denmark, France, Germany, Italy, the Netherlands, Norway, and the UK fall into this group. In Denmark, France, Germany, Norway, and the UK, the levels of Left government go from very low (often 0) to very high (often 100) depending on the election. In Italy and Netherlands, on the other hand, the levels only fluctuate between low and intermediate.

It is clear that a high degree of temporal variation is present in our sample. Unlike Tables 4.1 to 4.3, however, it is difficult to find patterns when looking at the levels of Left government. There are countries that display a considerable amount of stability. This is certainly the case in Canada, Japan, Switzerland, and the USA at the low level, and Finland and Sweden at the intermediate and high levels of Left government. But the cabinet participation of social democratic parties in other countries seems dependent on the results of particular elections and not necessarily subject to temporal trends.

4.2.2. Employment Protection

As I have explained in previous chapters, the differences between insiders and outsiders (and the influence over social democratic parties) can be either mitigated or exacerbated by the levels of employment protection insiders enjoy. When insiders lose their insulation to unemployment and become more like outsiders, social democratic parties will be more likely to promote labor market policies.

Employment protection was one of the three policies explained in the dependent variable section. Now, it also becomes an explanatory variable. The analysis below is developed in two steps. First, I explore the influence of government partisanship on pro-insider (employment protection) and pro-outsider policies (ALMPs and PLMPs). Secondly, I analyze the intermediating effects of existing levels of employment protection and corporatism on the relationship between government partisanship and labor market policy. In its role as a dependent variable, the employment protection measure used in this analysis was described in detail. I refer readers to Table 4.1 and the discussion that accompanied it.

4.2.3. Corporatism

While employment protection has a straightforward effect on insider vulnerability to unemployment, corporatism is a more ambiguous factor. What I have called the economic insider–outsider framework emphasizes the role of corporatism as a set of institutional arrangements that protect the interests of insiders. The Olsonian interpretation of corporatism, on the other hand, emphasizes the effects of institutional encompassment. In this view, corporatist arrangements are believed to facilitate the consideration of outsider interests by insiders and, therefore, social democratic parties. These alternative interpretations imply different predictions about the influence of government partisanship on policy. The economic insider–outsider view would lead us to expect higher levels of social democratic government to be associated with more resources dedicated to labor market policy only when corporatism is low (and the influence of insiders is, therefore, minimized). The Olsonian view implies exactly the opposite. Higher levels of social democratic government should be associated with more resources dedicated to labor market policy only when corporatism is high (and insiders are, therefore, less likely to free ride).

My conceptualization of corporatism is influenced by Katzenstein (1985), Traxler (1999), and Kenworthy (2003). In the words of Kenworthy,

corporatism consists of various types of institutional arrangements whereby important political-economic decisions are reached via negotiation between or in consultation with peak-level representatives of employees and employers (and/or other interest groups and the state). (Kenworthy 2003: 11)

Table 4.5. Corporatism in industrialized democracies, 1970–94

Country	1970	1975	1980	1985	1990	1994
Australia	0.27	0.2	0.13	0.2	0.2	0.13
Austria	0.96	0.96	0.96	0.96	0.96	0.96
Belgium	0.8	0.66	0.66	0.66	0.66	0.66
Canada	0.17	0.1	0.03	0.03	0.03	0.03
Denmark	0.83	0.76	0.76	0.76	0.61	0.61
Finland	0.9	0.9	0.83	0.9	0.9	0.83
France	0.5	0.43	0.43	0.36	0.36	0.36
Germany	0.84	0.84	0.84	0.76	0.76	0.76
Italy	0.4	0.4	0.47	0.4	0.4	0.4
Japan	0.73	0.73	0.8	0.8	0.8	0.8
Netherlands	0.74	0.67	0.6	0.53	0.53	0.53
Norway	0.99	0.99	0.99	0.99	0.92	0.92
Sweden	0.99	0.99	0.99	0.99	0.85	0.78
Switzerland	0.55	0.55	0.55	0.55	0.55	0.55
UK	0.21	0.28	0.07	0.07	0.07	0.07
USA	0.15	0.08	0.01	0.01	0.01	0.01

Notes: Corporatism is measured as an index ranging from 0 to 1.
Source: Hicks and Kenworthy (1998).

As was mentioned in Chapter 3, the measure for corporatism used in this book encapsulates a number of economic characteristics: the centralization and coordination of unions, business, and wage-setting; the cooperation between government and interest groups; the existence of tripartite organizations, the degree of cooperation among economic actors, etc. (see Hicks and Kenworthy 1998 for details). The variable ranges from 0 to 1 (where higher values mean more corporatism) and reflects a continuum across countries and through time. There are two important advantages to this corporatism measure. First, it is not a dichotomous variable and it allows for a great degree of variation among countries. Second, while other measures of corporatism are country-specific, this does vary through time. This within-country temporal variation is optimal for my analysis, since I am interested in how the changing characteristics of corporatism constrain the actions of social democratic government.

Table 4.5 provides the levels of corporatism for all countries included in this chapter's analysis from 1970 to 1994.[14] Three differentiated clusters can be identified: a low corporatism group (levels under 0.3), an intermediate one (levels between 0.3 and 0.7), and a high one (levels over 0.7). Australia, Canada, the UK, and the USA belong to the first group. The USA, Canada, and the UK are the countries with the lowest levels of corporatism in this group (starting in 1980, it is 0.01 in the USA, 0.03 in

[14] The data are available only until 1994.

Canada, and 0.07 in the UK). Australia reaches the highest level in this group (0.2). In the intermediate group, we can include Belgium, France, Italy, the Netherlands, and Switzerland. France, Italy, and Switzerland have relatively stable levels that always stay within the boundaries I have set for intermediate corporatism. Belgium and the Netherlands, however, have higher levels in 1970 and then fall into the intermediate level for the rest of the period. There are seven countries in the last group. Austria, Denmark, Finland, Germany, Japan, Norway, and Sweden all have high levels of corporatism. Sweden, Norway, and Austria (0.99, 0.99, and 0.96, respectively, for most of the period) have the highest levels in the sample. Denmark and Germany, on the other hand, have the lowest levels in this group. In fact, Denmark, with a level of 0.76 from 1975 to 1985, falls into the intermediate group starting in 1990 (with a level of 0.61).

The table also makes clear that corporatism has decreased substantially in most of the countries. Corporatism experiences a decline in Belgium, Canada, Denmark, France, Germany, the Netherlands, Sweden, the UK, and the USA. It also experiences a general decline with a slight recovery in Australia (the recovery takes place in 1985 and 1990). Although corporatism remains relatively stable in five countries (Austria, Finland, Italy, Norway, and Switzerland) it can only be said to increase in one (Japan, from 1975 to 1980).

4.2.4. *Other Explanatory Variables*

4.2.4.1. LABOR MARKET INSTITUTIONS

As I explained in more detail in Chapter 2, the behavior of unions is a relevant factor in a government's policy orientation. I expect pressure from unions to make either pro-insider or pro-outsider policies more likely. I use corporatism as an aggregate index of the characteristics of a labor market in the interaction analysis of the factors that can affect the relationship between government partisanship and policy (see details below). For the direct analysis of the influence of partisanship on policy, I use two additional measures: wage bargaining coordination and union density.[15]

The measure used in my analysis to capture wage bargaining coordination is provided by Kenworthy (2001). It ranges from 1 to 5, with higher

[15] This is a practical decision. Ideally, I would include corporatism in these analyses as well. But the data for wage bargaining coordination and union density is more extensive (corporatism data are only available until 1994).

values representing more coordination.[16] The union density measure is provided by Golden, Wallerstein and Lange (2006). It represents employed union members as a percentage of employed labor force.

4.2.4.2. TRADE AND FINANCIAL OPENNESS

There are two opposing accounts of the effects of internationalization on partisan politics. There is first a large literature suggesting that growing levels of trade and financial openness diminish the ability of social democratic parties to produce Leftist policy and therefore weaken partisan differences.[17] Then there are some authors who argue either that international forces do not affect some partisan differences (like Garrett and Lange 1991; Boix 1998a) or that they actually have strengthened the influence of partisanship on policies and economic outcomes (Garrett 1998). The results presented in the following pages do not address whether international dependence limits the autonomy of governments. Rather, they look at the great variance in policy within the sample and try to assess the factors that are responsible for it. I expect that, once the influence of internationalization is controlled for, insider–outsider differences will account for whether partisanship affects policy or not.

Trade openness is measured as imports plus exports as percentage of GDP (European Commission 2006). Financial openness, or lack thereof, is measured as the absence, or existence, of capital account restrictions (Prasad et al. 2003).

4.2.4.3. GOVERNMENT DEFICIT

Deficits are introduced into the analysis as a measure of the limitations a government faces when deciding policy strategies. The general argument

---

[16] Kenworthy (2001: 79) explains the coordination scores for different wage bargaining arrangements as follows: 1, fragmented wage bargaining, confined largely to individual firms or plants; 2, mixed industry- and firm-level bargaining, with little or no pattern setting, and relatively weak elements of government coordination such as setting of basic pay rate or wage indexation; 3, industry-level bargaining with somewhat irregular and uncertain pattern setting and only moderate union concentration, government wage arbitration; 4, centralized bargaining by peak confederation(s) or government imposition of a wage schedule/freeze, without a peace obligation, informal centralization of industry- and firm-level bargaining by peak associations, extensive, regularized pattern setting coupled with a high degree of union concentration; and 5, centralized bargaining by peak confederation(s) or government imposition of a wage schedule/freeze, with a peace obligation, informal centralization of industry-level bargaining by a powerful, monopolistic union confederation, extensive, regularized pattern setting, and highly synchronized bargaining coupled with coordination of bargaining by influential large firms.

[17] See e.g. Scharpf (1991); Kurzer (1993); Moses (1994); Iversen (1996); Scharpf and Schmidt (2000).

is that governments with higher deficits have fewer resources at their disposal and therefore would encounter more difficulties when trying to expand their spending. One widely accepted interpretation of the policy changes of the early 1980s, for example, is that many governments had reached unsustainable levels of public debt (see Schwartz 1994, among others). I use a variable measuring annual deficits as a percentage of GDP (Armingeon et al. 2005). I include this measure only in the regressions with labor market policy as the dependent variable (since any relationship between resource limitations and legislation affecting employment seems unlikely).

4.2.4.4. UNEMPLOYMENT

Some authors have argued that policy levels simply respond to increasing needs (whether demographic, economic, or other).[18] I engage these arguments, at least partially, by controlling for the effects of unemployment. It is important for the validity of my conclusions that the results of the influence of partisanship over policy are not affected by increasing needs. We want to be able to conclude, for example, that social democratic governments do not promote higher levels of ALMPs regardless of the size of unemployment. The unemployment rate also acts as a partial proxy for the number of outsiders in an economy. It is essential that the results control for the size of the outsider group, since the insider–outsider partisanship model maintains that social democratic governments will appeal to insiders even when outsiders are numerous. I use the Eurostat definition of unemployment (European Commission 2006).

4.2.4.5. GDP GROWTH

Most analyses of economic policy include a measure of economic growth. This is particularly relevant because it is important to control for the effects of growth on the policy decisions of partisan governments. I use a variable measuring real growth of GDP as percentage change from previous year (European Commission 2006).

4.3. Methodology and Results

I use annual data from 16 industrialized democracies and present OLS results. The countries are Australia, Austria, Belgium, Canada, Denmark,

---

[18] See e.g. Wilensky (1975).

Finland, France, Germany, Italy, Japan, the Netherlands, Norway, Sweden, Switzerland, the UK, and the USA. The countries for which the data are available depend on the dependent variable. For the analysis of the determinants of employment protection, the time period available extends from 1970 to 1998 (except for Switzerland, where employment protection is only available from 1991). For the analysis of the determinants of ALMP, we have data for a more reduced time series. For most countries the data are available from 1980 to 1998. For Belgium, Germany, and Norway, however, they are only available starting in 1985; for Austria, Italy, and Japan, only from 1990 to 1998 (Switzerland is again an exception since the series starts in 1991). The availability for the last dependent variable, social policy, is slightly better. All countries provide data from 1980 to 1998 (except Norway, 1988–98, and Switzerland, 1991–8).

The pooled time-series cross-sectional nature of the data significantly increases the number of observations and therefore allows the testing of more complex causal models. There are, however, some complications. The first one has to do with the dynamic nature of the data. Beck, among others, has pointed out that '(m)odern time-series analysts model the dynamics directly as part of the specification' (Beck 2001: 279). One of the most convenient ways to do this is to estimate a single equation error correction model. The estimation of an error correction model is appropriate when we are interested in the rate at which the dependent variable returns to equilibrium in response to changes in the explanatory variables. There are two important advantages to error correction models: (*a*) they allow us to estimate the short- and long-term effects of the explanatory variables, and (*b*) they are a solution to issues of nonstationarity in pooled time-series cross-sectional data (see Beck and Katz 1996; Beck 2001).[19]

To estimate an error correction model, I take first differences of the dependent and the explanatory variable of interest (government partisanship). The specification adopted in the empirical analysis is as follows:

$$\Delta\text{POLICY}_{it} = \beta_0 + \beta_1 \text{POLICY}_{it-1} + \beta_2 \Delta\text{PARTISANSHIP}_{it}$$
$$+ \beta_3 \text{PARTISANSHIP}_{it-1} + \beta_4 X_{1it} + \ldots + \beta_n X_{nit} + \varepsilon_{it}$$

where *i* and *t* refer to the particular countries and years, β_0 represents a general intercept, POLICY is the dependent variable (and the explanatory lagged dependent variable), PARTISANSHIP is the explanatory variable of interest (introduced into the model as first difference and as a lag), and

---

[19] For two applications of error correction models similar to the one in this chapter, see Iversen and Cusack (2000) and Keele (2007).

X_1 to X_n are the other explanatory variables, β_1 to β_n are the slopes of the explanatory variables, and ε_{it} denotes the errors.

As I mentioned above, an error correction model allows the estimatation of the short- and long-term effects of the explanatory variables. More specifically, in this model the slope of the first difference, β_2, captures the immediate or contemporaneous effect of government partisanship on policy. The slope of the lag, β_3, captures the long-term or equilibrium effect of government partisanship on policy. The long-term effects, moreover, take place at a rate determined by the slope of the lagged dependent variable, β_1.[20]

The existence of country-specific factors not included in the analysis (country-specific omitted variables) could affect the accurate estimation of the model. Like most analyses in comparative political economy, it is reasonable to assume that there are a number of country-specific effects that cannot be introduced explicitly into my model (specific historical circumstances, difficult to capture institutional developments, etc.). To deal with these variables I produce a set of estimates with random effects.[21]

Finally, Beck and Katz (1995, 1996) have proposed a method that produces consistent standard errors estimates in the presence of panel heteroscedastic errors. Since their recommendations have been widely followed in the recent comparative political economy literature (see, e.g. Garrett 1998; Hall and Franzese 1998; Iversen 1998), I also present the results estimating panel-corrected standard errors.

4.3.1. *The Determinants of Employment Protection—ALMPs and PLMPs*

The following pages contain the results of the regressions. The model with panel-corrected standard errors and the one with random effects are presented side by side. For each variable, I present the estimates of the coefficients, their standard errors, and p values from two-sided t tests of significance. To make the interpretation of the results easier, the significance levels of the estimates are also indicated by the asterisks in the usual manner (*** if p value < .01, ** if < .05, and * if < .1). In all cases I present the estimates of the constant and the lagged dependent variable first, immediately followed by the main variable of interest: cabinet partisanship (as first difference and as a lag). Then I produce the estimates for the rest of the explanatory variables.

---

[20] The long-term effect of an explanatory variable can be calculated by dividing the slope of its lag by the minus slope of the lagged dependent variable. For government partisanship, this would mean: β_3/β_1. See Bannerjee et al. (1993) and Keele (2007) for details.

[21] For details on estimating random effects with panel data, see Hsiao (1986).

Table 4.6. The determinants of employment protection, 1970–98

	Panel-corrected standard errors	Random effects
Constant	**.031*****	**.061*****
	(.007)	(.014)
	.000	*.000*
Lagged dependent variable	**−.016*****	**−.038*****
	(.006)	(.008)
	.007	*.000*
Δ **Left government**	**−.0001**	**−.0001**
	(.0001)	(.0001)
	.372	*.188*
Lag of Left government	**.0002*****	**.0001*****
	(.0001)	(.0001)
	.006	*.018*
Union density	**−.027***	**−.034**
	(.014)	(.024)
	.052	*.150*
Wage bargaining coordination	**.001**	**.004***
	(.002)	(.002)
	.651	*.080*
Trade openness	**.002**	**−.0002***
	(.007)	(.0001)
	.253	*.089*
Lack of financial openness	**.0000**	**.010***
	(.0001)	(.006)
	.879	*.064*
Lag of unemployment rate	**−.003*****	**−.003*****
	(.001)	(.001)
	.000	*.001*
GDP growth	**.001**	**.001**
	(.001)	(.001)
	.378	*.129*
N	425	425
R^2	.16	.12

Notes: Employment protection is measured as an index ranging from 0 to 2, higher values mean more employment protection.

Source: Baker et al. (2004).

All entries are OLS estimates. Numbers in bold are estimated coefficients; numbers in parentheses are standard errors; numbers in italics are p values from two-sided t tests.

The asterisks signify statistical significance in the usual manner (*** if p value $< .01$, ** if $< .05$, and * if $< .1$).

Table 4.6 presents the results for the determinants of employment protection. The pro-insider orientation of social democratic governments seems obvious when examining the estimates in the table. Leaving aside the constant, only three factors are significant at better than the traditional 95 percent level of confidence: the lagged dependent variable, the long-term effect of Left government, and the previous year's unemployment rate. The most important finding for this chapter's arguments is that, as expected, social democratic governments are significantly associated with higher levels of employment protection in the long term (the contemporaneous effect is insignificant). This result is confirmed by both models (with panel-corrected standard errors and with random effects). During the period of time under analysis, the long-term effect of Left government has been a significant increase in employment protection for insiders. This result is all the more meaningful when we remember that in many OECD countries unemployment increased dramatically during this period. As indicated by the estimate for the lagged dependent variable, the long-term effects of social democratic government, moreover, take place at a rate of 16 percent (in the panel-corrected standard error model) or 38 percent (in the random effects model) per year.

The only other explanatory variable which reaches significance at more than the 95 percent level of confidence is the previous year's unemployment rate. Higher levels of unemployment reduce the employment protection of insiders. Since this variable represents a pool of potential competitors for insiders, it is not surprising that greater levels of unemployment reduce the power of insiders to demand employment protection.

The substantive significance of the findings is perhaps best illustrated by calculating the long-term effects of a change in government partisanship while keeping the other variables constant. Using the estimates for the lag of Left government in Table 4.6, we can find the long-term effect that would result from a gain from 0 to 100 percent of cabinet seats. Let me first point out that this kind of electoral victory by Left parties is not an unreasonable scenario to use as an illustration. Many countries in the sample experience similar victories (the Left coming to power and forming a government on their own after being in the opposition). The estimates in the table show that such a change in Left government would be associated with an increase in employment protection equal to 1.25, using the results with panel-corrected standard errors. To put this increase in context, we can look at the employment levels of a particular country. Looking back to Table 4.1, it was shown that in Australia the employment protection index was 0.5 in 1995. A change in Left government of the magnitude suggested above would therefore be associated with a 250 percent long-term increase in employment protection in Australia.

I have explored the robustness of the employment protection conclusions described above in related work. Rueda (2005) uses two different definitions of government partisanship (a cabinet ideological center of gravity measure and one based on party manifesto data) but confirms the findings in Table 4.6 in a number of different ways. It shows that these alternative measures of partisanship do not affect the results. It also indicates that a model with country fixed effects corroborates the findings in Table 4.6. The analysis in Rueda (2005) indicates that the results are robust to several specifications of the government partisanship lag as well.

Tables 4.7 and 4.8 present the results of the analysis of active and passive labor market policies. If Table 4.6 made clear the pro-insider orientation of Left governments when examining the determinants of employment protection, Tables 4.7 and 4.8 make equally obvious their lack of attention to outsider interests. The most important findings regarding the insider–outsider model relate to the estimates for Left government. The tables show, as hypothesized, the lack of any long-term partisanship effect on the levels of either active or passive labor market policy. In the long-term, social democratic government has no effect on ALMPs or PLMPs (this is confirmed by both the panel-corrected standard errors model and the one with random effects). The tables also show that the immediate effects of Left government on PLMPs is statistically insignificant.[22] Table 4.7 indicates, moreover, that the immediate effect of social democratic government on ALMPs is significant but negative. Increasing levels of Left government are in fact associated with decreasing levels of ALMP in the short term. It is important to emphasize that these results contradict the conventional wisdom, and much of the existing literature, regarding the influence of partisanship on active policies (see, e.g. Janoski 1990, 1994; Boix 1998a; Swank and Martin 2001). These results reinforce the conclusions of the insider–outsider model: when insiders do not share the goals of outsiders, social democratic governments do not promote pro-outsider policies.[23]

The substantive significance of the findings in Table 4.7 can be illustrated by performing a calculation similar to the one in the discussion of Table 4.6. Using the estimates for the first difference of Left government in Table 4.7, we can calculate the immediate effect resulting from a gain by the Left from 0 to 100 percent of cabinet seats. Such a change in Left government would be associated with an immediate decrease in ALMPs equal to 0.13. We can once again put this effect in context by looking at the ALMP levels of a particular country. In Table 4.2, we see that in Germany, for example, ALMPs represented 0.7 percent of GDP in 1985.

---

[22] All results in Table 4.8 are confirmed by an analysis using a more restrictive measure of passive labor market policy only including unemployment benefits.

[23] Other authors have observed similar results to those presented in Tables 4.7 and 4.8. See Moene and Wallerstein (2003) for a comparative analysis and King (1995) for one of the UK.

Table 4.7. The determinants of active labor market policy, 1980–98

	Panel-corrected standard errors	Random effects
Constant	**−.023**	**−.023**
	(.040)	(.048)
	.560	.625
Lagged dependent variable	**−.088***	**−.088***
	(.045)	(.027)
	.050	.001
Δ **Left government**	**−.0013****	**−.0013****
	(.0006)	(.0004)
	.042	.011
Lag of Left government	**.0002**	**.0002**
	(.0004)	(.0003)
	.648	.586
Employment protection	**.028**	**.028**
	(.030)	(.032)
	.351	.384
Union density	**.085**	**.085**
	(.065)	(.072)
	.193	.242
Wage bargaining coordination	**.006**	**.006**
	(.011)	(.012)
	.588	.603
Trade openness	**.0007***	**.0007**
	(.0004)	(.0005)
	.093	.127
Lack of financial openness	**.033**	**.033**
	(.025)	(.031)
	.196	.295
Lag of unemployment rate	**.003**	**.003**
	(.004)	(.004)
	.424	.449
Government deficit	**−.012****	**−.012***
	(.005)	(.004)
	.011	.001
GDP growth	**−.012****	**−.012****
	(.005)	(.006)
	.025	.037
N	232	232
R^2	.18	.18

Notes: ALMPs are measured as a percentage of GDP.

Source: Armingeon et al. (2005).

All entries are OLS estimates. Numbers in bold are estimated coefficients; numbers in parentheses are standard errors; numbers in italics are p values from two-sided t tests.

The asterisks signify statistical significance in the usual manner (*** if p value < .01, ** if < .05, and * if < .1).

The suggested change in Left government would therefore be associated with a whopping 19 percent immediate decrease in ALMPs in Germany.

Tables 4.7 and 4.8 also show that other explanatory variables reach significance at more than the 95 percent level of confidence. Government

Table 4.8. The determinants of passive labor market policy, 1980–98

	Panel-corrected standard errors	Random effects
Constant	**2.115*****	**2.188*****
	(.262)	(.246)
	.000	*.000*
Lagged dependent variable	**−.043*****	**−.045*****
	(.012)	(.013)
	.000	*.001*
Δ **Left government**	**.000**	**.000**
	(.002)	(.002)
	.849	*.854*
Lag of Left government	**.002**	**.002**
	(.001)	(.001)
	.149	*.199*
Employment protection	**.102**	**.122**
	(.125)	(.139)
	.413	*.381*
Union density	**.270**	**.328**
	(.247)	(.322)
	.273	*.307*
Wage bargaining coordination	**−.075**	**−.083**
	(.049)	(.053)
	.127	*.116*
Trade openness	**.002**	**.002**
	(.002)	(.002)
	.374	*.414*
Lack of financial openness	**.025**	**−.004**
	(.140)	(.134)
	.857	*.974*
Lag of unemployment rate	**−.051****	**−.059*****
	(.022)	(.021)
	.018	*.004*
Government deficit	**−.042****	**−.045*****
	(.019)	(.016)
	.028	*.004*
GDP growth	**−.290*****	**−.286*****
	(.030)	(.026)
	.000	*.000*
N	259	259
R^2	.48	.48

Notes: PLMPs are measured as a percentage of GDP.

Source: Armingeon et al. (2005).

All entries are OLS estimates. Numbers in bold are estimated coefficients; numbers in parentheses are standard errors; numbers in italics are p values from two-sided t tests.

The asterisks signify statistical significance in the usual manner (*** if p value < .01, ** if < .05, and * if < .1).

deficits and GDP growth are significant determinants of both ALMPs and PLMPs. The previous year's unemployment rate, on the other hand, is only significant as a determinant of PLMPs. Unsurprisingly, the results suggest that increasing levels of government deficit and unemployment reduce the resources dedicated to labor market policy (although in the case of unemployment the effect is only significant on PLMPs). It is perhaps less straightforward that GDP growth is also associated with decreasing levels of ALMPs and PLMPs.

In Rueda (2005, 2006), I use a number of different specifications for the variables and the models to further explore the relationship between government partisanship and labor market policy. The two alternative definitions of government partisanship in Rueda (2005, 2006), a cabinet ideological center of gravity measure and one based on party manifesto data, confirm the findings in Tables 4.7 and 4.8. These analyses also indicate that a model with country fixed effects does not make any difference to the substantive results, and neither do several specifications of the government partisanship lag.

4.3.2. The Mediating Effects of Employment Protection and Corporatism

To analyze the mediating effect of employment protection and corporatism on the relationship between government partisanship and labor market policy, I introduce a set of interactions in the model. I estimate interactions for employment protection and corporatism separately. The models follow the same specifications as those explained above. As before, I estimate single equation error correction models but in this case, the lag and first difference of Left government is interacted with the variables capturing either employment protection or corporatism.

Tables 4.9 and 4.10 present the results for the interactions with employment protection. Table 4.9 contains the analysis of ALMPs and Table 4.10 of PLMPs. I will focus on the effects of the interaction between Left government and employment protection (since the estimates for the other explanatory variables are not that different from the ones in the non-interactive models). Regrettably, the results in Tables 4.9 and 4.10 do not offer us a particularly intuitive way of understanding the effects of the interaction. The statistical significance of the lower-order coefficients, in particular, does not tell us much about the relationship between the interacted variables.[24] To illustrate the effects of the interacted terms and to simplify the assessment of their statistical significance, I calculate conditional effects. Having identified the range of variation in employment protection in Table 4.1, I define a low and a high value. Low employment protection is defined as a score of 0.4 (this is not a particularly low level,

---

[24] In the political science literature, the meaning of interactions is commonly misinterpreted. For some illustrations of this, see Braumoeller (2004).

Table 4.9. The determinants of active labor market policy, 1980–98 (interaction with employment protection)

	Panel-corrected standard errors	Random effects
Constant	**−.021**	**−.021**
	(.040)	(.048)
	.603	.664
Lagged dependent variable	**−.086*****	**−.086********
	(.044)	(.027)
	.053	.002
Δ **Left government**	**.001**	**.001**
	(.001)	(.001)
	.233	.337
Lag of Left government	**.001**	**.001**
	(.001)	(.001)
	.225	.262
Employment protection	**.058**	**.058**
	(.035)	(.040)
	.101	.146
Δ **Left government***	**−.002*****	**−.002*****
Employment protection	(.001)	(.001)
	.050	.051
Lag of Left government*	**−.001**	**−.001**
Employment protection	(.001)	(.001)
	.370	.313
Union density	**.089**	**.089**
	(.065)	(.072)
	.170	.217
Wage bargaining coordination	**−.003**	**−.003**
	(.012)	(.014)
	.788	.813
Trade openness	**.0008******	**.0008*****
	(.0004)	(.0005)
	.040	.077
Lack of financial openness	**.039**	**.039**
	(.027)	(.032)
	.150	.220
Lag of unemployment rate	**.001**	**.001**
	(.005)	(.005)
	.806	.806
Government deficit	**−.012******	**−.012*******
	(.005)	(.004)
	.010	.001
GDP growth	**−.011*****	**−.011*****
	(.005)	(.006)
	.039	.057
N	232	232
R^2	.20	.20

Notes: ALMPs are measured as a percentage of GDP.

Source: Armingeon et al. (2005).

All entries are OLS estimates. Numbers in bold are estimated coefficients; numbers in parentheses are standard errors; numbers in italics are p values from two-sided t tests.

The asterisks signify statistical significance in the usual manner (*** if p value < .01, ** if < .05, and * if < .1).

Table 4.10. The determinants of passive labor market policy, 1980–98 (interaction with employment protection)

	Panel-corrected standard errors	Random effects
Constant	**2.113*****	**2.254*****
	(.259)	(.259)
	.000	*.000*
Lagged dependent variable	**−.042*****	**−.046*****
	(.012)	(.014)
	.001	*.001*
Δ **Left government**	**.000**	**.000**
	(.007)	(.007)
	.973	*.950*
Lag of Left government	**.007****	**.005**
	(.003)	(.004)
	.030	*.157*
Employment protection	**.230**	**.235**
	(.140)	(.175)
	.100	*.180*
Δ **Left government*** **Employment protection**	**−.000**	**.000**
	(.005)	(.005)
	.968	*.942*
Lag of Left government* **Employment protection**	**−.004***	**−.004**
	(.003)	(.003)
	.080	*.283*
Union density	**.294**	**.409**
	(.243)	(.348)
	.227	*.240*
Wage bargaining coordination	**−.116****	**−.116***
	(.055)	(.061)
	.036	*.058*
Trade openness	**.002**	**.002**
	(.002)	(.003)
	.233	*.352*
Lack of financial openness	**.061**	**−.008**
	(.142)	(.138)
	.667	*.953*
Lag of unemployment rate	**−.062*****	**−.074*****
	(.023)	(.022)
	.006	*.001*
Government deficit	**−.043****	**−.048*****
	(.019)	(.016)
	.026	*.003*
GDP growth	**−.288*****	**−.281*****
	(.030)	(.026)
	.000	*.000*
N	259	259
R^2	.49	.49

Notes: PLMPs are measured as a percentage of GDP.

Source: Armingeon et al. (2005).

All entries are OLS estimates. Numbers in bold are estimated coefficients; numbers in parentheses are standard errors; numbers in italics are p values from two-sided t tests.

The asterisks signify statistical significance in the usual manner (*** if p value < .01, ** if < .05, and * if < .1).

Table 4.11. The determinants of active labor market policy, 1980–98 (conditional on employment protection levels)

	Panel-corrected standard errors		Random effects	
	Low employment protection	High employment protection	Low employment protection	High employment protection
Δ **Left government**	**.001**	**−.002****	**.001**	**−.002****
	(.001)	(.001)	(.001)	(.001)
	.524	*.019*	*.627*	*.002*
Lag of Left government	**.001**	**−.000**	**.001**	**−.000**
	(.000)	(.001)	(.001)	(.001)
	.206	*.679*	*.270*	*.574*

Notes: ALMPs are measured as a percentage of GDP.

Source: Armingeon et al. (2005).

All entries are OLS estimates. Numbers in bold are estimated coefficients; numbers in parentheses are standard errors; numbers in italics are p values from two-sided t tests.

The asterisks signify statistical significance in the usual manner (*** if p value < .01, ** if < .05, and * if < .1).

Canada, the UK, and the USA all display lower levels of employment protection throughout the period). High employment protection is defined as a score of 1.7 (again, this is not an unrealistically high level—Italy, throughout the period, and Sweden, in the 1980s, have higher levels of employment protection). I then calculate the long-term and immediate effects of Left government conditional on these two levels of employment protection. Tables 4.11 and 4.12 present the results.

Table 4.11 presents the effects of Left government on ALMPs and Table 4.12 on PLMPs. Each table presents conditional effects for both model alternatives (the one estimating panel-corrected standard errors and the one with random effects). When analyzing Table 4.7, I pointed out that social democratic government had no long-term effect on ALMPs and that its immediate effects were in fact negative. Table 4.11 confirms the long-term results, the lag of Left government is an insignificant determinant of ALMPs whether employment protection is high or low. In line with the expectations of the insider–outsider model, the immediate effects of Left government are contingent on the levels of employment protection. Table 4.11 shows that high employment protection is entirely responsible for the effects we saw in Table 4.7. While social democratic government is insignificant in low employment protection countries, it is statistically significant and negative when employment protection is high. It is indeed the case that insiders who experience high levels of employment protection do not pressure social democratic parties to

Table 4.12. The determinants of passive labor market policy, 1980–98 (conditional on employment protection levels)

	Panel-corrected standard errors		Random effects	
	Low employment protection	High employment protection	Low employment protection	High employment protection
Δ **Left government**	**.000**	**−.000**	**−.000**	**.000**
	(.005)	(.003)	(.005)	(.004)
	.976	.973	.955	.947
Lag of Left government	**.005****	**−.001**	**.004**	**−.001**
	(.002)	(.002)	(.003)	(.003)
	.029	.677	.133	.794

Notes: PLMPs are measured as a percentage of GDP.

Source: Armingeon et al. (2005).

All entries are OLS estimates. Numbers in bold are estimated coefficients; numbers in parentheses are standard errors; numbers in italics are p values from two-sided t tests.

The asterisks signify statistical significance in the usual manner (*** if p value < .01, ** if < .05, and * if < .1).

promote ALMPs. In fact, when insiders are well insulated from unemployment, social democratic governments are associated with lower (rather than higher) levels of ALMPs.

Turning now to the effects of partisanship on PLMPs, the general conclusion of the non-interactive model was that Left government was not a significant determinant of social policy. Table 4.12 offers a more subtle picture. When we look at the effects of social democratic government conditional on the levels of employment protection, we can see that partisanship does have a long-term effect but only when employment protection is low. The lag of Left government is significant at better than a 95 percent level of confidence in the panel-corrected standard error model.[25] Again in a manner that supports this book's arguments, the table suggests that when insiders have little employment protection, they do become more interested in social policy (like outsiders). As a consequence of this, social democratic governments promote higher levels of PLMPs, but only when employment protection is low.

To explore the mediating effects of corporatism on the relationship between government partisanship and labor market policy, I introduce interactions in the model in the same way as in the employment protection analysis. Tables 4.13 and 4.14 present the results for the interactions with corporatism. Table 4.13 contains the analysis of ALMPs and

[25] This result is not confirmed by the random effects model.

Table 4.13. The determinants of active labor market policy, 1980–94 (interaction with corporatism)

	Panel-corrected standard errors	Random effects
Constant	**−.025**	**−.025**
	(.047)	(.060)
	.603	*.679*
Lagged dependent variable	**−.070**	**−.070****
	(.063)	(.034)
	.272	*.040*
Δ **Left government**	**.000**	**.000**
	(.001)	(.002)
	.873	*.890*
Lag of Left government	**.001**	**.001**
	(.001)	(.001)
	.100	*.116*
Corporatism	**.012**	**.012**
	(.109)	(.098)
	.914	*.904*
Δ **Left government*** **Corporatism**	**−.003**	**−.003**
	(.002)	(.002)
	.119	*.130*
Lag of Left government* **Corporatism**	**−.002**	**−.002**
	(.001)	(.001)
	.268	*.162*
Employment protection	**.049**	**.049**
	(.055)	(.050)
	.367	*.326*
Union density	**.157***	**.157**
	(.088)	(.100)
	.073	*.116*
Trade openness	**.001**	**.001**
	(.001)	(.001)
	.238	*.283*
Lack of financial openness	**.014**	**.014**
	(.038)	(.039)
	.724	*.729*
Lag of unemployment rate	**−.004**	**−.004**
	(.008)	(.007)
	.601	*.559*
Government deficit	**−.016*****	**−.016*****
	(.006)	(.004)
	.009	*.000*
GDP growth	**−.003**	**−.003**
	(.006)	(.007)
	.568	*.632*
N	168	168
R^2	.21	.21

Notes: ALMPs are measured as a percentage of GDP.

Source: Armingeon et al. (2005).

All entries are OLS estimates. Numbers in bold are estimated coefficients; numbers in parentheses are standard errors; numbers in italics are p values from two-sided t tests.

The asterisks signify statistical significance in the usual manner (*** if p-value < .01, ** if < .05, and * if < .1).

Table 4.14. The determinants of passive labor market policy, 1980–94 (interaction with corporatism)

	Panel-corrected standard errors	Random effects
Constant	**1.612*****	**1.612*****
	(.238)	(.246)
	.000	*.000*
Lagged dependent variable	**−.023***	**−.023**
	(.013)	(.014)
	.082	*.105*
Δ **Left Government**	**.014****	**.014****
	(.007)	(.007)
	.035	*.043*
Lag of Left government	**.005****	**.005***
	(.002)	(.003)
	.042	*.083*
Corporatism	**.308**	**.308**
	(.421)	(.387)
	.465	*.427*
Δ **Left government*** **Corporatism**	**−.015***	**−.015**
	(.009)	(.011)
	.092	*.144*
Lag of Left government* **Corporatism**	**−.003**	**−.003**
	(.004)	(.005)
	.501	*.565*
Employment protection	**−.165**	**−.165**
	(.169)	(.168)
	.329	*.326*
Union density	**.105**	**.105**
	(.254)	(.378)
	.678	*.781*
Trade openness	**.001**	**.001**
	(.002)	(.003)
	.694	*.722*
Lack of financial openness	**−.031**	**−.031**
	(.149)	(.159)
	.834	*.844*
Lag of unemployment rate	**−.032**	**−.032**
	(.042)	(.033)
	.444	*.328*
Government deficit	**−.041***	**−.041****
	(.021)	(.018)
	.057	*.021*
GDP growth	**−.284*****	**−.284*****
	(.032)	(.029)
	.000	*.000*
N	195	195
R^2	.49	.49

Notes: PLMPs are measured as a percentage of GDP.

Source: Armingeon et al. (2005).

All entries are OLS estimates. Numbers in bold are estimated coefficients; numbers in parentheses are standard errors; numbers in italics are p values from two-sided t tests.

The asterisks signify statistical significance in the usual manner (*** if p value < .01, ** if < .05, and * if < .1).

Table 4.15. The determinants of active labor market policy, 1980–94 (conditional on corporatism levels)

	Panel-corrected standard errors		Random effects	
	Low corporatism	High corporatism	Low corporatism	High corporatism
Δ **Left government**	**−.000**	**−.003****	**−.000**	**−.003****
	(.001)	(.001)	(.001)	(.001)
	.787	.014	.813	.002
Lag of Left	**.001**	**−.000**	**.001**	**−.000**
government	(.000)	(.001)	(.000)	(.001)
	.120	.591	.138	.517

Notes: ALMPs are measured as a percentage of GDP.

Source: Armingeon et al. (2005).

All entries are OLS estimates. Numbers in bold are estimated coefficients; numbers in parentheses are standard errors; numbers in italics are p values from two-sided t tests.

The asterisks signify statistical significance in the usual manner (*** if p value < .01, ** if < .05, and * if < .1).

Table 4.14 of PLMPs. Two things must be pointed out before analyzing the results in the tables. First, since corporatism is introduced into the model, the measure of wage bargaining coordination (encapsulated now by the more encompassing measure of corporatism) is excluded from the analysis. Second, the measure for corporatism is available only up to 1994, which reduces the number of observations in the analyses.

I will focus my attention on the influence of the interaction between Left government and corporatism. To illustrate the effects of the interacted terms, I will once again calculate conditional effects. Having described the range of variation in the sample (when analyzing Table 4.5), I define a low and a high corporatism value. Low corporatism is defined as a score of 0.15 (not an unrealistically low level, since Canada, the UK, and the USA display lower levels of corporatism during most of the period under analysis). High corporatism is defined as a score of 0.9 (again, not an unrealistically high level, Austria, Norway, and Sweden have higher levels throughout the period). I then calculate the long-term and immediate effects of Left government conditional on these two levels of corporatism. Tables 4.15 and 4.16 present the results.

Table 4.15 presents the effects of Left government on ALMPs and Table 4.16 on PLMPs. When analyzing Table 4.7, I pointed out that social democratic government had no long-term effect on ALMPs and that its immediate effects were in fact negative. Table 4.15 confirms the long-term results found in the non-interactive model (Table 4.7) and the

Table 4.16. The determinants of passive labor market policy, 1980–94 (conditional on corporatism levels)

	Panel-corrected standard errors		Random effects	
	Low corporatism	High corporatism	Low corporatism	High corporatism
Δ **Left government**	**.012****	**.000**	**.012****	**.000**
	(.006)	(.004)	(.006)	(.004)
	.031	*.901*	*.034*	*.917*
Lag of Left government	**.004****	**.002**	**.004****	**.002**
	(.002)	(.002)	(.002)	(.003)
	.019	*.339*	*.046*	*.421*

Notes: PLMPs are measured as a percentage of GDP.

Source: Armingeon et al. (2005).

All entries are OLS estimates. Numbers in bold are estimated coefficients; numbers in parentheses are standard errors; numbers in italics are p values from two-sided t tests.

The asterisks signify statistical significance in the usual manner (*** if p value < .01, ** if < .05, and * if < .1).

interactions with employment protection (Tables 4.9 and 4.11). The lag of Left government is an insignificant determinant of ALMPs whether corporatism is high or low. The immediate effects of Left government, however, are contingent on the levels of corporatism. Just as when analyzing employment protection, Table 4.15 shows that while social democratic government is insignificant in low corporatism countries, it is statistically significant and negative when corporatism is high. It is indeed the case that insiders in countries characterized by high levels of corporatism do not pressure social democratic parties to promote ALMPs. In fact, in these countries, social democratic governments are associated with lower (rather than higher) levels of ALMPs. These results challenge the widely accepted Olsonian understanding of corporatism and support the opposing economic insider–outsider views.

When looking at PLMPs, the general conclusion in the non-interactive model had been that Left government was not a significant determinant of social policy. As was the case when making the distinction between high and low employment protection, the consideration of corporatist levels transforms this view. Table 4.16 makes clear that social democratic government does have both a long-term and an immediate effect on PLMPs, but only when corporatism is low. The first difference and the lag of Left government are significant at better than a 95 percent level of confidence in both the panel-corrected standard error and the random effects models. Social democratic government promotes higher levels of

PLMPs only in countries where insiders are not protected by high levels of corporatism. When corporatist arrangements exist, the influence of Left government is highly insignificant. This result suggests, as in the case of ALMPs,[26] that the economic insider–outsider interpretation of corporatism may be more accurate than an Olsonian one. The table suggests that when insiders do not have corporatist arrangements to protect them, they do become more interested in social policy (like outsiders). As a consequence of this, social democratic governments promote higher levels of PLMPs, but only when corporatism is low.

---

[26] This was also the conclusion of the individual analysis in Chapter 3.

5

Partisan Government and Employment Protection

Perhaps the best way to start this second part of the book is by providing a very brief reminder of some of the reasons why case studies are important to my argument. The case comparisons provide a detailed analysis of the relationship between government partisanship and policy. Although the quantitative results that I presented in previous chapters are powerful evidence supporting the insider–outsider partisanship model, the case studies clarify the influence of electoral considerations (affecting insiders, outsiders, and upscale groups) on the policy choices of social democratic and conservative parties in three country cases. In a clearer way than the previous general chapters, the country analyses allow us to examine political (as well as policy) developments as they evolved after 1970 and to trace the causal processes affecting the outcomes of interest. They also facilitate the assessment of political agency (the interplay of actors, including parties and social partners, their motivations, and strategies) and institutional constraints (the mediating effects of corporatist arrangements or labor market vulnerability) in a way that is difficult to capture in the aggregate analyses presented in previous chapters.

The analysis of the Spanish case in this chapter will show that the social democratic party [*Partido Socialista Obrero Español* (PSOE)] was decidedly pro-insider in the period under analysis. Facing increasing economic challenges (unemployment, inflation, etc.), the PSOE responded by staunchly maintaining the high protection of insiders and by facilitating the entry into the labor market of outsiders. The following pages will also show that unions are an even stronger defender of insiders in Spain. Their goals were not only the defense of insider employment protection, but also the increase of insider wages (which put them at loggerheads with the PSOE governments, more interested in promoting wage moderation to combat inflation). Also in agreement with this book's arguments, this chapter will show that the conservative party [*Partido Popular* (PP)] attacked insider protection when it got to power.

In the Netherlands, the analysis will show very similar developments to those described in the Spanish analysis. The Labor Party [*Partij van de Arbeid* (PvdA)] has defended the interests of insiders by making high employment levels for standard employment its most important objective. As in the case of Spain, unions attempted to defend insider employment protection and also to increase insider wages but the promotion of both these goals became difficult by the early 1980s. Conservative parties in the Netherlands are less powerful than in Spain or the UK. The Christian Democratic Party (CDA) and the Liberal Party (VVD)[1] have not been able to attack insider protection. In a way that reflects the opportunities and limitations present in a corporatist environment, they have focused instead on promoting insider wage moderation (in a much more successful way than in Spain). The creation of a large pool of outsiders has also been the result of labor market policy in the Netherlands. In Spain, this was accomplished mostly through the use of fixed-term employment, in the Netherlands through part-time employment.

Finally, the analysis of the UK is all about the consequences of unfettered conservative government. In the 1980s and 1990s, Thatcher and Major engineered a dramatic attack on insiders in the UK. This chapter will also show that Labour's return to power has meant a very timid attempt to promote insider protection. Unlike in Spain and the Netherlands, given the nature of the attack on insiders (among other things through the weakening of unions) and the traditional lack of interest in coordination by the social partners, wage moderation has received very little attention in the UK.

5.1. Some Background: Labor Market Institutions

This book's theoretical claims are fundamentally affected by the nature of the labor market and the influence of the social partners on parties. It is therefore necessary to provide some introductory remarks about labor market institutions in Spain, the Netherlands, and the UK before developing my analysis about the political determinants of employment protection.

[1] *Christen Democratisch Appèl* (CDA) and *Volkspartij voor Vrijheid en Democratie* (VVD).

5.1.1. *Spain*

The two most important unions in Spain are the *Unión General de Traba-jadores* (UGT), traditionally linked to the Socialist Party, and the *Comisiones Obreras* (CCOO), traditionally close to the Spanish Communist Party. The dominance of these two unions drives Führer (1996: 206) to declare that, because of their strength and legal privileges, UGT and CCOO 'determine, at every level, the worker side of labor relations in Spain'.[2] Since employers cannot choose to engage in collective bargaining with just one recognized union, as is the case in other countries, the Spanish system of worker representation has promoted multiunionism in most negotiating forums (see e.g. Milner and Metcalf 1994). In spite of the prominence of multiunionism, its effects are severely limited by single table bargaining.[3]

One of the most relevant characteristics of Spanish trade unionism is its low membership figures, but many observers have argued that the influence of trade unions in Spain is more related to their performance in works council elections than to membership (see Milner and Metcalf 1994; Führer 1996). The results of these elections constitute the only criteria by which legal representation rights and public subsidies are bestowed upon unions. The laws concerning 'most representative' union status determine that a union needs to obtain 'at least 10 percent of the works council delegates or staff representatives nationwide (or 15 percent in a particular region if the union is regionally based) to be able to negotiate on the relevant sector bodies' (Milner and Metcalf 1994: 20). Election results also govern the financing of unions (which is dependent on the state, given the paucity of membership dues).

Another characteristic of Spanish unions relevant to my analysis is the fact that membership is almost entirely composed of insiders and that only those with stable employment tend to participate in works council elections. Although reliable membership data is quite difficult to obtain,[4] there is a general consensus among observers that insiders constitute the overwhelming majority of both CCOO and UGT's members. An exact figure is hard to estimate[5] but it is generally agreed both that most members are insiders and that unions have made few efforts to

[2] My translation.
[3] Although the preeminence of UGT and CCOO has been maintained, since the early 1980s public sector unions have experienced very significant growth.
[4] For a more detailed explanation, see Führer (1996: 132–46).
[5] In interviews, union officials informally declared that more than 90 percent of members are insiders.

integrate outsiders into their ranks (Estivill and de la Hoz 1990; Dolado and Bentolila 1992; Rhodes 1997). As for participation in works council elections, the unemployed are automatically excluded and those with temporary contracts tend neither to vote nor to run. It is also important to point out that, by law, only workers in companies with more than ten workers can participate in works council elections.[6] Abellán, Felgueroso and Lorences calculate that this limitation precludes the participation of up to a third of Spanish workers in elections to collective bargaining bodies (1997: 253).

In the period under analysis, Spanish collective bargaining has taken place at three levels: national, sectoral, and company. Although most agreements are signed at the company level, most workers are affected by collective bargaining at the sectoral provincial level (Jimeno 1996; Abellán, Felgueroso, and Lorences 1997). More specifically, while from 1981 to 1999 between 65 and 72 percent of agreements were signed at the company level and the rest at the sectoral level, between 80 and 90 percent of workers were covered by sectoral collective bargaining (both at the national and provincial level). This means that since the early 1980s, Spanish collective bargaining has been characterized by an intermediate level of centralization/coordination (Aragón Medina and Gutiérrez Benito 1996).

As for the actors involved in collective bargaining, they are the unions and the employer associations, sometimes with the participation of the government when national pacts are negotiated. The participation of unions in collective bargaining is exclusively dependent on the results of works council elections. This system results in the two major unions, CCOO and UGT, negotiating the agreements of as much as 95 percent of workers affected by collective bargaining (Abellán, Felgueroso, and Lorences 1997). Employers, on the other hand are mostly organized in two related associations: *Confederación Española de Organizaciones Empresariales* (CEOE) represents large companies and *Confederación Española de Pequeña y Mediana Empresa* (CEPYME) medium and small companies. CEPYME is a member of CEOE, but it has its own constitution. Although there is a lack of reliable data, CEOE and CEPYME are estimated to represent about 90 percent of Spanish companies and to participate in collective bargaining negotiations affecting as many as 80 percent of workers (Martínez Lucio 1991; Abellán, Felgueroso, and Lorences 1997).

---

[6] In companies with more than ten workers but less than fifty, there are elections for *delegados de personal* and in companies with fifty workers or more there are elections for *comités de empresa* (see Ministerio de Trabajo y Asuntos Sociales 1998).

Regarding coverage, a very high proportion of workers are affected by collective bargaining agreements in Spain. According to most estimates, between 80 and 85 percent of the salaried labor force is covered by agreements (Abellán, Felgueroso, and Lorences 1997). Once an agreement is signed by unions and employers, it is automatically extended to all companies within its functional level irrespective of their participation in collective bargaining.

5.1.2. The Netherlands

The level of union density in the Netherlands is not very high by international standards. About 30 percent of Dutch workers are members of a trade union.[7] The three most important federations are the *Confederation of Dutch Trade Unions* (FNV), the *Christian-National Union Confederation* (CNV), and the *Union of White Collar and Senior Staff Associations* (VHP). Although formal affiliations between the unions and the parties do not exist, the FNV is the union with connections to the Labor Party[8] and the CNV to the Christian Democratic Party. In 1996, there were 1.9 million union members in the Netherlands, 63 percent were affiliated to the FNV, 18 percent to the CNV, and 9 percent to the VHP. In spite of the spectacular increase in part-time employment experienced in the Netherlands since the 1970s (more on this below), unions mainly represent full-time workers with stable contracts. Figures for 1995/96 show that 81 percent of union members are employed, 81 percent work more than 35 hours a week, and 95 percent have a standard (not flexible or fixed-term) contract (Visser and Hemerijck 1997: 86). Women, young people, and immigrants are underrepresented in Dutch unions.

As for employers, between 60 and 70 percent of private sector employees work for companies that belong to an employers' association (Visser 1992). The Federation of Dutch Industry and the Dutch Federation of Christian Employers (VNO-NCW) organizes large and medium size employers, MKB-Nederland companies with less than fifty workers, and LTO Nederland agricultural companies.

The wage setting process in the Netherlands is highly centralized and coordinated. Every year there are attempts by unions and employers to

---

[7] Union density was about 40 percent in the 1950s and 1960s, slowly declined in the 1970s and dramatically fell to 25 percent in the 1980s. In the 1990s, union density has increased to about 30 percent. For more details, see Ebbinghaus and Visser (1996).

[8] As with Spain's PSOE, some union leaders have had successful political careers in the PvdA. The most notable example since the early 1970s is Wim Kok, FNV leader in the 1970s, PvdA Finance Minister from 1989 to 1994, and Prime Minister from 1994 until 2002.

reach a national wage agreement at the National Labor Council. Since 1964, these efforts have been mostly unsuccessful at setting formal wage increases at the national level but they have often produced guidelines and recommendations for negotiations at the sectoral level (de Neubourg 1990: 88). Wage bargaining negotiations take place at the industry and company levels. Most collective agreements are signed at the industry level but the proportion of company agreements has been rising. In 1990, 82 percent of workers were covered by industry agreements and 18 percent by company agreements. In 1975, the proportion of those involved in company agreements had been only 14.6 percent (Teulings and Hartog 1998: 269). Agreements are extended to all workers in the company (union, nonsigning union, and nonunion members).[9]

Unions have no exclusive jurisdiction over collective bargaining and single table bargaining with employers is the rule (Visser 1998). Employers do not have an obligation to negotiate and there are no recognition rules for unions. Any union can enter collective bargaining negotiations and employers can sign an agreement with any union involved in bargaining. This means that unions always face a threat of exclusion from agreements, a threat that is carried out often enough to be credible (Teulings and Hartog 1998). Unions have an interest in avoiding exclusion from negotiations not only because of the loss of representation rights and legitimacy as worker representatives, but also because signing agreements enables the unions to receive a fee from employers—as compensation for the extension of agreements to all workers within the company (Visser and Hemerijck 1997).

There are two elements that promote moderation and cooperation on the employer side as well. First, collective agreements in the Netherlands contain a no-strike clause preventing unions that have signed them to engage in labor unrest. Only unions that sign the agreement are covered by the no-strike clause, so employers have strong incentives to cooperate and try to involve as many unions as possible (Visser 1998). Second, collective bargaining in the Netherlands is subject to mandatory extensions by the government. This means that the Ministry of Social Affairs (and Employment) has the authority to impose collective agreements on firms that did not sign them. Extensions 'can be granted if employers that are party to the agreement (directly or as member of a signing association) employ at least 55 percent of the workers in the industry' (Freeman,

---

[9] Some workers are excluded. Although it is difficult to find data on exclusion rules, this group mostly consists of low-paid workers in noncore activities like cleaning, catering, doormen, etc. (Hartog, Leuven, and Teulings 1999).

Hartog, and Teulings 1996: 1). Extensions require that at least one party that signed the agreement request them. Mandatory extension applied to about 17 percent of all companies and 9 percent of employees in the private sector in the mid-1990s (Visser and Hemerijck 1997: 90). In order to avoid the imposition of agreements in which they have had no say, employers (and unions) are motivated to participate in collective bargaining.

5.1.3. *The UK*

Until the 1970s industrial relations in the UK were characterized by a steady increase in union membership, an increase in the scope of collective bargaining, and growing involvement by unions in the implementation of social and economic policy (Edwards et al. 1992). Since the late 1970s, however, union membership in the UK has drastically declined. From a peak of 52 percent of the labor force in 1978, the proportion of union members declined to 45 percent in 1985 to 39 percent in 1990 and to 27 percent in 1995.[10] New union recognitions are rare (Metcalf 1994).

The structure of unions in the UK has been described as 'a complex pattern with no underlying logic' (Edwards et al. 1992: 32). In 1989, there were 313 trade unions with slightly more than 10.1 million members. While the 10 largest unions organized more than 60 percent of members, 76 percent of unions organized about 3 percent of members. Disparities in terms of members and resources are considerable. Moreover, the domain of a number of unions overlaps at any one sector or company. Within the minority of firms that recognize a union, for example, those with more than 1,000 workers have commonly recognized more than four unions. Multiunionism in the UK has a number of negative consequences (Addison and Siebert 1993). Among them are centrifugal tendencies (that have been associated with labor unrest), demarcation disputes among unions, and more complicated collective bargaining.

There is only one central confederation, the Trade Union Congress (TUC), but a number of unions (about 20 percent of the total) do not belong to it. The TUC does not have a bargaining mandate. It does not have the resources or organization to coordinate either collective bargaining or industrial disputes. As Batstone notes, 'the British TUC has a structure which imposes serious limits upon its ability to act as the representative of the union movement—it has very limited resources and few powers to impose sanctions or to control the actions of member unions'

---

[10] Data from Ebbinghaus and Visser (2000).

(1989: 242). In terms of staff, resources, and finances, the TUC is one of the weakest federations in Europe (Visser 1990*b*). The main role of the TUC has been as a powerbroker among other unions (some of them with more staff and resources than the TUC). The Bridlington Rules (adopted in 1939) determine that affiliated unions commit themselves not to infringe on the rights of other members and give the power to intermediate to the TUC. Increasing differences among TUC affiliates, however, have considerably diminished the intermediation power of the TUC in recent years.

As for the composition of union membership in the UK, Metcalf explains that the 'probability of belonging to a union is higher for full-timers than for part-timers, for men than for women, for manuals than for nonmanuals, in manufacturing than in services, in large workplaces than in small ones, in northern Britain than in southern' (1994: 130). The great majority of union members are employed. Union members in the UK do not keep their membership when they lose their jobs and the unemployed are very unlikely to become members of a union (Edwards et al. 1992: 31). The decline in membership since the late 1970s has affected the TUC most. TUC unions had almost 12 million members in 1979 but in 1993 the number had reduced to only 6.8 million (Visser and Van Ruysseveldt 1996: 64).

Unions have traditionally been strongly connected to the Labour Party. There are historical reasons for this close relationship. While in many European countries social democratic parties helped to create unions, in the UK it was the unions that contributed to the creation of the Labour Party. Until the end of the 1970s, this connection was translated into a significant amount of union participation in the policymaking process when Labour was in power.[11] Today, most large unions are affiliated to the Party and control a considerable number of votes at the annual Labour Party Congresses.

Employers in the UK are unusual in the European context for several reasons. First, the UK has a large number of employers' organizations (more than 250). Membership in these associations is, however, very low compared to most other European countries. Companies belonging to an employers' association account for less than 50 percent of the total number of companies and fewer than 70 percent of employees work in companies belonging to an association (Visser and Ruysseveldt 1996). Second, the UK's employers are also uncommon in having turned their backs on multiemployer bargaining (Edwards et al. 1992: 17). The fact

---

[11] See Minkin (1992) and Ludlam and Taylor (2003) for a detailed analysis.

that most collective bargaining in the UK is done by single employers significantly diminishes the incentives for employers to join associations. The Confederation of British Industry (CBI) comes closest to being a peak employers' organization in the UK. The CBI, however, mainly serves as a lobbying group both in London and in Brussels (Longstreth 1979). It does not negotiate on behalf of its members or sign agreements.

The collective bargaining system in the UK has been described as one in which managers and workers reach 'an accommodation within the workplace without a framework of rules laid down either by the state or by industry-wide agreements' (Edwards et al. 1992: 4). In this system shop stewards are very important both in their role as intermediaries for worker grievances and also as mobilizers of workers for union actions. Before the 1980s, few restrictions existed either on unions to strike or on employers to use lockouts. Since Thatcher's first electoral victory in 1979, as will become clear in the following pages, the number of restrictions promoted by the government has grown significantly. As a consequence of these restrictions, the coverage of collective bargaining has substantially decreased and nonunionism is becoming the norm in the UK. The absence of unions in a company means the lack of collective bargaining agreements. Unlike the other two cases examined in this chapter, in the UK there are no provisions to extend collective bargaining agreements to companies that did not sign them. Also unlike Spain or the Netherlands, in the UK there is no distinction between the side of industrial relations having to do with works councils and the one having to do with union actions. In the 1970s, unions, feeling at the peak of their powers as worker representatives, defended 'single channel' representation and rejected proposals to introduce works councils and worker representation in company boards (Visser and Van Ruysseveldt 1996: 44).

5.2. Employment Protection in Spain in the 1980s and 1990s

I have divided the analysis of labor market legislation in Spain into three main periods. The first (1980–6) can be characterized as one influenced by the legacy of the Francoist past and by the existence of some degree of coordination. In this period, employment protection in Spain was characterized by very high firing costs for those enjoying stable employment and by the emergence of outsiders. The second (1986–95) can be best described as one in which the connection between social democratic government and the promotion of outsider labor was confirmed and in which national coordination was abandoned. And the final one (1996–2000) is most clearly identifiable by the existence of a conservative government and the beginning of a reduction in insider protection.

5.2.1. *1980–6: Coordination*

According to most scholars analyzing the Spanish case, labor market legislation at the beginning of the democratic era was greatly influenced by the practices, policies, and institutions set up during the Francoist period (Segura 2004). Under Franco, labor militancy had been kept in check by numerous concessions to permanent workers, chief among them were very high firing costs (both in terms of the payments to be received by the worker and of the procedures needed to grant authorization).[12] During the dictatorship, labor relations had been regulated by the *ordenanzas laborales* and the transition to democracy marked the emergence of a legal framework for collective bargaining, first through the Moncloa Pacts (1977) and then through the approval of the Workers' Statute (*Estatuto de los Trabajadores*) and the Employment Law (*Ley Básica de Empleo*) in 1980.

The Workers' Statute and the Employment Law of 1980 did not significantly alter some fundamental characteristics of previous regulations but rather added to them. The Workers' Statute promoted a reduction in the scope of national legislation determining individual workers' rights and an increase in the role of collective bargaining (Recio 1998). Regarding worker representation, these laws introduced the basis for a dual model characterized by unions and workers' committees (or works councils).

Two characteristics of the 1980 legislation are most relevant to my argument. Through the Workers' Statute and the Employment Law, the *Unión de Centro Democrático* (UCD)[13] government modified the requirements needed to dismiss individual workers and introduced new contracts for temporary employment.[14] Regarding firing costs, the 1980 Employment Law expanded the definition of termination with cause (cause was now understood to include technological and economic motives), allowed for termination without cause (meaning due to the worker's shortcomings, once these shortcomings were demonstrated), and, in some cases, reduced severance pay (Morán 1996). In reality, however, the effects of these measures were very limited. Firing costs remained mostly untouched and, some would argue, were even reinforced by the elimination of some of

---

[12] See e.g. Rhodes (1997).   [13] Center-Right party in power until 1982.

[14] In the following pages, temporary employment is used to describe fixed-term contracts (as opposed to the standard indefinite contracts of Spanish permanent workers).

the wage flexibility and overtime regulations of the Francoist period and by the introduction of new limitations on functional and geographical mobility (Rhodes 1997: 107).

Equally significant for subsequent insider–outsider dynamics, the 1980 Workers' Statute and the Employment Law brought about the legalization of several new forms of temporary employment. As Morán points out, the Workers' Statute did not take away any of the regulatory benefits of the standard stable/indefinite contract but it accepted the need to promote temporary employment as a solution to cyclical economic problems (1996: 23, also see Recio 1998: 120–1). Fixed-term contracts (whether *temporal, en prácticas,* or *en formación*) were therefore given legal status and the door was opened for the government to use them in some circumstances (e.g. to promote the employment of those looking for a first job).

The government change in 1982, when the PSOE led by Felipe González won the general elections by an overwhelming margin, did not result in any reversal of labor market legislation. In fact, the massive increase in unemployment experienced in the early 1980s culminated in the decision by the González government to extend the use of temporary contracts in 1984. The PSOE government even introduced a new form of temporary contract (the *contrato de fomento de empleo,* or contract for the promotion of employment) that made it possible for employers to use a temporary contract for up to three years without having to provide a reason.

Since the early 1980s, therefore, the Spanish labor market has been characterized by high firing costs for those enjoying stable employment and increasing flexibility for those stuck with temporary employment. Since this is an important point in my analysis, I will provide a more detailed explanation. At that time, there were four kinds of contracts with different dismissal costs attached to them.[15] First, there was the standard indefinite contract. For a standard contract to be terminated with cause, the employer needed only to send a letter and pay compensation. This compensation consisted of twenty-days' salary per year worked in the job, up to a maximum of twelve months' salary. However, the worker could challenge the dismissal in court and, if the termination was considered without cause, a judge could reinstate the worker or increase the compensation to forty-five-days salary per year worked, to a maximum of forty-two months' salary. As pointed out by Rhodes, the threat of court action increased the average compensation for dismissal to more than the regulated twenty days per year (1997: 108). Collective dismissals, on

---

[15] This follows the explanation provided by Toharia (1993).

the other hand, were defined as those involving more than two workers (regardless of firm size) and they required authorization from the Ministry of Labor (not a judge). The procedure was long (between fifty and seventy-five days), the administrative red tape was considerable and great flexibility was granted to the authorities. According to Toharia, the Ministry of Labor had a tendency to consider all collective dismissals/restructurings that did not have worker support 'arbitrary' (1993: 123). Second, there was the ordinary temporary contract (*temporal ordinario*), which was a contract for a particular activity of a temporary nature. There were no time limits and when it was over the worker obtained no compensation for time worked and had no right to a legal challenge. Third, there was the temporary contract for the promotion of employment, which lasted a minimum of six months and could be renewed for a maximum of three years (if extended over this period of time, they automatically became indefinite contracts). When the contract was over, the worker had no right to a legal challenge but compensation equal to the salary of twelve days per year worked was granted. Finally, there were the training contracts (*contrato en prácticas* or *contratos para la formación*). They were contracts for people younger than twenty years of age or who had just finished studying. These were like the temporary contracts for the promotion of employment but the worker received no compensation upon termination and they did not become permanent contracts if extended over the maximum time allowed by law.

The nature of labor market legislation was therefore highly protectionist of those with stable employment (see Toharia 1993; Jimeno 1996; Rhodes 1997). So much so that the real costs of dismissals in Spain quite possibly were the highest in Europe (Jimeno 1996: 6). More importantly, the introduction of flexibility was limited to a very intense promotion of temporary contracts. The most obvious consequence of this process was the promotion of profound insider–outsider differences in Spain.

Insider protection in Spain at this time was also affected by the behavior of unions. UGT had emerged from the dictatorship in a condition of clear inferiority in comparison to CCOO. Numerous authors have argued that UGT's cooperative stance since 1977 was motivated by its need to gain legitimacy and, therefore, support (see e.g. Morán 1996: 26). Regarding labor market legislation, the modernization in labor relations defended by UGT also represented the setting up of a legal context in which UGT could challenge the near hegemony in worker representation enjoyed by CCOO. This was the case particularly with the Union Freedom Law of 1985 (*Ley Orgánica de Libertad Sindical*) which strengthened the position of the two largest trade unions through the provision of state subsidies, of compensation for losses since the Civil War, and of facilities from the old Francoist unions (Maravall 1995: 222–4).

Because it served to strengthen UGT as an alternative to CCOO, it was with respect to wage bargaining that UGT's willingness to coordinate was most consequential during the 1980–6 period. After the Moncloa Pacts, wage bargaining coordination was promoted in a series of national social pacts. The *Acuerdo Marco Interconfederal* (AMI), signed in January of 1980, was the first. The AMI was valid for 1980 and 1981 and it was signed by UGT and CEOE. At this time the relationship between UGT and PSOE was quite close (the PSOE representatives in Parliament, for example, had adopted all of UGT's suggestions for their proposed amendments to the Workers' Statute)[16] and participation in national coordination was seen by the UGT leadership as a way to attract members (and voters in works council elections). The main characteristic of AMI was the agreement by the cosigners to keep salary increases within a 13 to 16 percent band in 1980 and an 11 to 15 percent band in 1981 (Duréndez Sáez 1997). There was also a 'dropping-out clause' (*claúsula de descuelgue*) specifying the conditions under which a company would be allowed not to follow the wage recommendations. As Royo points out, although CCOO had not taken part in the agreement and opposed its implementation in the workplace, the AMI was successfully applied in the lower levels of bargaining (2000: 78). It is, in any case, clear that the strategy of cooperation, moderation, and responsibility paid off for UGT. By the time the first works council elections took place later in 1980, UGT greatly improved its position by obtaining 30 percent of representatives while CCOO experienced a setback (considering its previous position) and obtained only 31 percent of representatives.

Wage bargaining coordination continued with the *Acuerdo Nacional sobre el Empleo* (ANE), which was signed by UGT, CCOO, CEOE, and the UCD government in June of 1981 but would take effect in 1982. The ANE contained a salary increase recommendation (a 9 percent to 11 percent band) but also introduced unions (and the employers' association) in some governmental institutions (Social Security, Employment Agency, etc.). The participation of CCOO in the ANE was no doubt affected by the success of UGT's moderate strategy in the previous works council elections. But all social partners were also strongly influenced by the attempted *coup d'état* in February 1981. Despite CCOO's participation,

---

[16] See Hamann (1999: 13–14).

the results of the works council elections in 1982 confirmed the growth of UGT (with 37 percent of representatives) and the more sluggish performance of CCOO (which obtained 33 percent).

As was the case with labor market legislation, the electoral victory of PSOE in 1982 did not represent a change for wage bargaining coordination. As Bermeo and García-Durán have argued, the PSOE government was like the UCD one 'in that both parties were interested in using incomes policy as a means of controlling inflation and promoting investment' (1994: 110). From very early on, the González governments emphasized wage moderation and temporary employment as the way to international competitiveness (Recio and Roca 1998).[17] The *Acuerdo Interconfederal* (AI) was signed in 1983 by both unions and CEOE.[18] Although the government did not sign the agreement it was an active organizer of the negotiations and, once it was agreed, a supporter of it. The AI established limits for salary increases (between 9.5 percent and 12.5 percent) and also contained a number of clauses (about productivity, security in the work place, absenteeism, etc.) that were taken from the AMI.

No national agreement was signed to cover 1984. Although there had already been a drift between the government and the unions because of the industrial restructuring policies proposed by González, the lack of a social pact was mainly caused by the insurmountable differences between the unions and the employers' views on salary increases. Boyer, the PSOE's Finance minister, had declared that his goal was to reduce inflation to 8 percent by limiting wage increases to at most 6 percent (Royo 2000: 84). The unions strongly rejected this proposal and when, in their negotiations with the CEOE, employers would not accept an increase above 6.5 percent, no agreement was reached (Morán 1996: 30).

For 1985, however, a final attempt to coordinate wage demands was successful. The *Acuerdo Económico y Social* (AES) was signed in October 1984, to take effect during the following two years. The objective had been clearly stated by González in public statements that preceded the agreement: the control of wages was considered a fundamental weapon in the control of inflation (Duréndez Sáez 1997: 164). The belief that a more confrontational strategy was more beneficial at this stage for

---

[17] In effect, the PSOE government tried to offer a deal to stable workers: the high levels of employment security that they enjoyed would be continued and in return they would moderate their wage demands. As the following paragraphs will make clear, this trade-off in fact dominated PSOE's employment policies until 1996 when they lost power.

[18] UGT's participation is hardly surprising but CCOO's seems to be the result of its leadership not wanting to publicly oppose a socialist party that had just won the elections by a surprising majority.

117

membership and works council election goals, caused CCOO leaders to abandon the negotiations and reject the agreement once it had been signed by UGT, CEOE, and the government. The AES included salary objectives for 1985 and 1986 and a set of government intentions about the size of the public sector, unemployment benefits, and the reform of labor relations law (to make it more similar to that of other European nations). This last clause was one of the most controversial aspects of the agreement because it was interpreted by employers to mean the lowering of dismissal costs and the end of administrative authorization for dismissals. Between October and December of 1986, works council elections took place. UGT obtained 41 percent of the representatives while CCOO obtained 35 percent. Although these elections confirmed UGT as the most powerful confederation in Spain, when the results were analyzed in more detail it became clear that there was a decrease in UGT support in big companies, the public sector, and other areas in which the power of Spanish unions had traditionally rested. This turn of events, as Morán argues, convinced the UGT leadership that the subordination of their strategies to the policies of the PSOE government endangered the subsequent success of the union (1996: 33, see also Maravall 1995: 226). The age of (partial) coordination was over.

5.2.2. 1987–95: End of Cooperation and Promotion of Outsiders

Two important developments took place during this period. First, the end of coordination affected the influence of insiders on union strategies. Higher levels of coordination can limit the ability of insiders to free ride. Coordination in the labor market promotes the consideration of non-particularistic goals by the social partners. The collapse of coordination in Spain intensified the differences between insiders and outsiders and made the interests of insiders all the more important to unions and the social democratic party. Second, the changes in employment legislation described in section 5.2.1 became the engine for an enormous increase in temporary employment. As insiderness was being reinforced, therefore, outsiderness became a defining characteristic of the Spanish political economy.

Up to 1985 there had been some degree of cooperation between the unions (at least as far as UGT was concerned) and the socialist government. From 1986 on, however, the attitude of the social partners shifted away from national coordination quite dramatically. Coinciding with an upswing of the economy, the PSOE government declared that its main concern was still inflation, and to control it, endorsed an extremely strict monetary policy. The government's tight monetary policies had already caused friction between UGT and PSOE but it became even more divisive when the economy was growing. The determination of the González administration in its anti-inflationary objectives was considered by the unions to imply a tight control of wage increases. Union officials, on the other hand, wanted the better economic circumstances to be coupled by an increase in wages and public spending. The insistence of the government on inflation as the most relevant macroeconomic goal and on the moderation of wage demands as the way to reduce it made the collaboration of unions complicated (Recio and Roca 1998). This was particularly clear in the failure of conversations between the government and the unions after González's economic team had declared their intention to recommend wage increases below the predicted level of inflation (Morán 1996: 33).

Different explanations have been provided for the breakdown of coordination. Some authors (see e.g. Maravall 1995) have argued that the end of coordination was influenced by the consolidation of democracy in Spain, others (like Recio and Roca 1998) that the UGT leadership became convinced that the government was not committed to cooperating with the union and had rather used it to rubber-stamp measures previously taken. These are undoubtedly important factors but it is my contention that UGT's decision to conclude cooperation was also significantly influenced by two additional issues. First was the consideration that whatever legitimacy and institutional gains were to result from cooperation, they had already been obtained.[19] The strategy of cooperation and responsibility had already paid off with workers (in the works council elections of 1980, 1982, and 1986) and with the government (by benefiting from legislation, like the 1985 Union Freedom Law, that favored UGT as the alternative to CCOO).

As for the second factor, I would argue that in the Spanish labor relations context (characterized by union competition for members, low union density, and intermediate collective bargaining centralization) the presence of a social democratic party in government, instead of a conservative one, may have made agreement less rather than more likely. Union leaders seemed to believe they needed to radicalize their

---

[19] This was made very clear by Nicolás Redondo, the General Secretary of UGT, when in the 1987 Confederal Committee meeting he declared: 'coordination is no longer possible, it was possible during the democratic transition because we were looking for political legitimacy' (quoted by Morán 1996: 49, my translation).

positions to distinguish what they offered to prospective members/voters from what could simply be obtained from the social democratic government. Attracting union members and works council voters is a vital necessity for a Spanish union and this is difficult to do if the demands of UGT seem indistinguishable from the objectives of the governing social democratic party. If members and potential members do not feel that there is some 'value added' to a union's demands there is no reason to support that particular union. The need to radicalize demands in a direction consistent with the interests of the most numerous constituency of unions (insiders) is particularly strong when a 'rival' union (in this case, CCOO) can attract members/voters by catering to those interests. Following this logic, the cooperation of UGT with the PSOE government from 1982 to 1985 was incidental, the result of the need to obtain some political legitimacy and institutional advantages to improve the situation in which the union found itself at the end of the dictatorship. Once these were accomplished, separating union demands from the objectives of a social democratic government was paramount. The relevance of this interpretation is emphasized by the following exchange between Felipe González and Antón Saracíbar, UGT's secretary of organization, during the PSOE's Federal Committee meeting in October 1987. According to Maravall, González asked what was needed for UGT's cooperation and Saracíbar answered, 'all unions want coordination but mainly with a conservative government. With a social democratic government, a union like UGT has no vital necessity for coordination' (1995: 227).[20]

The attitude of the other social partners toward coordination was equally negative at this time. CEOE officials were ready to admit that national pacts were 'mortally wounded' (Duréndez Sáez 1997: 188). Although employers had been strong supporters of coordination, the experience of the previous years had made them much less enthusiastic. They were dissatisfied in particular with the ineffectiveness of national recommendations to moderate wage increases, with the Spanish wage structure (in which fixed components dominate variable ones to the detriment, in the employers' view, of productivity), and with the unwillingness of the government to address dismissal costs. The CCOO leadership, on the other hand, had never been a convinced participant in coordination and in fact regretted having participated in the 1982 and 1983 pacts. Agustín Moreno, secretary of the *Acción Sindical* section in CCOO's Confederal Committee until 1995, recognized that participation in these pacts

[20] My translation.

generated problems between CCOO's leadership and the rank-and-file and lower-level union officials (Moreno 1989).

The breakup of cooperation and the increasing animosity between UGT and the PSOE government culminated with the organization of a general strike by UGT and CCOO in December of 1988. The strike was very successful and enjoyed a great degree of popular support. According to some analysts the final straw that precipitated the strike was the introduction of a *Plan de Empleo Juvenil* (Youth Employment Plan), which proposed a further flexibilization of contracts for young people as the method to combat unemployment (Adelantado, Noguera, and Rambla 1998). But, as the preceding paragraphs make clear, the reasons for the breakdown of coordination had accumulated and promotion of employment precariousness (an important element of the PSOE's strategies since 1982) does not seem the most significant motivation.[21]

As coordination collapsed, the economy experienced a significant amount of growth and unemployment started to decline. Because of the legislation changes described in section 5.2.1, however, the overwhelming majority of the employment created at this time was characterized by temporary contracts. According to Dolado and Bentolila, between 1986 and 1990 total employment increased by 3 percent per year but a whopping 98 percent of all contracts registered at employment offices were temporary ones (Dolado and Bentolila 1992: 12). As a result, by 1992 over one third of all employees worked under temporary contracts. Moreover, temporary contracts had not only become the main form of entry into the labor market but also the main form of exit from it. The role of unemployed people as the insiders' buffer against economic downturns is clearly reflected by labor market exit figures. As Richards and García de Polavieja point out, even in 1991, when unemployment was at its lowest since 1982 and the economic cycle was at its peak, 60 percent of unemployment and 65 percent of long-term unemployment had been originated by the termination of fixed-term contracts (1997: 16).

The general strike and the decrease in electoral support suffered by the PSOE in the elections held in the fall of 1989 (when the socialists lost the absolute majority they had enjoyed since 1982) promoted a temporary lull in labor market policy. By 1991, the government was engaged in unsuccessful negotiations with the social partners to convince

---

[21] Different analysts have argued against the interpretation of the Youth Employment Plan as the most important reason for the general strike (see the collection of *El País* articles in Juliá 1988). The PSOE's continued emphasis on wage moderation and the proposed austerity in public spending seem to be more important factors influencing the strike.

them of the need for a Competitiveness Pact that would promote further labor market flexibility and a commitment to wage moderation. In spite of this failure, the beginning of an economic downturn and the prerequisites for the Maastricht Treaty provided the excuses needed to design these policies without union support. In 1992, the government approved a Convergence Plan whose main characteristic was the reduction of public spending on unemployment benefits (the conditions to receive them became more exclusionary). Then in 1993, immediately after the general elections that had confirmed PSOE rule but again with a decrease in support, the González government started a dialogue with unions and employers about labor market reforms. This dialogue did not prove productive and, in January of 1994, UGT and CCOO organized a second general strike against the proposed labor market legislation. Although the general strike was again quite successful (although less so than the one in 1988), the PSOE government did not change its approach and approved a Law-Decree modifying the Workers' Statute (Cachón Rodríguez 1997: 87).

The 1994 labor market reforms contained five basic changes: (*a*) the creation of two new kinds of contracts with very little social protection, the learning contract (*contrato de aprendizaje*) and the part-time contract (*contrato de tiempo parcial*);[22] (*b*) the legalization of temporary employment agencies; (*c*) the legalization of private hiring intermediaries; (*d*) the transformation of existing regulations to provide employers with greater discretion in matters such as geographical mobility and the length of the working day (Recio and Roca 1998: 148); and (*e*) the transformation of some of the requirements for worker dismissal. The two most relevant legislative changes for my analysis are those related to the further flexibilization of temporary employment and those affecting firing costs.

About the extension and facilitation of temporary contracts, it seems clear that three out of the five areas of change directly address this issue. The government attempted to promote the use of temporary contracts by creating two new contracts with very low levels of protection and, therefore, employers' contributions (see Martín and Santos 1994; Recio and Roca 1998). Part-time contract holders, for example, were not covered for ordinary sickness and received no unemployment benefits (Rhodes 1997: 111). In addition, temporary contracts were not only made cheaper but also more available by the legalization of temporary employment and private hiring companies. These measures can only be interpreted as a sign

---

[22] The training contract (*contrato de formación*) was abolished. Since the learning contract did not have fiscal incentives (like the reduction of social security contributions), it was hoped it would contribute to the control of the budget (Alba Ramírez 1996: 17).

of the PSOE government's willingness to promote a further increase in 'precarious' employment (an almost insignificant portion of the contracts signed were indefinite).

The decisiveness that dominated the reforms concerning temporary employment was not present, however, in the labor market measures affecting the employment protection of insiders. The 1994 legislation initiative included: the acceptance of organizational and production reasons as valid justifications for collective dismissals; a more restrictive redefinition of collective dismissals; and the specification of fifteen days as the maximum length for the labor authorities to consider a collective dismissal application. The effectiveness of these changes was questioned by the CEOE, and more drastic reforms (like eliminating the need for authorization altogether) were again demanded, but the González government had no interest in lowering the protection of insiders. I agree with Rhodes' argument that lowering the firing costs for those enjoying permanent employment would have undoubtedly been a 'major vote loser' for the PSOE government (1997: 109). The words of Marcos Peña Pinto, General Secretary of Employment and Labor Relations in the Ministry of Labor, leave little doubt regarding the intentions of the 1994 reforms. Together with the promotion of temporary employment described above, Peña defines the objective of the reforms as '(t)o protect employment by maintaining the procedures for the dismissal of workers as rigid as possible' (Peña Pinto 1994: 52).

Most observers would agree that the effects of the 1994 labor market reforms on firing costs were minimal. This is first because collective dismissals still required administrative approval in a way that, according to Jimeno, obligated employers to accept greater compensation than that stipulated by law in return for the unions' agreement (1996: 8–9). Then there is the fact that a great number of the individual dismissals that went to court resulted in the worker receiving more compensation than established by law for terminations with cause. Since the job protection of insiders remained practically untouched but temporary employment was significantly extended, the 1994 labor reforms did not do anything to reverse (in fact, they reinforced) the growth of outsiderness in Spain (Jimeno 1996: 9). As Jimeno and Toharia argue, it is clear that since 1982 the PSOE governments had opted for the flexibilization of the labor market in a very peculiar way: 'reducing the job security of new entrants into employment (if they were hired under fixed-term contracts) without reducing the job security of those already employed under permanent full-time contracts' (Jimeno and Toharia 1994: 109).

5.2.3. 1996–2000: Conservative Government and Decline in Insider Employment Protection

With the narrow victory of PP in the general elections of 1996 a new period for insider employment protection begins. The most significant conservative legislation of this period was the 1997 labor market reforms. The 1997 reforms were substantially different from those attempted by the previous PSOE governments for one main reason: the protection of insiders is lowered for the first time. Also, unlike the PSOE government's 1994 reforms (vocally opposed by the unions), the PP government actively sought the participation and eventual acceptance of the social partners.[23]

In April of 1997, CCOO, UGT, and CEOE signed three pacts under the tutelage of the PP government. These were the *Acuerdo Interconfederal para la Estabilidad del Empleo* (AIEE), the *Acuerdo Interconfederal sobre Negociación Colectiva* (AINC), and the *Acuerdo Interconfederal de Cobertura de Vacíos* (AICV). The AINC represented an effort to once more reshape collective bargaining in Spain. While the 1994 legislation represented changes in collective bargaining directed to transform national law, the 1997 changes were meant to promote change from within the collective bargaining system itself (del Rey Guanter et al. 1998). The AINC was meant to provide better guidelines for the issues discussed at each level of bargaining and to promote sectoral bargaining without taking away from the autonomy of company bargaining (CES 1997: 344–56). The AICV, on the other hand, represented the continuation of a set of pacts (starting with the Workers' Statute) directed to substitute the regulations that existed in the pre-democratic period (*Ordenanzas Laborales* and *Reglamentaciones de Trabajo*).

It is, however, the AIEE that most relevantly affects the insider–outsider arguments presented in this chapter. The basic idea guiding the AIEE reforms was that the promotion of stable employment can only be obtained by reducing the protection of insiders. As Sáez points out, a reduction in dismissal costs was expected to produce more employment stability (1997: 322). At the same time, some of the conditions for temporary employment became more limited. More concretely, a new indefinite contract was created. The 'contract for the promotion of

---

[23] I would argue, however, that the cooperative attitude of the conservative government resulted from the limited nature of their electoral victory. Although this situation would change in 1999, when the conservative party was confirmed in power by a majority as overwhelming as the one enjoyed by the PSOE in 1982, Aznar's first government was weak enough (needing the support of the regional parties to pass legislation) to be interested in attaining a degree of consensus before transforming the basis of labor market regulations.

indefinite employment' (*contrato de fomento de empleo indefinido*) was to be used by individuals who had experienced difficulties entering the labor market and by those holding temporary contracts.[24] Because of the lower dismissal compensation of the new indefinite contracts, the AIEE agreement was expected to reduce average dismissal costs by approximately 25 percent for an employee with ten years of experience (Sáez 1997: 322). Temporary employment was expected to decrease as a result of new legislation providing employers with fiscal and social security incentives for creating indefinite jobs. It was also limited by a reduction of the kinds of activities covered by ordinary temporary contracts (those signed until the completion of a particular task) and the transformation of the learning contract (the *contrato de aprendizaje* created in 1994) back into the previously abolished training contract (*contrato para la formación*). The training contract was not to be used as a contract to promote employment but rather for the provision of training for workers between 16 and 21 years of age.[25] Finally, the AIEE further improved temporary employment by increasing the levels of protection of part-time contracts.

The attitude of the conservative party toward these reforms is not hard to understand within my insider–outsider framework. A lowering of the protection of insiders benefits employers and as such is one of the main strategies hypothesized in my argument. Limiting the use of temporary employment, as well as the improvement in protection for part-time employment, seems also reasonable (if coupled with a general decrease in insider protection). A conservative party without a clear electoral advantage would, logically, be interested in attracting outsider support.

The reasons why this pact was signed by unions characterized by the staunch defense of insiders are more difficult to explain.[26] Schwartz argues that, at this point,

unions confronted the evidence of their separation from public opinion, since the majority of people were convinced that legislation seeking to protect stable workers doomed many to unemployment. Something needed to give way on the side of the privileged. Union leaders would have paid a very high price in terms

[24] The only difference between this contract and the standard indefinite contract is that the compensation for termination without cause was lower (thirty-three days per year worked, up to twenty-four months).

[25] Its maximum length was two years unless extended by collective bargaining to a maximum of three.

[26] The rejection by insiders of even these concessions was reflected in the vocal opposition to the pact by Izquierda Unida (the Communist lead coalition party) and a critical sector of CCOO headed by Agustín Moreno. This opposition was particularly clear in the public demonstrations of May 1, 1997 (see *El País* of May 2, 1997).

of reputation and support if it had become obvious that they were responsible for the breakdown of the negotiations.   (Schwartz 1997, my translation)

There is some truth to this. It is also the case that, even after these reforms, unions could argue that they had been once more successful in defending the protection of insiders. Cándido Méndez, General Secretary of CCOO, and Antonio Gutiérrez, General Secretary of UGT, strongly emphasized in their evaluations of the pact how the dismissal compensation of those holding standard indefinite contracts had not changed at all (see e.g. *El País* of April 17, 1997 and *El País* of April 23, 1997).

Finally, the victory of PP in the general elections of March 2000 (which resulted in an absolute conservative majority) immediately resulted in proposals to further reduce dismissal costs. In October 2000, the second PP government proposed an extension to all new contracts of the regulations limiting the compensation for termination without cause to thirty-three days per year worked, up to twenty-four months. Unencumbered now by the limited electoral support of their first administration, members of the new conservative government hinted first to employers and then to the general public that this time they would not wait for the agreement of unions and that they would pass the proposed legislation without union cooperation (*El País*, October 25, 2000 and interview with Rodrigo Rato, Minister of Finance, in *El País*, October 29, 2000).[27]

5.3. Employment Protection in the Netherlands

To understand employment protection in the Netherlands from 1970 to 2000, we need to explore its close relation to insider wage demands. As was the case in Spain, insiders (and the unions that represent them) want both employment protection and wage increases. The analysis below will show that, in increasingly challenging circumstances, however, governments can only offer insiders the continuation of high levels of employment protection in return for wage moderation. The development of employment protection in the Netherlands can be divided into two periods: the 1970s, characterized by the success of insiders in securing both high levels of employment protection and high wages; and the 1980s and 1990s, when insiders sacrificed wages to maintain high employment

---

[27] The reforms did in fact take place just as predicted, without union support, in 2001.

protection levels and outsiders emerged as an extremely significant portion of the labor market.

5.3.1. Protection and Wages: The 1970s

The starting point in my analysis is one that is favorable to insiders. In the 1970s, insiders in the Netherlands enjoyed high levels of employment protection and increasing wages. I will analyze these two factors separately.

Levels of employment protection increased considerably in the early 1970s, as in many other OECD countries, through numerous legislative initiatives (Van Peijpe 1998). Most Dutch jobs are covered by a contract of unlimited duration (De Neubourg 1990: 102). The costs of ending these contracts are generally high. After systematically reviewing legislation, Mosley (1994) concludes that the Netherlands belongs in the group of OECD countries with the most restrictive dismissal regulations. The Dutch case is grouped with Spain, Italy, Portugal, and Greece.[28]

These high levels of employment protection are not so much the consequence of the regulated dismissal costs that employers must pay but of the 'complex and lengthy procedures necessary to effect individual or collective dismissals for economic reasons' (De Neubourg 1990: 105). In the Netherlands, a preliminary procedure has to be followed before any dismissal can be implemented. An employer needs an 'acceptable' reason to lay off workers and, under the Extraordinary Labor Relations Act of 1945, the prior approval of the director of the regional employment office for nearly all types of dismissal (Gorter and Poot 1999). For individual dismissals, although the employment office accepts a great majority of applications, the prior approval process entails a written request, a written defense (sometimes also an oral hearing) and consultations with representatives of employers and unions. In addition to the approval process, employers have to give a period of notice that can be as high as twenty-six weeks for workers over forty-five years of age (Van Peijpe 1998: 141). A number of other special groups (like pregnant women, absentee or sick workers, and members of work councils) are entitled to greater protection. Moreover, after the decision is made by the regional employment office, workers can challenge dismissals in court. In some cases, an alternative approach to individual dismissals has been for employers to apply directly

---

[28] In the less detailed quantitative analysis in Chapter 4, the Netherlands belonged to the group with intermediately high levels of employment protection (using the measure in Baker et al. 2004).

to a court. The judge decides on the amount of compensation to be paid to the worker. In this case, the process is generally faster but compensation is also higher.[29] Because of the relative gain in procedural ease, this approach to dismissals is increasingly popular in the Netherlands (Gorter and Poot 1999: 7).

The process is even more complicated for collective dismissals. The period of notice is longer since laying off twenty or more workers (within a three-month period) requires the employer to officially notify not only the regional public employment office but also the works council and the trade union. The employment office's regional director then gives a month to all actors involved to reach a 'social plan' (Visser and Hemerijck 1997: 139). In addition to this, contract suspensions are legally discouraged. Like Spain, and unlike some other countries with relatively high levels of protection (e.g. Sweden or Norway), firms in the Netherlands cannot adjust employment through temporary lay-offs or short-term work (see De Neubourg 1990 for details).

Until the 1970s, wage moderation had been an essential part (if not the most essential part) of Dutch corporatist politics and economic performance (see e.g. Wolinetz 1989). In the 1950s and 1960s, the government used the Dutch corporatist structure to promote the participation of the social partners in the design and implementation of incomes policies. In an economic context characterized by an expanding world economy and stable mass production, a low-wage strategy based on effective incomes policies was very successful (Hemerijck 1995). However, Wolinetz convincingly argues that corporatist wage moderation 'became increasingly difficult in the full employment economy of the 1960s and impossible in the highly polarized 1970s' (1990: 419). Starting in the 1960s, then, the dam burst and the near universal compliance with tripartite economic indications that had been the norm since 1945 could no longer be taken for granted (Gladdish 1991: 139). By 1970, after general rises, the Netherlands had become a high wage economy and the Dutch were quite wealthy (in international terms). The wage moderation that had followed World War II was now not easy to accomplish (Braun 1986).

The collapse of wage moderation in the 1970s was influenced by a number of factors. Following the general elections of 1972, the most leftist government of the postwar period was formed. Despite the lack of strong

---

[29] Because of the long notification periods and prior consent requirements, Dutch law provides no statutory right to severance pay in case of dismissal (Van Peijpe 1998: 145). The judicial practice of awarding damages (one month salary for every year worked) has become a kind of unlegislated severance pay.

parliamentary support, the Den Uyl (PvdA) administration committed itself to, in the words of Hemerijck, an ambitious program characterized by the 'redistribution of wealth, knowledge, and power' (1995: 206). Facing the consequences of the first oil crisis, Den Uyl opted for a Keynesian strategy of fiscal stimulation. His objective was a corporatist deal exchanging fiscal stimulation for wage restraint but the radicalized Dutch unions wanted more than the government, with weak support from the Christian Democrats, could offer (Hemerijck, Unger, and Visser 2000: 211). Unable to promote wage moderation, the Den Uyl government imposed wage and income freezes in 1974 and 1976 but the effects were minimal (Hemerijck, Van der Meer, and Visser 2000: 260). Den Uyl's problems with increasing wage levels were exacerbated by two factors. First, Den Uyl saw the support of the unions as the key to political survival and was reluctant to antagonize them (Visser 1992). Second, since 1967, unions had been able to secure the inclusion of automatic price escalators in collective agreements. According to Visser and Hemerijck, by 1980 automatic price escalators determined 75 percent of annual wage increases (1997: 96).

5.3.2. The 1980s and 1990s: The Return of Wage Moderation and the Emergence of Outsiders

Although the unemployment rate had grown from about 2.3 percent in 1973 to more than 6 percent in 1980, a vicious circle of high wages and protection for insiders and increasing unemployment for outsiders dominated the 1970s. The deadlock was broken by the conservative government that took office in 1982. Led by Ruud Lubbers, the new CDA-VVD coalition considered the slowdown of economic and employment growth to be the result of high labor costs and public expenditures, low profits, and excessive levels of government intervention (De Neubourg 1990: 2). Although the Lubbers government is often referred to as a 'no nonsense austerity coalition',[30] its conservative orientation is evident. Gladdish, for example, declares that 'there can be no doubt that the alliance between the CDA and the Liberals proved a crucial point in the complexion of recent politics, for it shifted the balance manifestly to the right' (1991: 61). It was also important that the VVD had almost as high a percentage of the vote as the CDA in the 1982 elections and consequently occupied six ministries (eight for the CDA) and had eight state secretaries (as many as the CDA).

---

[30] See e.g. Visser and Hemerijck 1997.

The key objective in the CDA-VVD government's strategy was to decrease labor costs, which would increase profitability, investment, and employment (De Neubourg 1990: 3). To accomplish this, pressure was applied on the social partners to come to an agreement that would secure wage moderation. First, the government signaled a break from the policies of the past by announcing the suspension of price compensation payments and the freezing of public salaries, social benefits, and the minimum wage (Visser and Hemerijck 1997: 100). Then it made known that 'it would intervene directly in the wage bargaining process should the social partners (. . .) fail to work out a meaningful program for wage moderation at the national level' (Jones 1998: 2–3). This threat prompted the social partners to negotiate earnestly and on November 24, 1982, the *Wassenaar* Accord was signed.

First and most importantly, *Wassenaar* signified the commitment of the social partners to wage moderation in exchange for working time reductions. On wage moderation, the agreement recommended unions to 'forego nominal wage increases and suspend the payment of cost-of-living adjustments'. On working time, it recommended employers not veto negotiations regarding a reduction of working time from 40 hours per week (Visser and Hemerijck 1997: 81). *Wassenaar* also started the transformation of the wage bargaining system in the Netherlands from one characterized by high centralization and ineffectiveness (in the 1970s) to a more decentralized but very coordinated one (Visser 1990*a*).

The results of *Wassenaar* were consequential. First, *Wassenaar* promoted wage moderation and therefore improved the price competitiveness of Dutch products (Hemerijck, Unger, and Visser 2000). Between 1982 and 1985, average real wages fell by 9 percent (Visser and Hemerijck 1997: 101). Also by 1985, cost-of-living and escalator clauses had become very rare in collective agreements (Visser 1992). Average unit wage costs from 1983 to 1987 declined by 20 to 30 percent compared to the average for the 1975–80 period, and the profitability of manufacturing firms increased by more than 30 percent (De Neubourg 1990: 3–4). *Wassenaar* also resulted in some significant working time reductions. The working week for civil servants, for example, fell from 40 to 38 hours and twelve extra vacation days per year were added (Andeweg and Irwin 1993: 193).[31] Between 1987 and 1997, the average working week for

---

[31] For a critical analysis of the degree to which shorter working time arrangements took place (or did not) after 1982, see Visser (1989: 240–1).

the whole economy was brought down from 40 to 37.5 hours (Hemerijck and Van Kersbergen 1997: 267).[32]

The reasons why Dutch unions signed the *Wassenaar* Accord, especially after more than a decade of refusing to engage in wage moderation, need to be explored in more detail. One of the most important factors undoubtedly had to do with the trade-off included in the agreement. As the paragraph above indicates, the working-time reduction obtained in exchange for wage moderation was an attractive feature for unions worried about the reaction of insiders (Hemerijck 1995: 218–9). The uncertainty about increasing unemployment may be another reason. The restructuring process that the country was going through contributed to the willingness of insiders to sacrifice wages to maintain the levels of employment protection. As De Beer argues, it seems logical to assume that union members were prepared to accept wage moderation 'in order to save their jobs' (1999: 5). A third reason has to do with union legitimacy. By signing the agreement, the unions retained their role as the legitimate representatives of the employed and therefore maintained their influence over policymaking and, in particular, social policy (Wolinetz 1989; Jones 1998). Also influential in the change of union strategy, finally, were the losses in membership experienced in the late 1970s and early 1980s. During this time, unions failed to attract new and especially young members.

In 1986, the general elections can be considered a referendum on the Lubbers government. The results seemed to indicate that there was a high degree of popular support for the conservative government's policies. Although the Labor Party increased their share of the vote from 30.4 percent in the 1982 elections to 33.3 percent, they were 'overshadowed by the striking success of the CDA which represented the first significant advance of the Christian grouping since the 1960s, and made the CDA the largest party in the Second Chamber' (Gladdish 1991: 65). The election allowed the CDA and the VVD to recreate their coalition with a majority of twelve seats. The distribution of seats in the cabinet reflected the fact that support for the VVD had declined (nine ministers for the CDA vs. five

---

[32] Although one of the publicly acknowledged reasons why working time was being reduced for those with stable employment was the reduction of unemployment, it was soon very clear that the effects were minimal. According to a 1985 survey of companies working in the Netherlands, no employment effects had resulted in 78 percent of all firms which had introduced shorter working hours since 1982 (Visser 1989: 241). This was not surprising. According to Visser, a policy pursuing working-time reduction to promote employment would have to be matched by vacancy refilling and recruitment measures (1989: 241). This was not the case in the Netherlands.

for the VVD), but the policies pursued by the new conservative coalition did not change.

The return to wage moderation as a fundamental feature of the Dutch political economy was so generally accepted from the first Lubbers government until 2000 that there is little to say about developments after the 1986 elections. As a result of the 1989 election, the Christian democrats formed a coalition with the social democrats but the attitude of the new CDA-PvdA government did not change regarding the desirability of wage moderation.[33] The only transformation concerned the exchange behind wage restraint. While previously, wage moderation had been 'traded' for shorter working hours it now was accompanied by 'lower taxes for workers and lower social contributions for employers, made possible by improved public finances and a broader tax base' (Hemerijck, Unger, and Visser 2000: 221).

The participation of the Labor Party in a government that made wage restraint its most important goal may seem surprising (especially when compared to the policies of the PvdA in the 1970s). During the 1980s, however, the Labor Party had changed its attitude and had become much more pragmatic (for details, see Hillebrand and Irwin 1999). A conscious attempt to make themselves into acceptable partners for the Christian democrats was reflected in a very moderate election program in 1989. Once the cabinet was formed, the fact that Wim Kok (now leader of the PvdA but previous chairman of the FNV) took the Finance Ministry also hinted at the new expediency of the social democratic party. The emphasis on wage moderation in fact continued after the formation of the first and second 'purple'[34] coalitions led by Prime Minister Wim Kok, from 1994 to 1998 and from 1998 to 2002 (see Hoogerwerf 1999: 162).

Turning now to employment protection, the pattern we encountered in Spain in the 1980s is repeated in the Netherlands: wage moderation is offered to governments by insiders as a way to maintain their employment protection. Mosley points out that dismissal regulations have remained significantly unchanged through the 1980s and early 1990s (1994: 79). The OECD's overall strictness of protection against dismissals index confirms these observations. The index is constructed

---

[33] At this time, however, union membership decline had stopped and the unions were feeling confident enough to organize a series of strikes in the industry, transport, education, and health sectors.

[34] In 1994 and 1998, the PvdA formed a governing coalition with VVD and D66. It is referred to as the purple coalition because of the mixing of the social democratic red with the conservative blue.

by averaging the scores obtained by each country in three categories: 'procedural inconveniences which the employer faces when trying to dismiss employees; notice and severance pay provisions; and prevailing standards of and penalties for unfair dismissal' (OECD 1999: 54). The score for the Netherlands is 3.1 for the 1980s and also for the 1990s. As a way to compare, the index scores for Italy and Sweden are 2.8 in both decades, Germany's is 2.7 in the 1980s and 2.8 in the 1990s, while the UK's is (not surprisingly) a low 0.8 for both periods.

The influence of government partisanship on employment protection levels is not obvious. There have been very few initiatives to modify employment protection since the late 1970s. Before the 1994 election, there was talk about eliminating prior approval 'on the grounds that existing procedures were cumbersome, costly, over-protective and inhibiting flexibility' (Visser and Hemerijck 1997: 162). This has been the argument frequently presented by the OECD, and favored by Dutch employers, in its recommendations to Dutch governments (see e.g. OECD 1996). The debate encountered strong opposition from the unions and, after the 1994 elections, the PvdA-led governing coalition did not produce any substantial changes in employment protection regulations. The second PvdA-led governing coalition (elected in 1998) did produce some changes. In 1999, a mild reduction of statutory dismissal protection for standard contracts was enacted. The approved measures (which expanded the justification for negotiated dismissals, but with the possibility of legal appeal), however, were not very substantial.

One of the reasons why high employment protection levels have not been more hotly debated is that in the Netherlands (as in Spain) flexibility in the labor market has taken the form of increasing numbers of nonstandard contracts since 1980. Nonstandard work (especially part-time) has become a shockingly large proportion of employment in the Netherlands. Part-time work rose from 16.6 percent of total employment in 1979 to 36.5 percent in 1996 (Visser and Hemerijck 1997: 30).[35] Between 1980 and 1984, the beginning of the wage moderation and employment growth that typify the 'Dutch miracle', full-time employment decreased by 12 percent and part-time employment increased by almost 28 percent (Visser 1989: 232). It is therefore clear that the extraordinary growth in part-time employment in the Netherlands is to a great extent responsible for the decrease in unemployment. Hemerijck,

---

[35] The Netherlands has become the country with the highest proportion of part-time employment in the OECD.

Unger, and Visser calculate that 67 percent of the jobs created since 1982 have been part-time jobs (2000: 229). Salverda provides an even starker picture by looking at a different period and including in the analysis fixed-term employment. On balance, he argues, the great majority of Dutch employment growth between 1979 and 1997 consisted of part-time and flexible jobs—in a ratio of 3 to 1 (1999b: 5).

The composition of part-time employment since 1980 has also been very specific: young people and, especially, females are almost exclusively represented in the growing part-time sector (Hemerijck 1995; van Oorschot 2004). For Dutch men, part-time employment is very occasional (restricted to the beginning or end of their work careers, see Goul Andersen and Bendix Jensen 2002). Making the connection between female participation, part-time employment, and the decrease in unemployment, Hemerijck and Van Kersbergen argue that female part-time employment is the most conspicuous factor in the improvement of the Dutch labor market since 1980 (1997: 263).

Part-time workers, however, were entitled to few employment rights.[36] In the 1980s, unions showed little interest in part-timers. Employment rights and benefits favored full-time workers. More specifically, legal employment protection, coverage by works councils and social insurance entitlements did not extend to those working less than 14 hours per week in the Netherlands (Visser 1989; Maier 1994). This is particularly meaningful given the fact that a considerable number of female employees work very short hours (17 percent of all female workers worked less than 12 hours per week in 1994).[37] Moreover, it is difficult to assess what proportion of part-time employment is truly voluntary (Visser 1989: 232).[38]

The second kind of nonstandard work that has become an important part of the job growth story in the Netherlands is fixed-term employment. In the Dutch context, fixed-term contracts are used for the replacement of regular workers on sick leave or holiday, and for seasonal work or specific jobs (De Neubourg 1990: 99). There are also 'flexi-contracts' (also known as call-up contracts, minimum–maximum contracts and zero-hour contracts) for work to be done whenever it is needed by the employer. The terms of a fixed-term contract (especially duration) are predetermined

---

[36] In Chapter 7, I analyze in more detail the relationship between hours worked and social benefits.

[37] For details, see Visser and Hemerijck (1997: 30–1).

[38] A survey in the Netherlands posed the question of whether we should talk about part-time employment or part-time unemployment (OECD 1996). In other words, are the Dutch voluntary part-timers or part-timers who cannot find full-time employment?

and cannot be changed as a result of collective bargaining. In theory, if a fixed-term contract is renewed after its conclusion, it does not expire automatically any longer and it is subject to the standard rules for dismissal. In practice, employers have evaded the legal procedures. After a fixed-term contract expires, the worker is often hired on a temporary basis through a temporary work agency, and after that a 'new' fixed-term contract is signed (and so forth). The combination of fixed-term contracts and temporary work has become known as the 'revolving door' (Van Peijpe 1998: 136). As indicated by Salverda (1999*b*) and Visser and Hemerijck (1997), fixed-term employment has become a very important part of the employment growth picture in the Netherlands. This is particularly true since 1993. While females are disproportionately represented in part-time work, fixed-term employment is especially high among young people.[39]

In terms of benefits and employment rights, precariousness has also been the rule for fixed-term contracts and what I have referred to above as flexi-contracts. Flexi-contracts were not covered by Dutch legislation and carried little legal protection (de Neubourg 1990: 101). As for fixed-term employment, Gorter and Poot show that workers on fixed-term contracts in the Netherlands had access to unemployment benefits in less favorable terms than workers with stable contracts (1999: 7).

Some improvements of the benefits and protection of part-time and temporary employment were promoted in the 1990s. In 1993, the legislation that excluded part-time employment from minimum wage requirements was abolished and in 1995 the first collective agreement for temporary workers was signed (Visser and Hemerijck 1997: 43–4). Then in 1999, a 'Flexibility and Security' proposal was passed by parliament and the right to continued employment, pension and social security was granted after two years of work (Hemerijck, Unger, and Visser 2000: 227). These changes were relatively minor (no measure was taken, for example, to limit the use of the fixed-term/temporary employment revolving door) and took place too late to modify the general sense that in the Netherlands nonstandard employment was second class employment for most of the 1980s and 1990s.[40]

How did governments promote the emergence of outsiders in the Netherlands? Two interpretations are possible. Visser and Hemerijck have

---

[39] Flexible work is also concentrated among those with the lowest educational levels (van Oorschot 2004).

[40] For evidence showing that flexible employment is still not socially protected in the Netherlands, see van Oorschot (2004).

argued that government policies did not have much to do with the promotion of part-time employment. 'The development towards the one-and-a-half jobs model,' they explain, 'is an example of *fortuna*, policies which prosper because they accord with the circumstances.' In support of their argument they quote the Minister of Social Affairs and Employment, Ad Melkert, who declared that part-time employment growth 'just came our way' (1997: 43). This does not seem to tell the whole story. I don't mean to deny that a number of factors unrelated to government design affected the emergence of part-time work in the Netherlands. Because of higher education attainment, smaller families, changing societal norms, and labor market uncertainty, more females wanted to enter the labor market starting in the 1970s. Part-time work became the predominant way of participating in the labor market for many women because of the absence of a comprehensive childcare system (Hemerijck, Unger, and Visser 2000: 217). Part-time work also turned out to be an attractive option for employers. Visser and Hemerijck argue that part-time employment was ideal for employers because it 'allows differentiation across groups of workers, disconnects operating hours from working hours, brings actual and contractual working hours nearer as part-time workers tend to be sick in their own time, and is reversible' (1997: 34–5).

This interpretation underestimates, however, the influence of government policy. First, although demographic pressures certainly demanded an expansion of employment, it is not clear that entry into the labor market for women and young people had to take the form of nonstandard employment. As was the case in Spain, the existence of highly protected jobs promoted the use of flexible nonstandard contracts for new workers. In many ways, insiderness created the need for outsiderness when demographic and economic circumstances changed in the 1970s. Maintaining the levels of insider employment protection was a choice made by policymakers and they are, therefore, also responsible for the increase in nonstandard employment. Second, it is also important to point out that one of the generally recognized reasons for the increase of part-time employment and the overwhelming number of female part-timers is the absence of a childcare system (Hemerijck, Unger, and Visser 2000). The absence of a government effort to promote day-care facilities and family-oriented services clearly influenced the emergence of part-time work (see Visser and Hemerijck 1997). Finally, some analysts argue that since the early 1980s part-time employment has been promoted directly by governments, if in often informal ways (see e.g. Andeweg and Irwin 1993: 193). Part-time employment was publicly encouraged, for example, in a 1987 government memorandum and it was later promoted by a 1989 tripartite recommendation (Salverda 1999*b*: 28).

5.4. Employment Protection in the UK

The analysis of employment protection in the UK is mostly about the consequences of conservative government. It has been divided into three sections. The first shows how insiders were successful in securing employment protection while not committing to wage moderation in the 1970s. The second illustrates how Thatcherism meant a dramatic attack on insiders in the 1980s. The third describes the continuation of conservative anti-insider government in the 1990s and Labour's return to power (and its weak attempts to promote insider protection).

5.4.1. *The 1970s: Protection and Lack of Wage Moderation*

Starting after World War II, efforts directed to promote wage moderation as a way to control inflation have had a long tradition in the UK. From 1948 to 1950 the Labour government led by Attlee negotiated voluntary wage restraint with the TUC. According to some analysts, this first episode of incomes policy was in fact much more successful than any of those that would follow it (Brown 1994: 33). The success was no doubt influenced by the fact that, at this time, collective bargaining in the UK was characterized by a small number of national, industry-wide agreements. The increase in inflation of the late 1950s suggested the need for the sort of incomes policy arrangement that had been so successful in 1948 but attempts to resuscitate wage moderation were not successful. To promote wage moderation in the 1960s, Harold Wilson's Labour government created the National Board for Prices and Incomes (NBPI) in 1964. The NBPI was a tripartite body not only in charge of promoting wage restraint but also of making sure that collective bargaining resulted in stable prices. The Board's independent emphasis on wage restraint, however, soon embarrassed a government more interested in exchanging pay increases for political acquiescence from labour.

In terms of employment protection, by the end of the 1960s, insiders were protected by a dismissal cost system that compared favorably with those in most other European countries. Redundancy payments had existed in the UK since 1965 when the Redundancy Payments Act was passed during Wilson's Labour government. At this time, the average payment amounted to about 12 weeks' pay, although in real terms it was perhaps as much as 15 or 16 weeks' pay because redundancy payments were not taxed (Bosworth and Wilson 1980: 97–8).[41] Insiders were also looked after by influential unions that interacted with employers in a relatively unrestricted industrial relations context.

In 1970, the Conservative Party won the election and its leaders tried to implement legislation that would transform collective bargaining, industrial disputes, and union behavior following the American model (Weekes et al. 1975). The effects of the 1971 Industrial Relations Act, however, were intensely and effectively resisted by unions (Smith 1980). Heath's electoral program had been explicitly against incomes policy. As the Conservative Party's 1970 manifesto declared: '(o)ur theme is to replace Labour's restrictions with Conservative incentive. We utterly reject the philosophy of compulsory wage control. (...) Labour's compulsory wage control was a failure and we will not repeat it' (Conservative Party 1970). One of the first measures to be taken by the Heath government therefore was the abolition of the NBPI. The conservatives' disdain for coordinated wage moderation, however, 'lasted only two years' (Brown 1994: 35). In 1972, having failed to win TUC support to combat an ever-increasing inflation rate, Heath implemented a compulsory incomes policy with penalties for employers that did not follow wage guidelines. This approach was unsuccessful and early in 1974, coal miners engaged in strikes to protest against the wage limitations established by the government. Challenging the miners, Heath called a general election and lost.

In 1974, Labour returned to power and repealed the 1971 Act (Brown, Deakin, and Ryan 1997). The Trade Union and Labour Relations Act of 1974 and the Employment Act of 1975 not only reversed the Industrial Relations Act but also strengthened unfair dismissal provisions. These acts expanded the rights of workers regarding redundancy and unfair dismissal, and established additional rights in relation to minimum pay, sick-leave pay, maternity rights, union membership, and union duty (Bosworth and Wilson 1980: 110).

Although the Labour Party publicly disputed the virtues of incomes policies at this point,[42] Wilson was determined to recreate a voluntary

---

[41] The number of people entitled to redundancy, however, was small. Workers younger than 18 years and those who had been in the job for less than 2 years were automatically excluded. Even in 1971, during the recession, they amounted to about 12 percent of registered unemployment (Bosworth and Wilson 1980).

[42] See Dawkins (1980) for details.

agreement with the unions to promote wage moderation. At the center of Labour's income strategy was the 'Social Contract', a policy package negotiated with the TUC. The TUC agreed to promote wage restraint in exchange for favorable legislation—initially, a repeal of the 1971 Industrial Relations Act as well as price and rent controls (Dawkins 1980). In spite of inflation levels that reached 25 percent in 1975, however, the TUC could not deliver on its commitment to wage moderation.[43] The government had then to request the IMF's assistance to protect the British pound.

As a part of the IMF package, the government made sure that wage growth limits were adhered to in the public sector but it did not implement any legislation to guarantee that the guidelines were followed in the private sector. Wages increased by as much as 17.5 percent in 1975–6. Although the IMF loan had been followed by a temporary fall in inflation, given the lack of success of voluntary wage restraint the government tried establishing a more formal wage increase objective (only 5 percent). This attempt encountered passionate opposition from the unions, which engaged in growing levels of contestation (Artis, Cobham, and Wickham-Jones 1992). This was particularly the case in the public sector, which, unlike many private companies, had suffered a substantial amount of involuntary wage moderation (Brown 1994: 36). A number of very visible public sector strikes took place in the winter of 1978–9 (the 'winter of discontent'). The collapse of wage moderation was marked by the defeat of union leaders publicly committed to it (like Jack Jones of the Transport and General Workers' Union) in the debate about continuing cooperation with the government (Edwards et al. 1992). Eric Deakins, who from 1974 to 1979 was Under Secretary of State for Trade and for Health and Social Security, describes Labour's interpretation of union behavior at this time as both 'reactionary and lunatic'. '(F)or the sake of marginal gains in real income,' he argues, 'trade unions showed themselves prepared to take the serious risk of the return of a Tory government' (1988: 12). The winter of discontent significantly damaged the government. As Deakins noted '(r)otting rubbish in the streets, sewage in the rivers, ambulance services disrupted, bodies piling up in the mortuaries: such examples undermined Labour's claim to be able to deal with the trade unions' (1988: 12).

---

[43] According to some observers, the absence of wage restraint was not so much the result of a lack of commitment by the TUC but of its inability to control the demands of local unions.

5.4.2. The 1980s: Anti-Insider Thatcherism

Insider protection was to drastically change in 1979 when Margaret Thatcher won the elections with a strongly antiunion message. The goals of the incoming government have been explained by Charles Bellairs (Consultant Director in the Conservative Political Centre) as follows: 'to deal with abuse of the trade union "closed shop", to protect individual trade union members against exploitation by the trade union bureaucracy and generally to correct the imbalance of power in favor of trade unions in such matters as pay negotiations' (1985: 6). The Conservative Party election manifesto declared that 'by heaping privilege without responsibility on the trade unions, Labour have given a minority of extremists the power to abuse individual liberties and to thwart Britain's chances of success' (Conservative Party 1979). The manifesto proposed limiting picketing, the closed shop, and striking as measures to reverse this tendency (Conservative Party 1979). In 1979, the context for these proposals could not have been more favorable as the popularity of unions had reached unprecedented lows (Edwards et al. 1992: 12).[44]

The Employment Act of 1980 represented the first step in the attack on insiders by the Thatcher government. Fulfilling Thatcher's election promises, the Act contained measures to: restrict the closed shop (providing compensation for people excluded from a closed shop and requiring that at least 80 percent of workers covered approved the creation of a new closed shop); limit picketing; remove provisions for obligatory arbitration when unions were trying to obtain recognition; and reduce dismissal costs (Simpson 1981). The reduction of employment protection is particularly important to my argument. As Edwards et al. have argued, the Thatcher government 'viewed employment protection provisions not as essential minimum standards but as "burdens on business" (particularly in respect of small employers) which acted as a deterrent to the employment of more people' (1992: 13). The 1980 Employment Act reduced dismissal costs in three ways: it eroded the rights of employees who had been subject to termination without cause, removed the employers' burden of proof for cause, and reduced maternity rights regarding reinstatement.

The 1980 Act was soon followed by the 1982 Employment Act, which moved further in the antiunion direction. This act restricted the definition of lawful union action to those having to do directly with the relationship between union and employer. Disputes 'not mainly' about specific

---

[44] In a survey conducted in 1978, 82 percent of respondents believed that unions had too much power (Visser and Van Ruysseveldt 1996: 49).

conditions (pay, work, jobs, etc.) were excluded from the definition, as were those that did not directly involve the workers in a particular job place. Occupations and sit-ins at the place of work were also made illegal. The immunity of trade unions from civil actions was ended and unions could now be sued for the damages that had resulted from illegal strikes. The closed shop was further limited by requiring an 85 percent approval vote (Visser and Van Ruysseveldt 1996).

The three subsequent electoral victories of Mrs Thatcher in 1983, 1987, and 1989 did not represent any change in the orientation of labor market legislation. The power of unions and insiders continued to be attacked by several legislative decisions. With the 1984 Trade Union Act, the conservative government made it more difficult for unions to defend insiders. Legal immunity was further reduced; now it not only applied to illegal actions but to any union decision to strike that had not been supported by a previous secret ballot).[45] The 1984 Act also required a vote every five years to elect union executive bodies and every ten years to decide whether the union should have political funds. The 1988 Employment Act made post-entry closed shop (and any strike to enforce it) illegal. It also abolished unions' legal rights to discipline members for crossing a picket line during a lawful strike and it extended secret voting to any union election. The 1989 Employment Act, finally, abolished legislation extending some labor market regulations to small companies (Brown, Deakin, and Ryan 1997). It also eliminated the Training Commission (created in 1988 to substitute the Manpower Services Commission (MSC)) and removed unions from training boards. The 1989 Act also reduced the administrative costs of dismissals by making it unnecessary for employers to provide a reason for dismissals unless the employee had been continuously employed for two years (it had been six months before).[46]

In terms of coordination with the social partners, Thatcher's electoral victories represented, in essence, the end of any attempt to promote wage moderation in the UK. Given the systematic weakening of unions promoted by the conservative governments, this is hardly surprising. The market-oriented policy of the Thatcher governments, largely relying on tight monetary policy to control inflation, marked the end of more or less formal incomes policies (Chater, Dean, and Elliott 1981: 1). The

---

[45] This had become a particularly important issue after previous strikes by coal miners that had not been voted on.

[46] Through the 1980s, in addition to the developments already mentioned, legislation changes had added a number of new factors (like company size or administrative problems) to the already long list of circumstances that could be considered by Industrial Tribunals when deciding the unfairness of a dismissal.

Conservative Party believed that a tight monetary policy would make coordination unnecessary, since trade unions would soon realize that the consequences of irresponsible wage bargaining was unemployment for their members (Rhodes 2000: 41).

5.4.3. *The 1990s: More Anti-Insider Conservative Government and New Labour*

The arrival of John Major at 10 Downing Street in 1990 did not modify the labor market policy orientation of the Tory government. The 1990 Employment Act effectively abolished the pre-entry closed shop by making the refusal of employers to hire nonunion members illegal (Brown, Deakin, and Ryan 1997). The 1990 Act also made it legal to dismiss workers who had participated in any unlawful industrial action (immunity was also removed from union officials taking actions on behalf of those dismissed for having participated in these actions).

In 1993, Major implemented the Trade Union Reform and Employment Rights Act. This Act made it legal for employers to offer employees financial enticements not to join a union. It also stipulated that employers were to get seven days warning in case of industrial action and that all prestrike votes were to be postal and to be subject to an independent count. It abolished arrangements that allowed employers to deduct union contributions directly from wages unless they were confirmed in writing every three years. The Arbitration Commission was no longer required to encourage collective bargaining and Wages Councils (and therefore any remaining minimum wage stipulations) were abolished. In addition to the fact that the UK was now the only European country without a minimum wage, the abolition of Wages Councils had important implications for the coverage of collective bargaining. The coverage of collective bargaining agreements had already drastically declined from 1984 (when it was 64 percent of employment) to 1990 (when it was only 47 percent). The disappearance of Wages Councils meant that regulated conditions for work and pay had now been eliminated for an additional 20 percent of employed workers (Visser and Van Ruysseveldt 1996: 69).

Perhaps trying to prevent their imminent electoral defeat, in 1996 the Major government seemed to soften, but not fundamentally modify, the degree of anti-insider and antiunion measures. The 1996 Employment Rights Act made it possible for employees who had received notice to be allowed to take time off (and to be remunerated for this time) to look for another job or to get training conducive to getting another job. The

Act established provisions for antenatal care and it instituted that time off and remuneration would be granted to employee representatives for the performance of their duties. An unremunerated period of fourteen weeks for maternity leave (as well as the right to return to work after it) was also specified. As for dismissal costs, the 1996 Employment Rights Act established a minimum notice period of a week for those who had been in the job for less than two years and a week per year worked (up to a maximum of twelve weeks) for other workers. The Act also recognized the right of every worker not to be unfairly dismissed, although it allowed for a very loose interpretation of what constituted fair dismissal and did not apply to those employed for less than two continuous years or above the retirement age. It also stipulated the amount of compensation to be provided by employers for unfair dismissals. Compensation consisted of a basic award (equal to 1 or 1.5 weeks of pay per continuous year worked up to twenty years) and a compensatory award (to be at most equal to the basic award) to be determined by a judge.

The electoral victory of Tony Blair in 1997 and the return to office (after eighteen years) of the Labour Party resulted in timid reversals of some of the conservative attacks on insiders. Many analysts have argued that New Labour emerged as a political option sharing many Thatcherite characteristics. This was certainly the case regarding unions and wage bargaining. McIlroy argues that for New Labour trade unions had become an 'electoral handicap', a 'constraint on the development of new support', a 'barrier to a rational-efficient party' and a 'potential impediment to the optimal operation of the market and to successful government' (1998: 539). Crouch notes that New Labour shares the view that '(w)orkers' rights are a drag on entrepreneurial freedom, or inconvenient sops offered to keep trade unions quiet, not extensions of citizenship to the workplace which are quite likely also to improve employees' contribution to efficiency' (1999b: 69). As early as 1995, Blair had declared to the TUC that conservative antiunion legislation would be maintained not only because of electoral reasons (Blair believed the general public supported union limitations) but also because of conviction and economic effectiveness (quoted by McIlroy 1998: 542).[47] In 1996, the theme of stakeholder capitalism (a system more similar to the Rhine model with more participation of unions in enterprises

---

[47] Dorey colorfully describes New Labour's attitude toward unions as follows: 'Ernest Bevin famously remarked that the Labour Party grew out of the bowels of the trade union movement, but today, it is New Labour which seems to view the trade unions as excrement' (1999: 190).

and policymaking) was publicly rejected by Blair (Norris 1999). In any case, after years of Thatcherism, the unions were too weak to impose any priorities on the Labour Party. Arthur Scargill bluntly described the feelings of the TUC about New Labour's lack of interest in promoting union goals. Regarding Tony Blair's speech, he declared to the 1995 TUC: 'Tony Blair effectively turned around and told this Congress: "Get stuffed." The tragedy was that, having done that, you applauded what he said' (quoted by McIlroy 1998: 550). Cooperation, if there was going to be any, would have to be based on unions giving way to New Labour.

Regarding employment protection, nevertheless, some policies promoted by the Blair government differ from those endorsed by conservatives since 1979. In some respects, Blair's government has timidly promoted some pro-insider policies (although the degree to which 'insiderness' remains after Thatcher is open to question). To begin with, very soon after the elections Blair signed to the European Social Charter and accepted the European Working Time Directive.[48] Then in 1998, the Employment Rights (Dispute Resolution) Act was passed. The Act set up an arbitration system for unfair dismissals.[49] It amended previous trade union and labor relations acts and made it possible for the Advisory, Conciliation, and Arbitration Service (ACAS) to provide an arbitration scheme in case of unfair dismissals, sex discrimination disputes, etc. The Act also established settlements for redundancy cases and internal appeal procedures for unfair dismissals. In the same vein, the Blair government also passed in 1998 the National Minimum Wage Act. The Act instituted a minimum wage and established the Low Pay Commission as the governmental agency in charge of setting and implementing the minimum wage. Rhodes calculates that, although there have been significant implementation problems, minimum wage legislation has resulted in wage increases of up to 40 percent for about 2 million workers (2000: 60). The 1999 Employment Relations Act, finally, tried to reverse some of the policies developed by the previous conservative governments regarding collective bargaining. The Act promoted the recognition of unions (40 percent of the vote needed for recognition and automatic union

---

[48] The initial impression that New Labour would embrace more comprehensive worker rights through European Union channels was, however, soon corrected. Taking the side of employers, the Blair government was strongly against the establishment of more formal consultation and information mechanisms (a part of the Social Charter).

[49] The ambitious program of increasing employment rights that Kinnock and Smith had espoused was, however, downplayed by Blair (McIlroy 1998: 543).

recognition where 50 percent of workers belong to a union),[50] attempted to abolish discrimination by employers of union members (e.g. by making the use of blacklists illegal and dismissal for union activities unfair), and allowed union participation in training schemes. Some protection against unfair dismissal was also extended to all workers after twelve months of service.

While Blair's first government could be considered to have taken a few measures in favor of insider protection (even if faint-hearted), it was clear that New Labour had no interest in promoting wage moderation as a policy objective. There have been occasional vague references about creating some sort of national forum where ministers, trade union leaders, and employers would discuss pay arrangements. But they have not resulted in any specific proposals. The main reason for this is that New Labour does not believe in the centralization or coordination of wage bargaining as a way to control inflation. As Mandelson and Liddle made clear, New Labour believes that centralized incomes policies are no longer appropriate. Instead, they continue, the Labour government 'should promote increased flexibility in the setting of employee rewards that genuinely relate pay to performance' (quoted by Dorey 1999: 197). As far as coordination goes, New Labour seems to share the neoliberal views of the previous conservative governments and to defend tight monetary policy as the best way to control inflation.

The absence of any attempt to promote wage moderation in the UK since the end of the 1970s is, I would argue, understandable. In Spain and the Netherlands, wage moderation was offered by insiders as a concession to governments so that employment protection levels could be maintained. In the UK, conservative governments had already decided to attack insider employment protection in 1979. They had no incentives to promote coordinated wage moderation when they were convinced that union weakness was a better outcome (it reduced the power of insiders and promoted unregulated wage determination). In addition, in the UK neither unions nor employers have traditionally supported coordination.

Focusing on the interests of unions first, the rhetoric of 'free collective bargaining' has been very attractive to unions in the UK. Historically, unions have been against any intervention that interfered with their collective bargaining role or their internal affairs. This, according

---

[50] The effects of these measures, however, were estimated to be very limited given the low levels of support for unions. Automatic union recognition if 50 percent of workers are union members, for example, was calculated to affect only 2 percent of workplaces without union recognition (see Cressey 1999: 185).

to Mayhew, 'is the problem with an incomes policy: to some degree it diminishes the collective bargaining role of the union' (Mayhew 1981: 32). As a consequence, as Edwards et al. point out, '(e)xcept in periods of exceptional economic crisis (1948–50, 1975–6) British unions have always vigorously resisted any notion of wage restraint' (1992: 46). Ken Gill, the General Secretary of the Amalgamated Union of Engineering Workers and member of the General Council of the TUC in 1981, candidly describes the approach of unions in the UK to wage moderation. 'The *raison d'être* of the trade union,' he explains, 'is to improve, or at least to safeguard, the real value of the salaries and conditions of its members' (1981: 184).

As for employers, they have strongly opposed any restraints on their autonomy (Mayhew 1981). Dermot Glynn, the Economic Director of the Confederation of British Industry in 1981, expounds on this point by noting that the inevitable disadvantage of incomes policies 'is the reduction of the employer's discretion to pay the levels of wage and salary that market forces make necessary' (1981: 210). Although wage restraint is theoretically attractive, employers have therefore been firmly against incomes policy in the UK. This has been particularly the case since 1979, when labor market legislation substantially increased their bargaining power with unions and employees.

6

Unemployment Vulnerability and Active Labor Market Policies

The aim of this chapter is to explore the effects of government partisan-ship and employment protection on ALMP. Chapter 5 has shown that a strong relationship exists between the partisan nature of governments and the employment protection enjoyed by insiders. In two of my coun-try cases, Spain and the UK, Left government is characterized by the steadfast support of high protection for insiders. Conservative govern-ment, on the other hand, promoted immediate (and sometimes dramatic) decreases in insider protection. My analysis also showed that corporatist arrangements in the Netherlands muted to some extent the influence of partisanship on insider protection but facilitated the coordination of wage moderation (in a way that was impossible in Spain or the UK).

In the first half of this book, I have argued (and shown some systematic evidence to support) that social democratic governments are not willing to promote labor market policy unless it is accompanied by a decline in insider protection. Chapter 3 demonstrated that insiders feel sufficiently protected from unemployment not to feel labor market policy is worth its costs. It also showed that when employment protection levels go down, insiders become more like outsiders and therefore more likely to support ALMPs. In Chapter 4 we saw that social democratic governments promote policies in accordance with the preferences of insiders. Left government is in fact associated with low levels of ALMPs unless employment pro-tection is low. A more detailed analysis of the developments in Spain, the Netherlands, and the UK since 1970 will shed some light on the causal processes affecting the relationship between government partisan-ship and ALMP and the intermediating effects of insider employment protection.

This chapter's analysis of the Spanish case shows that government partisanship does not affect ALMPs. I suggest that social democratic governments in Spain have not promoted higher levels of ALMP than conservative ones. Insider employment protection remained high throughout the period of PSOE rule and outsiders became a high proportion of the labor market, effectively buffering insiders from unemployment threats. As the following pages show, the promotion of precarious employment was in fact understood by the PSOE leadership as the main weapon to combat unemployment. The behavior of the social democrats is, therefore, perfectly understandable from an insider–outsider perspective. The conservative governments (starting in 1996) represented something of a change. Employment protection was reduced, and the demand for ALMP increased. The PP governments did not increase active measures in a significant way (training and public employment services remain very weak) but they did reduce the preponderance of temporary employment in the Spanish labor market.

This chapter will also show that developments in the Netherlands are remarkably similar to those in Spain. Although the levels of ALMP are higher through the period under analysis, they are not influenced by partisanship in a clear way. As made clear in Chapter 5, in the Netherlands, just like in Spain, insider employment protection does not decline and outsiders emerge as a significant buffer for insiders. This mutes the vulnerability of insiders to unemployment and the influence of insider–outsider differences on social democractic governments. Also as in Spain, this results in a general disregard for public employment service and training.

The analysis of the UK case, finally, shows a clear temporal division. During the 1970s and 1980s, government partisanship does not affect a general disinterest in ALMP. Employers did not want them, unions had incentives not to pay too much attention to them, and Conservative and Labour governments had no reason to favor them. The UK analysis demonstrates how high levels of insider protection made the Labour Party indifferent to ALMPs until the arrival of Margaret Thatcher. The decrease in insider protection promoted by the conservative governments of Thatcher and Major, however, facilitated a new interest in ALMPs by insiders and the emergence of Blair's Third Way (defined as a Labour strategy with employment promotion as a preeminent goal). Although the nature of ALMPs has changed (having acquired conditionality requirements not envisioned by traditional social democracy), New Labour has been characterized by an emphasis on active measures.

6.1. Active Labor Market Policies in Spain

ALMP is an area where there are not many detailed analyses of the Spanish case. Using the data available, a number of authors have argued, however, that Spain clearly belongs to the group of OECD countries where ALMPs have traditionally been given very little attention. This can easily be appreciated by comparing the ALMP levels in Spain with those of some other OECD countries. Table 6.1 presents ALMPs for a sample of countries considered to reflect the existing diversity in the OECD.

The measure for ALMP in Table 6.1 is the same as the one used in the analysis in Chapter 4. I mentioned then that the OECD data encompass the following five areas: (*a*) public employment services and administration, (*b*) labor market training, (*c*) youth measures, (*d*) subsidized employment, and (*e*) measures for the disabled. When I examined the existing cross-national diversity in ALMPs in Chapter 4, I placed countries into three general groups: those with high, intermediate, and low levels of active policies. I have chosen one country in each of these groups to compare Spain with. From the group characterized by low levels of ALMPs, I have selected Canada (others in this group were Australia, Austria, Italy, Japan, Switzerland, the UK, and the USA). I have included Finland from the second group (the only other country with intermediate levels was Norway). The representative from the group with high levels of ALMP is Sweden (the others were Belgium, Denmark, France, Germany, and the Netherlands).

As the figures in Table 6.1 indicate, Spain has dedicated considerably fewer resources to ALMPs than most of the OECD countries in the sample. In fact, the 0.18 percent and 0.33 percent of GDP that Spanish governments dedicated to ALMPs in 1980 and 1985 were considerably lower than the levels in Canada (the representative of the

Table 6.1. Active labor market policy in Spain and a sample of industrialized democracies, 1980–2000

Country	1980	1985	1990	1995	2000
Spain	**0.18**	**0.33**	**0.83**	**0.51**	**0.93**
Canada	0.29	0.65	0.53	0.57	0.41
Finland	0.99	0.91	0.99	1.54	1
Sweden	1.21	2.12	1.67	2.23	1.31

Notes: ALMPs are measured as a percentage of GDP.
Source: Armingeon et al. (2005).

low ALMP group). The investment in ALMP experienced a significant increase in 1990, but, at that time, the level in Spain was still considerably lower than in Finland (the example of intermediate levels of ALMP) and less than half that of Sweden. While in 1995 ALMPs became once more a very low 0.51 percent of GDP (in Canada the figure at this time was 0.57 percent), in 2000 they climbed back to levels more similar to 1990. Even in 2000, however, Spain remained below Finland in terms of resources dedicated to ALMPs. It seems accurate, therefore, to include Spain within the group of OECD countries where ALMPs are not emphasized. The low levels of ALMPs in Spain are particularly meaningful when we consider that, since the Essen Summit of 1994, a consensus had been reached by EU members to encourage active policies. It is also important to point out that a significant part of the resources directed to ALMPs in Spain is in fact provided by the EU's structural funds and, concretely, by the European Social Fund (Alvarez Aledo 1997: 24).

One of the main objectives in this section is to explore the relationship between government partisanship and ALMPs. To do this we turn now to Figure 6.1. The figure provides a timeline for ALMP in Spain reflecting the

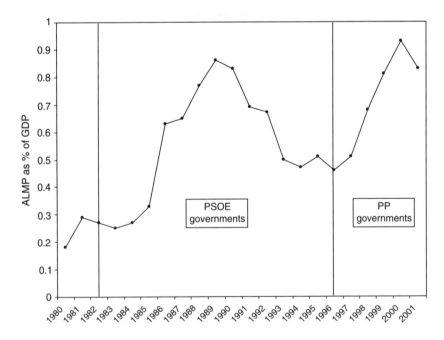

Figure 6.1. ALMPs in Spain, 1980–2001

partisan nature of the government in power. Two major periods can be distinguished, one characterized by PSOE government (1982–96) and the second by PP government (1996–2001).

It would be difficult to propose that a strong relationship between government partisanship and ALMPs exists after examining the numbers in Figure 6.1. While active measures received an increasing amount of resources from 1983 to 1989 (during the PSOE's first two terms), they experienced a dramatic decline from 1989 to 1996 (their last two terms in power). ALMPs increased from a dismal 0.27 percent of GDP in 1984 to a still relatively low 0.86 percent of GDP in 1989. From 1989 to 1996, ALMP levels dropped to 0.46 percent of GDP. Perhaps more importantly, the years of conservative government in Spain are characterized by an increase in the resources dedicated to active policy. As I've mentioned, by the end of PSOE's rule in 1996 the level of ALMPs was only 0.46 percent. Throughout the first term of conservative government in Spain, however, they climbed to 0.93 percent of GDP in 2000 (more than double the figure in 1996 and the highest level in our sample). I hasten to add that this increase needs to be put into the context of generally very low levels of ALMPs. In any case, it seems fair to say that social democratic government has not been associated with more ALMP in Spain.

The arguments presented in Chapters 1 to 3, however, emphasized that employment protection can mitigate the influence of insider–outsider differences. As insiders become more like outsiders, I argued, their support for ALMPs will increase. This may have been part of the story from 1996 to 2001, when the PP governments decreased the employment protection of insiders. But it was clearly not the case during the years of PSOE government in Spain. Two factors contribute to the insulation of insiders from unemployment from 1982 to 1996. First, the social democrats in Spain did not reduce the high levels of employment protection that insiders enjoyed. Second, while insiders continued to be significantly protected from unemployment, outsiders were becoming a vast portion of the labor market. From 1982 to 1996 unemployment and precarious employment grew radically. The average unemployment rate during this period exceeded 16 percent of the labor force and, by 1992, more than a third of all employees worked under temporary contracts. Unemployment, moreover, was concentrated in the two groups that came to represent outsiders in Spain: young people and women. The proportion of the unemployed under the age of 25 increased dramatically throughout the 1970s and 1980s, although (due to the use of temporary contracts) youth employment was highly cyclical and experienced significant increases in economic upswings (Alvarez Aledo 1997: 26).[1] A similar trend can be observed when analyzing unemployment in terms of gender. By 1991, women represented almost 52 percent of the unemployed and only one third of those employed (Jimeno and Toharia 1994: 35–7).

It is clear that the expectations of the insider–outsider partisanship model are supported by an analysis of aggregate ALMP expenditure in Spain. This general analysis, however, can be corroborated by a more detailed study of the labor market policies implemented since 1980. As a number of authors have pointed out, the absence of any coherent government effort defines the approach to ALMPs in Spain (see, e.g. Palacio 1991; Recio 1998). The attention paid to employment promotion by policymakers from all parties has been both disorganized and very limited. The other aspect that most observers would emphasize is the fact that most labor market policies in Spain have had the objective of increasing temporary and cheap employment (Cachón Rodríguez 1997; Chozas 2000; González Calvet 2002,).[2] In fact, the paragraphs below will suggest that the promotion of precarious employment was considered the only (or at least their main) objective of ALMP since 1980.[3] Any other aspect (including training) received little attention and few resources. I concentrate my analysis on three ALMP areas: the measures implemented to promote nonstandard employment, public employment services and administration, and training.

6.1.1. *General Promotion of Nonstandard Employment*[4]

Given the emphasis on the promotion of temporary employment by policymakers in Spain, it is inevitable that an explanation of ALMPs would outline some of the legislative measures that were the focus of Chapter 5. Very little can be said about ALMPs before 1980. There had been a series of short-term programs mainly directed to the integration of

[1] The high level of youth unemployment is even more dramatic when considering that the relative weight of young people in the labor force had fallen substantially in those years. This is both because of a decline in birth rates and because young people spent more time in education and entered the labor market later in life (Alba Ramírez 1996: 16).

[2] Turning temporary employment into the norm for labor market entry (particularly for young people and females) can certainly be considered the guiding principle of social democratic labor market policy throughout this period (Cachón Rodríguez 1997: 88).

[3] This was done with the acquiescence, if not active approval, of unions. In his analysis of active policies in Spain, Pérez-Díaz argues that UGT and CCOO 'have acted as if they represented workers in permanent jobs (increasing their purchasing power and defending their job security), and have adopted a confused and ultimately unsatisfactory strategy towards those in other kinds of employment' (1999: 212).

[4] This is a brief summary of a number of measures examined in more detail in Chapter 5.

young people into the labor market. These programs had been part of the 1977 Moncloa Pacts and were subsequently developed by the center-right UCD governments. In 1978, the *Instituto Nacional de Empleo* (INEM) was created as the main agency to design and implement labor market policies in Spain.

In 1980, the UCD government approved the Workers' Statute. This was a measure that, for the first time in Spain, explicitly presented temporary contracts as a tool for the promotion of employment. The 1980 Workers' Statute and the Employment Law created several new forms of temporary employment as a solution to cyclical economic problems. Fixed-term contracts (*temporal, en prácticas,* and *en formación*), in particular, were designed for those experiencing difficulties in the labor market.

The socialist victory in the 1982 elections promoted an important transformation of the Workers' Statute. The 1984 labor market reforms reflected the development of an employment promotion strategy that would be maintained with only minor changes until the end of the PSOE governments in 1996. This approach rested on two pillars: a relatively incoherent and underfinanced training plan (the *plan de formación e inserción profesional,* also known as *Plan FIP*),[5] and the promotion of temporary employment as the main way of introducing new workers into the labor market. With the 1984 labor market reform, the PSOE government introduced a new form of temporary contract (the *contrato de fomento de empleo,* or contract for the promotion of employment) that allowed employers to use a temporary contract of up to three years without having to provide a reason.

After the success of the general strike of 1988, the socialist government waited to introduce any further modifications in the labor market regulations. The 1994 labor market reform, however, confirmed and, in fact, extended the use of temporary contracts as the most important measure to promote employment. At a time when official unemployment figures had reached the astounding 24 percent mark, the PSOE government proposed once again to facilitate precarious employment (González Calvet 2002; Ferreiro Aparicio 2003). The 1994 labor market reforms created two new kinds of contracts with very little social protection: the learning contract (*contrato de aprendizaje*) and the part-time contract (*contrato de tiempo parcial*) (Martín and Santos 1994; Recio and Roca 1998). It also legalized temporary employment agencies and private hiring intermediaries.

---

[5] More on this topic below.

The final policy initiative that will be analyzed in this section is the 1997 labor market reform, implemented, this time, by the PP government. The 1997 legislation moderated some of the emphasis placed on temporary employment by the previous social democratic governments. The reforms provided fiscal and social security incentives for creating indefinite jobs. They also created a new kind of contract (the contract for the promotion of indefinite employment, *contrato de fomento de empleo indefinido*) to help individuals who had experienced difficulties entering the labor market and those holding temporary contracts. Moreover, the use of temporary contracts was limited by reducing the kinds of activities covered. Finally, they improved temporary employment by increasing the levels of protection of part-time contracts. The goal of these changes was to improve the quality of the labor market by reducing the prevalence of temporary employment (see, e.g. Cachón and Palacio 1999; Ferreiro Aparicio 2003). And they did enjoy a degree of success in turning the tide against the overwhelming use of temporary contracts in the Spanish labor market (for some evidence, see Martín 2004).

6.1.2. *Public Employment Services and Administration*

The INEM is the main governmental agency in charge of employment promotion in Spain. Since 1978, its role has been to organize employment services, promote employment, provide training, and administer unemployment subsidies (Jimeno 1993: 235). As mentioned in section 6.1.1, until 1994, the INEM had a monopoly on employment placement services. This meant that workers needing a job and employers needing to fill a vacancy had a legal obligation to use the INEM's services (Rodríguez-Piñero 1996). This was also the case in a number of OECD countries, but Spain was one of the few in which all job openings had to be notified to the government and in which private employment agencies were prohibited (Jimeno 1993: 242–3).

The monopoly on employment services of the INEM, however, did not produce a high degree of efficiency. It was in fact obvious very early on that the agency provided deficient placement services. In spite of its monopoly, the INEM only acted as an intermediary in 9 percent of the job offers that took place in the 1989–92 period, for example. The rest were job offers that the INEM simply processed, having reached the agency with a candidate already nominated by the employer (Jimeno 1993: 246). When we look at the average for the 1990s, the numbers are not much better. During this decade, the INEM administered only 13 percent of job offers (the average for public employment agencies in European Union countries was 25 percent).[6] Employers have repeatedly declared that using the INEM's services was a method that they seldom employed when looking for workers. As for the potential workers, in 1990, 90 percent of job seekers used the INEM as their main intermediary but, as shown above, only a very small percentage had any success (Alujas Ruiz 2002).

The low participation of the INEM in labor market placements and its lack of efficiency as an intermediary should not come as a surprise (see, e.g. Jimeno and Toharia 1994). It was the logical consequence of Spain being one of the OECD countries that, as was shown above, dedicated the fewest resources to ALMPs in general (and to public employment services in particular).[7] The 1994 reforms, legalizing temporary employment agencies and private employment services companies, did not change this general pattern. According to the legislation, private employment service companies needed to be nonprofit organizations and to develop a collaborative relationship with the INEM (see Alujas Ruiz 2002 for details). Employers were now free to fill vacancies without using the INEM; workers, on the other hand, were still required to sign up with INEM as the first step toward job searching. This turn to private intermediation was justified by the PSOE as an initiative to inject market dynamism and effectiveness into employment services (Casas and Palomeque 1994; Rodríguez-Piñero 1996). But private companies simply extended and facilitated the use of temporary employment.

The effect of the 1994 reforms was immediate. From 1995 to 1999, there was a dramatic increase in the use of temporary employment agencies. The proportion of temporary contracts administered by temporary agencies grew threefold and reached 16 percent of all temporary contracts registered in the INEM by 1999 (Malo and Muñoz-Bullón 2002). By 1997, there were more than 400 agencies and they processed about 2000 temporary contracts a day (Sáez 1997: 316). In 1996, however, the PSOE was defeated in the general elections and a new PP government came to power. This change in government partisanship had strong effects on employment protection legislation, as explained in more detail in section 6.1.1, but had few consequences in terms of public employment services. The role of the INEM continued to be that delimited by the 1994 legislation, with the exception of some power transferred from the

---

[6] For details, see Alujas Ruiz (2002: 408–9).
[7] Spain and Greece are, in fact, the countries with the lowest expenditure on public employment services in the OECD (Jimeno and Toharia 1994: 125).

national government to some regional ones in 1998,[8] and its efficiency did not seem to have improved substantially.

6.1.3. *Training*

Training in Spain is generally considered a policy area characterized by low funding and poor performance. Pérez-Díaz argues that vocational training is one of Spain's most serious problems, contributing to 'both the lack of adjustment between supply and demand for skilled labor, and the difficulties Spanish companies face in adapting to technical, organisational and product changes' (1999: 206). This is the case fundamentally because vocational training was designed as a 'lower-level secondary education for the children of families with fewer economic possibilities and/or less ambition to move up the social scale' (Pérez-Díaz 1999: 207).

In the 1980s, vocational training was considered mostly a negative choice for Spanish students (Meijer 1991: 15). Many of them failed general education courses and entered vocational training as a last resort. Vocational training opportunities were limited. For those not continuing with general education at 14 years of age, two options were open: vocational training through *Formacion Profesional* or to take a vocational course through the INEM (although students could not do this until they were 16, when they could legally enter the labor market). The main guidelines for this system were set up in the National Plan for Vocational Training and Entry into Working Life (*Plan Nacional de Formación e Inserción Profesional*) in 1985. According to most analysts, the effects of policies developed under this plan have been questionable. As Jimeno and Toharia argue:

Theoretically, the case for this type of policy is obvious (reducing mismatch reduces unemployment) (. . .). What would seem a bad strategy would be the introduction of these policies without identifying the mismatch and the nature of the training courses needed to solve the problem, in particular in terms of the adequate balance between classroom and on-the-job training. Unfortunately, this may have been the situation in Spain, where many courses have been offered but without substantial reference to the skills needed, and with an excessive emphasis on theoretical matters too remote from the practicalities of real-world job tasks'.

Jimeno and Toharia (1994: 127)

In general, training programs offered until 1993 lacked any degree of organization or coherence and were not well adjusted to the necessities of the labor market.

---

[8] For details, see Aragón Medina and Rocha Sánchez (2003).

The National Training Program (*Programa Nacional de Formación Profesional*) designed for the 1993–6 period was developed with the explicit objective of unifying and providing a coherent guide for the diverse training programs that existed in Spain (Garrido Medina 1996: 251). In this program, the existing training system (*Formación Profesional*) was divided and put under the control of three different agencies. The education ministry was in charge of vocational training as a part of an alternative secondary education, vocational training for the unemployed was to be coordinated by the INEM (and the regional governments that had this policy area within their responsibilities), and training for workers in employment was organized by a newly created agency (the FORCEM, *Fundación para la Formación Continua*).[9]

The main instrument intended to accomplish a degree of cohesion within training was the establishment of a national system of vocational qualifications. The reforms, however, did not result in any appreciable improvement. Examining the number of people who benefited by existing labor market policies in the 1993–6 period, Sáez (1997) observes that only the promotion of temporary employment seemed to have had any effect on employment. The influence of all measures in the National Training Program on the number of indefinite contracts was minimal (Sáez 1997: 319). The resources dedicated to the policies, moreover, were still surprisingly low, given the nature of the unemployment problem in Spain. This is especially the case when we consider that three quarters of the training programs were cofinanced by the European Social Fund.

The conservative electoral victory in 1996 was not followed by any significant change in training. In spite of the European Union emphasis on the necessity to improve ALMPs in Europe (clearly expressed in the Essen, Florence, and Amsterdam meetings, from 1994 to 1997), training in Spain was not substantially transformed. In 1998, a year after it was due (since the previous program had expired in 1996), the Second National Training Program was signed by employers, unions, and the government. The stated goals of the program were, once more, to promote the coordination and coherence of training programs, but the proposed measures were very limited. The agreement was more like a wish list of objectives and intentions than a package of concrete policies. A national system of vocational qualifications, nationally coordinated, and related to the concrete needs of the market, was again declared an important goal, as

---

[9] The FORCEM was created as a result of the National Agreement on Continuous Training (*Acuerdo Nacional de Formación Continua*) signed by employers and unions.

was a tighter collaboration between training centers and companies. But exactly how this was to be accomplished, or the amount of resources to be dedicated to these policies, was not clear (CES 1997: 311). It is true that a larger number of students entered vocational training at this time. But the weaknesses in the programs were still obvious. The analysis in Calero and Escardíbul (2005) puts in doubt that the vocational system in Spain after these reforms was well coordinated or well financed (in comparison with other European countries), or that the negative connotations associated with vocational training had been eliminated.

6.2. Active Labor Market Policies in the Netherlands

The levels of ALMP in the Netherlands can be put into context by comparing them to those in a sample of other industrialized democracies, just as was done in the Spanish analysis above. Table 6.2 presents Dutch figures for ALMPs together with those in three countries reflecting the existing diversity in the OECD. As in Table 6.1, Canada represents the countries with low levels of active policy, Finland those with intermediate levels, and Sweden those with high levels.

When comparing ALMPs across OECD countries in Chapter 4, I observed that the Netherlands belonged to a group characterized by high levels of ALMPs. The other nations in this group were Belgium, Denmark, France, Germany, and Sweden. I argued that, although there is a high degree of variation throughout the period for some of these countries, the averages for the members of this group tend to approach 1.2 percent of GDP. The figures in Table 6.2 support these assertions but they also make clear that ALMPs in the Netherlands have not received significant resources during the 1980s and early 1990s. ALMPs in the Netherlands are a greater percentage of GDP than those we saw in the Spanish case

Table 6.2. Active labor market policy in the Netherlands and a sample of industrialized democracies, 1980–2000

Country	1980	1985	1990	1995	2000
Netherlands	**0.58**	**1.01**	**1.09**	**1.11**	**1.47**
Canada	0.29	0.65	0.53	0.57	0.41
Finland	0.99	0.91	0.99	1.54	1
Sweden	1.21	2.12	1.67	2.23	1.31

Notes: ALMPs are measured as a percentage of GDP.
Source: Armingeon et al. (2005).

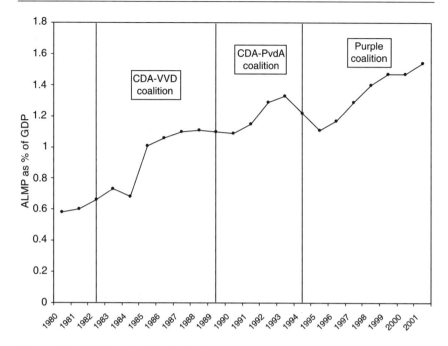

Figure 6.2. ALMPs in the Netherlands, 1980–2001

(see Table 6.1), but, from 1980 to 1995, they are closer to an intermediate level of investment (like in Finland) than to a high level (like in Sweden, or Belgium in Table 4.2). However, by 2000, ALMPs are 1.47 percent of GDP, which places the Netherlands solidly within the group of countries with high levels of active measures.

To analyze the relationship between government partisanship and ALMPs, we turn now to Figure 6.2. As we saw in the analysis of the Spanish case, the figure provides a timeline for ALMP that reflects the partisan nature of the government in power. There are three main coalitions reflected in the figure: the two CDA-VVD governments led by Ruud Lubbers from 1982 to 1989, the CDA-PvdA coalition (also under the leadership of Ruud Lubbers) from 1989 to 1994, and the two purple coalitions (PvdA, VVD, and D66) of Prime Minister Wim Kok from 1994 to 2002.

Figure 6.2 shows that the levels of ALMP in the Netherlands are consistently higher than those we saw in Spain.[10] During the first Lubbers term, ALMPs increased to about 1 percent of GDP (from a much lower level close to 0.6 percent in 1982). From then on, they experienced a relatively steady increase (only interrupted in 1994 and 1995). The increase in the

---

[10] As well as those I present below in the analysis of the UK case.

importance of active measures may have been influenced by the high levels of coordination in the Netherlands. However, it would be difficult to argue for a clear partisan effect in Figure 6.2. In addition to the difficulties inherent in distinguishing among the ideologies of very diverse coalitions, there is the fact that ALMPs increase in a relatively constant manner, apparently unaffected by the nature of government.

Regarding the influence of employment protection, the Netherlands is remarkably similar to the Spanish case. As in Spain, two factors significantly contributed to the insulation of insiders from unemployment. First, the employment protection of insiders remained more or less untouched throughout the period under analysis. Second, outsiders became an important part of the labor market. The unemployment rate in the Netherlands experienced a slow but steady growth during the 1970s (when it increased from 2.3 percent in 1973 to 5.4 percent in 1979) and a sudden explosion in the early 1980s (it reached almost 15 percent in 1984). Like in Spain, Dutch unemployment disproportionately affected females and young people. During the 1980s, female unemployment was consistently about 5 percentage points above male unemployment (sometimes more). Younger people were also overrepresented among the unemployed. The registered unemployment rate for those under 19 years of age, for example was as high as 49 percent in 1983 and it only fell to 30 percent by 1987.[11] The unemployment problem of these two groups (females and youths) is compounded by a tendency for high persistence. The number of long-term unemployed rose sharply in the early 1980s. In 1980, about 40 percent of those receiving unemployment benefits had done so for more than a year, by 1988 the figure had risen to almost 70 percent (Engbersen et al. 1993: 44).

The solution for the unemployment problem in the Netherlands was the emergence of nonstandard employment. Between 1980 and 1984, full-time employment decreased by 12 percent and part-time employment increased by almost 28 percent (Visser 1989: 232). Very soon, the Netherlands had become the country with the highest proportion of part-time employment in the OECD. The composition of part-time employment, moreover, had also been very specific: young people and, especially, females were almost exclusively represented in the growing part-time sector (Hemerijck 1995). Fixed-term employment has also become an increasingly important sector of the labor market in the Netherlands, particularly since 1993, and is concentrated on the young (Visser and

---

[11] The unemployment data in this paragraph are taken from De Neubourg (1990).

Hemerijck 1997; Salverda 1999*b*). From 1987 to the end of the 1990s, the number of young people in full-time jobs fell by 39 percent while the number of part-time and fixed-term jobs increased dramatically. This is the case even though a great majority of young people officially unemployed are looking for full-time employment.[12] Part-time and flexible jobs were, undoubtedly, the lion's share of employment growth between 1979 and 1997 (Salverda 1999*b*).

Given the increase of unemployment and the prevalence of nonstandard employment, it is surprising that ALMPs did not receive more attention. The following pages will address this issue and explore in more detail the development of ALMPs in the Netherlands.

6.2.1. The 1980s: The Need for ALMPs

ALMPs are widely recognized as a policy area that historically received little attention in the Netherlands. Before the 1970s, the success of a low-wage strategy suggested to policymakers that ALMPs were not really needed. There had been, to be sure, some criticism of the Public Employment Service. In 1967, for example, the OECD published a fairly negative report about the absence of a coherent ALMP framework in the Netherlands. But, as Visser and Hemerijck explain, in the tight labor market context of the 1960s politicians did not pay much notice (1997: 164). Since the existing Public Employment Service was considered more than adequate to deal with the then limited levels of unemployment, the only response to the report was the introduction of the social partners into the Social Economic Council in 1969.

Consistent with this general lack of attention to ALMPs, before the mid-1980s the main employment scheme had been 'the so-called *Loonsuppletie*, which offered a temporary wage supplement for all categories of unemployed people willing to accept a job with a wage below their previous wage level' (Van Oorschot 2004: 18). Unemployment, however, was becoming a much more visible problem at this time and policymakers started to search for alternatives. From 1979 to 1985, an effort was made (first by the coalitions led by Van Agt and then by the Lubbers government) to improve the Public Employment Service. The idea was to remodel the agency by following the suggestions of the Social Economic Council but, in practice, the restructuring of the service turned out to

---

[12] Wages have also declined. From 1977 to 1997, youth wages relative to adult wages have fallen from 67 to 55 percent (Salverda 1999*a*: 6). In other words, it seems that, as Salverda puts it, there is no 'Dutch miracle' regarding youth employment (1999*a*: 3).

be no more than 'an internal reorganization and facelift' (Visser and Hemerijck 1997: 164). Suggestions to turn the agency into a more effective and market conscious organization were not acted upon. At this time, the Public Employment Service was perceived (very much like the INEM, its Spanish counterpart) as a receptacle for unattractive vacancies. Employers, in particular, considered it the last place they would go to if they had a vacancy to fill (Visser and Hemerijck 1997: 165). The only change of any substance had been the creation of a temporary job agency within the employment service (called Start).

In the 1980s, the Lubbers governments did not change the fundamentals of ALMPs in the Netherlands. The conservative coalition's emphasis on fiscal austerity resulted, by 1985, in the elimination of job creation policies in the public sector and subsidies to firms in trouble (Visser and Hemerijck 1997: 160). Although some additional resources were dedicated to training for young unemployed people and handicapped workers, an overview of expenditures shows that the resources dedicated to active measures were very small. In 1985, the Lubbers government spent only about 1 percent of GDP on active policies (compared to the 3 percent of GDP spent on unemployment compensation) and, specifically, only about 0.2 percent on labor market training and youth employment programs.[13] This state of affairs makes Hemerijck and Vail describe the Public Employment Service during this period as a 'dormant state monopoly' which 'ran job-placement offices, shunned by employers and skilled workers and overrun by the unemployed for which little could be done' (2004: 21).

A number of reasons were presented to explain the high levels of unemployment experienced by the Netherlands in the 1980s (wage policies, labor costs, labor market inflexibility, female labor force participation, etc.). In an influential book, Therborn convincingly argued in 1986 that they were insufficient to explain Dutch unemployment in a comparative perspective. The high levels of unemployment were the results, in his view, of the lack of policies directed to promote employment (Therborn 1986). His argument was based on one main observation: the general philosophy of Dutch labor market policy was fundamentally passive. He supported this statement by pointing out that the Public Employment Service was part of a Ministry (Social Affairs) whose main objective was the distribution of social benefits and which lacked any independent resources for employment promotion (priority was given to passive measures). Other authors have added more elements to the list of employment

---

[13] See OECD, *Employment Outlook* (several issues) for details.

promotion weaknesses. Visser and Hemerijck point out that during the 1970s, the level of unemployment considered unavoidable by the government increased together with the growth in the actual unemployment rate so that employment targets slowly receded (1997: 159). In addition to the mostly passive nature of policies, they explain, those that were active mainly consisted of measures directed to job creation in labor-intensive sectors (like public infrastructure and construction) or to job preservation through subsidies to ailing sectors.

Given the dramatic increase in unemployment experienced in the 1970s and 1980s and the obvious deficiencies of public employment initiatives, it is surprising, according to Kurzer, that the Dutch governments, unions, and employers so consistently failed to improve ALMPs (1997: 114). An assortment of quotes can be offered to confirm the lack of attention that governments of all ideological origins paid to ALMPs.[14] Marcel Van Dam (PvdA Minister of Housing in two cabinets and confidant to PvdA Prime Minister Den Uyl) confessed that 'Therborn is right in saying that the Netherlands never had an active labor market policy.' Will Albeda (CDA Minister of Social Affairs from 1977 to 1981) agreed and declared that 'we remained passive when it went wrong.' Even the Director of the Public Employment Service stated that 'with hindsight, we can say to have probably made the wrong choices' by conducting an 'inconsistent labor market policy, with patchwork measures based on ad hoc recipes.' It is therefore clear that ALMPs did not rate highly on the priority list of Dutch governments compared to other goals like wage moderation and the reduction of the public deficit (Hemerijck 1995).

6.2.2. The 1990s

It has been widely argued that, starting in the late 1980s, a change in thinking about ALMPs took place (see e.g. Visser and Hemerijck 1997). I will explore in this section the extent to which ALMPs did receive more attention in the 1990s. It is true that the advent of the CDA-PvdA coalition (in power from 1989 to 1994) coincided with the conclusion of the deliberations about the remodeling of the Public Employment Service. The reform of the employment service had been discussed for years but two issues kept preventing any advance. There was first the participation of the social partners (the tripartization of the ALMP system had often been requested by unions and employers). Then there was the demand

---

[14] All the following statements are taken from Pieter Broertjes's *Getto's in Nederland* and are quoted by Visser and Hemerijck (1997).

for a more decentralized employment service (mainly by the Association of Municipalities and the governing bodies of big cities). Throughout the 1980s, decentralization had been an attractive option for Lubbers, given the CDA's interests in a reduction of the public sector. So was the idea of a tripartite employment service (given the need for cooperation with the social partners in a period when wage moderation was very important). The CDA Minister of Social Affairs and Employment had decided to promote both from very early on (during the first Lubbers government). But it took until almost a decade later for the CDA (now in a coalition with the PvdA) to reform the employment agency through the Employment Service Act of January 1991. The Act established that the employment service would be decentralized and subject to tripartite control. Unions, employers, and municipalities were to participate not only in the implementation but also in the design of ALMPs.[15]

Going back to Figure 6.2, ALMP levels from 1990 to 1994 seem to suggest that the 1991 reorganization of the employment service resulted in a slight increase in terms of resources. In 1990, active measures had been 1.09 percent of GDP and by 1994, they had become 1.22 percent.[16] Whether this increase did in fact result in more effective ALMPs is, however, questionable. In 1994, the remodeled employment service was reviewed by a government committee. The report (published in 1995) was very negative. The committee argued that the reorganization had been too expensive, 'decentralization had gone too far, finances were poorly managed, and decision-making procedures were unclear, slow and cumbersome' (Visser and Hemerijck 1997: 170; see also, Dercksen and de Koning 1995). The report explained, moreover, that policies directed to target groups (youth, long-term unemployed, and minorities) had failed and that the representatives of unions and employers had exhibited a tendency to act in the interest of their constituencies instead of promoting general goals.

The CDA tried to use the results of this report to put the design of ALMPs back in the hands of the central government but its attempts were interrupted by the 1994 elections and the formation of a new cabinet. Wim Kok (the prime minister of the resulting PvdA-VVD-D66

[15] Also of importance, the 1991 Employment Service Act legalized private employment intermediation agencies and temporary employment ones (requiring permits for particular activities).

[16] Data in the OECD *Employment Outlook* indicate that the increase in total ALMP levels was mainly instigated by a sharp rise in expenditures on public employment services and administration.

coalition) did not openly espouse the CDA reform but he did promote some changes. His purple coalition used the review (and the reactions to it) to propose a change in the legislation reducing the policy scope of the agency (Public Employment Service was to concentrate mainly on vulnerable groups in the labor market). Also in 1994, Ad Melkert (PvdA Social Affairs and Employment minister) announced cuts in the employment service but also some new job creation programs, again mainly for target groups. At the same time, a different development was weakening the Public Employment Service agency. In the words of de Koning, at this time '(s)ubsidized labor gradually became the most important active measure. As most people entitled to subsidized labor were clients of the municipal social services, and municipalities were an important provider of subsidized jobs, municipalities were made responsible for job creation schemes' (de Koning 2004: 2).[17]

In 1996, the PvdA-VVD-D66 government implemented a new Employment Services Act that introduced the final element in the Labor Party's ALMP strategy. The 'activating' side of social policy was promoted by requiring unemployment recipients to register in employment offices and to show that they were actively seeking to enter the labor market. The 1996 Law on Penalties and Measures, moreover, extended the sanctioning powers of social security administration agencies to 'activate' the unemployed. 'As van Oorschot explains,

(P)reviously, issuing penalties for non-compliance with job-search obligations was regarded as being within the competence of the administrative bodies, some of which acted quite leniently; with the new law, however, sanctioning became an obligation and penalties were nationally prescribed according to type of misbehavior; administrations were policed on their implementation.

(van Oorschot 2004: 19)

The eligibility and entitlement criteria for unemployment benefits were severely limited as well.

Independent of the Public Employment Service agency reforms, three additional policies became relevant to the analysis of ALMPs in the 1990s. They are labor pools, the Youth Work Guarantee Plan, and Melkert jobs. These three programs share one important feature: they are mostly directed at target groups.[18] In 1991, labor pools were introduced in the

---

[17] More on the use of municipalities for subsidized employment below.

[18] The targeted nature of active policies is in fact one of the most important characteristics of the Labor Party's strategy for job growth in the 1990s.

public sector for long-term unemployed people considered to have a low probability of finding a job. The program essentially facilitated minimum-wage jobs in the public sector (mostly in municipalities). The effectiveness of labor pools, however, was questionable. In practice, the outflow from labor pools to regular jobs was extremely limited. Between 1990 and 1995 less than 10 percent of those involved in labor pools left the public jobs for 'positive reasons' (Salverda 2000: 6). The Youth Work Guarantee Plan was established in 1992 and it offered 'a combination of training and work experience to school leavers up to the age of 23 who have not been able to find a job within six months and have less than one year previous work experience' (Visser and Hemerijck 1997: 173). As was the case with labor pools, however, very few youths participating in the Youth Work Guarantee Plan moved into other jobs. The effects in terms of assisting the transition between unemployment and work were not substantial (Salverda 2000). Melkert jobs received their name from PvdA Minister of Social Affairs and Employment, Ad Melkert. Some Melkert jobs (Melkert-I) were positions for the long-term unemployed in municipalities and health care institutions financed on a permanent basis by the central government. Others (Melkert-II) were jobs in the private sector that were made possible by reductions in taxes and social security contributions when the employer hired long-term unemployed or other vulnerable workers (see Salverda 2000; van Oorschot 2004 for more details). Melkert-I jobs were very similar to labor pools and they shared their effectiveness problem. They simply were not a successful policy tool to bring people from unemployment to standard work. There was an additional problem. Although the jobs were quite comparable to low-skilled 'normal' jobs, they received very low pay, were not covered by any pension rights, and had no protection over arbitrary management decisions. They in fact represented 'a separate and inferior labor market in which people become trapped' (Salverda 2000: 11). Melkert I and II jobs, in any case, were too few to cover more than a small portion of the groups at which they are targeted (van Oorschot 2004: 18).

6.3. Active Labor Market Policies in the UK

As in the two previous cases, it is revealing to put the levels of ALMP in the UK into context by comparing them to those in a sample of other industrialized democracies. Table 6.3 presents figures for ALMPs in the UK side by side with those in Canada (representing the countries with

Table 6.3. Active labor market policy in the UK and a sample of industrialized democracies, 1980–2000

Country	1980	1985	1990	1995	2000
UK	**0.56**	**0.73**	**0.59**	**0.44**	**0.36**
Canada	0.29	0.65	0.53	0.57	0.41
Finland	0.99	0.91	0.99	1.54	1
Sweden	1.21	2.12	1.67	2.23	1.31

Notes: ALMPs are measured as a percentage of GDP.
Source: Armingeon et al. (2005).

low levels of active policy), Finland (those with intermediate levels), and Sweden (those with high levels).

The table makes clear that, for much of the period, the UK has dedicated considerably fewer resources to ALMPs than all of the OECD countries in the sample. In the cross-national comparison of ALMP levels in Chapter 4, I argued that the UK belonged to a group characterized by low levels of ALMP. The other nations in this group were Australia, Austria, Canada, Italy, Japan, Switzerland, the UK, and the USA. Table 6.3 shows that the UK levels have been lower than those in Canada since 1995. It also shows that ALMPs in the UK have been about half as high as in Finland (the representative of the intermediate group) and just a third as high as in Sweden (in 1990 and 2000, much less than that). Compared with our two previous countries, the UK again distinguishes itself by its low ALMP levels. The resources dedicated to active measures in the UK are consistently lower than in the Netherlands (as expected). Perhaps more surprisingly, they are also considerably lower than those in Spain starting in 1990.

Once again I will use a timeline for ALMPs to explore their relationship with government partisanship. Figure 6.3 presents ALMP levels together with the partisan nature of the government in power. The period for which we have data can be divided into two sections: one characterized by Conservative government (from 1980 until 1997) and one by Labour governments (from 1997 to 2001).

Although conservative government is overrepresented during the years in our sample, it seems difficult to argue that the partisanship has greatly influenced the level of ALMPs in the UK. Figure 6.3 shows an increase in the resources dedicated to ALMP during the first two Thatcher terms, (from 1980 to 1987). In 1980, one year after Margaret Thatcher's first electoral victory, only 0.56 percent of GDP was dedicated to ALMP. By 1989, this figure had almost doubled (0.86%). Starting in 1987, however,

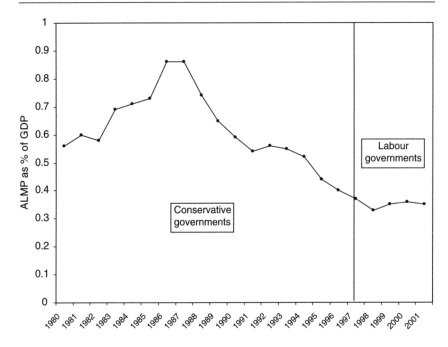

Figure 6.3. ALMPs in the UK, 1980–2001

there is a dramatic decline in ALMP until the end of conservative rule (by 1997, ALMPs were only 0.37% of GDP). The decrease in ALMPs was not strongly related to changes in unemployment levels. Figure 6.3 makes clear that the steepest decline in ALMP takes place from 1987 to 1991. Unemployment in 1987 was 10.3 percent of the labor force (admittedly, one of the highest levels during the period under analysis), but it was still quite a high 8.6 percent in 1991. It would then climb steadily up to 10.2 percent in 1993, when the level of active policy was as low as in 1991. More significantly, it is also unclear that social democratic government resulted in higher ALMPs. In spite of the emphasis given to active policy by proponents of the Third Way (see e.g. Giddens 1998), ALMPs remained at an extraordinary low level during the Labour governments starting in 1997 (around 0.4% of GDP).

The evolution of ALMPs depicted in Figure 6.3 is even more meaningful when we think about the effects of employment protection. As convincingly shown in Chapter 5, the UK experienced a radical decline in insider employment protection in the 1980s and 1990s. The decrease in ALMPs during the years of conservative government is expected (conservative governments are not in favor of active measures), but the lack of a significant increase during the years of Labour government is surprising. In the insider–outsider arguments presented in previous chapters, I have explained that decreasing levels of employment protection will make social democratic governments more likely to promote ALMPs. A more detailed analysis of these policies in the UK will illuminate this issue and show that the numbers in Figure 6.3 do not tell the whole story.

6.3.1. *Active Labor Market Policy before 1980*

As noted by Crouch, in 'the 1960s Britain had an apprenticeship model, but one in which weak employers' organizations, and trade unions more concerned with keeping up trainee wages than with improving the flow of skills, failed to provide high standards of training or an adequate supply of trained young workers' (1995: 298). The initial impetus for public training in the UK can be traced back to the 1964 Industrial Training Act establishing industrial training boards (ITBs). The boards were financed by a levy imposed on employers and they provided grants to firms that would engage in training following the guidelines established by the government (Bosworth and Wilson 1980). ITBs had a tripartite structure (both through participation in the boards and because they were overseen by the tripartite Central Training Council). In spite of the introduction of training boards, however, vocational education and training was provided for a very small portion of the workforce and most young people entered employment from general education. ITBs did not change the fact that training in the UK was rooted in the apprenticeship system (King 1995). As for the influence of government partisanship, Finegold and Soskice argue that '(t)hrough most of the postwar period, the use of ET [education and training] to improve economic performance failed to emerge on the political agenda' because both parties focused their efforts on general education and agreed that training was best left to industry (1988: 25).

In 1973, the conservative government led by Heath approved the Employment and Training Act, which created the Manpower Services Commission (MSC). The MSC was a tripartite agency (imitating similar ones in corporatist countries) with an equal number of union and employer representatives. The MSC was created to supervise the Employment Services Agency and the Training Services Agency. In Parliament, the Employment Secretary declared that the MSC 'will be able to take a national view of training needs, which no industrial training board can do' (quoted by King 1997: 393). However, because of the increasing unemployment problems of the early and mid-1970s and the lack of strong commitments from either Conservative or Labour governments, the MSC did not develop a comprehensive training program. As Finegold and Soskice point out, although funds increased, the MSC did little to improve skills, having to dedicate its resources to temporary employment, work experience, and short-course training (1988: 30).

The 1973 Act was followed by a number of active measures in the 1970s (Bosworth and Wilson 1980). Policies were implemented to provide training and on-the-job experience for young people, to increase the number of youths going into craft and technical training, and to create temporary jobs. A number of subsidies were also made available to companies that provided employment to targeted groups (the young, school leavers, etc.). The Job Release Scheme was started to promote the exit from the labor market of workers who were close to retirement. The Employment Service was reorganized. A network of Jobcentres was created that separated the provision of unemployment benefits from the promotion of employment, increased the number of notified vacancies, and seemed to increase the number of placements.[19] These measures, however, did not stop the unemployment rate from exceeding 15 percent in 1978.

6.3.2. *Active Labor Market Policy under Conservative Government*

The attitude of the Thatcher government toward training was most influenced by the interests of employers. As King points out, the Thatcher governments of the 1980s satisfied 'the employers' desire to have tripartism weakened and the levy removed' (1997: 395). A number of analysts have argued that these government programs provided cheap labor without providing training gains (see Finn 1987; Ainley and Corney 1990; King 1995, 1997). It is true that in the early 1980s, the conservative government increased the budget dedicated to training and extended the number of active policies (as shown in Figure 6.3). Crouch has argued that during the 1980s, the Thatcher governments used the MSC 'as a major policy instrument to introduce a more rigorous concept of VET [vocational education and training] into school and further education curricula, and to reduce youth wages' (1995: 298). This was particularly the case when Lord Young was the chairman of the MSC and a number of new training programs (e.g. for young and long-term unemployed) were

---

[19] The effectiveness of the Employment Service reorganization of the 1970s is highly disputed. Layard (1979) argues that the changes may have been partially responsible for the increase in unemployment experienced since 1966 (because, for example, of the reduced ability of governments to limit unemployment benefits for those not accepting 'satisfactory' job offers).

introduced. In 1987, these employment training initiatives were linked to the general reform of the education system promoted by the Thatcher government. Assistance to new labor market entrants was complemented by the development of technical education initiatives, the promotion of polytechnic centers, and the ensuing emergence of the Youth Training Program uniting all previous employment policies (Finegold and Soskice 1988). New antiunemployment initiatives like the New Job Training Scheme or the Youth Training Scheme were established and the budget for job formation policies increased from £1.1 billion in 1978–9 to £3.4 billion in 1987–8 (Boix 1998a: 177).[20] But this was to a great extent the consequence of the spectacular increase in unemployment experienced during this time. The old training problems remained. As Crouch (1995) also points out, Thatcher abolished most industrial training boards and therefore removed one of the only existing instruments for employers to improve training schemes. Then, when the apprenticeship system almost collapsed in the early 1980s, the conservatives failed to provide any coherent alternatives. In 1989, a government study reported that training was directed to short-term necessities and that most workers had not experienced any vocational training (King 1997: 396).

The main training program of the conservative governments, the Youth Training Scheme, was started in 1983. The Youth Training Scheme was designed to provide unemployed people under 18 years of age with some vocational training. In 1986, the Council for Vocational Qualifications was created to provide different levels of vocational attainment. The goal was to have at least 60 percent of workers qualified at the third level of vocational attainment by 2000 (Rhodes 2000: 48). This was complemented by the creation in 1988 of the National Vocational Qualifications and of General National Vocational Qualifications in 1992 (Cruz-Castro and Conlon 2001).[21] One of the goals of the youth scheme was to replace the failed apprenticeship system but, as Crouch notes, '(n)ot surprisingly, the standards of the replacement apprenticeship schemes were rather low' (1995: 299). The share of employees receiving some training increased from 8 to 14 percent between 1984 and 1994. But the effectiveness of the training programs has been generally questioned (many youths left the Youth Training Scheme without any qualifications)[22] and the resources

---

[20] It did then go down to £3.2 billion in 1989–90.

[21] This qualification system emerged as a way to assess performance. The government, however, did not specify how these standards were to be met. See Cruz-Castro and Conlon (2001) for details.

[22] See Rhodes (2000).

dedicated to these programs were less than impressive (as will become clear below). The actual effects of these training initiatives were also far from unambiguous. Lovering argues that instead of providing workers with skills for the market place, for many employers the main value of the Youth Training Scheme and Employment Training lied in 'providing them with the opportunity for extended recruitment procedures' (1994: 354).[23]

Regarding the public placement service, most analysts agree that it was not improved during the 1980s (see, e.g. Lovering 1994). Jobcentres handled only about a third of vacancies and became less involved in the labor market and less effective as the decade of Conservative government advanced. Private intermediation companies became very active in providing jobs, and other vacancies were mostly filled through the press and informal contacts. In addition to this, Jobcentres were severely limited by lack of resources. They lacked both the technology (e.g. no computerized records) and the staff to provide adequate employment services (Lovering 1994: 354). As their resources dwindled, Jobcentre workers saw their workloads increase and their salaries decrease. Their effectiveness was also limited by the government's decision not to allow Jobcentres to market themselves to employers. According to Finn (1988) and Lovering (1994), the public employment service had become more effective at funneling the unemployed into training programs (of dubious effectiveness) than at putting together potential employers and employees. As was the case in the analysis of the Spanish and Dutch public employment services, Jobcentres in the UK were not perceived by employers as an effective way to find workers. The Thatcher government's policies reinforced this perception. As Lovering argues, the more Jobcentres were seen as pushing unwilling claimants to apply for vacancies, the more reluctant employers were to use them (1994: 354).

In 1987, the TUC decided not to continue to cooperate with those programs administered by the MSC that were perceived to have as their main goal the reduction of youth wages (Crouch 1995). The government had already considered the idea of eliminating union participation from the MSC and in 1989 it decided to abolish the agency altogether. The 1989 Employment Act[24] eliminated the Training Commission (created in 1988 to replace the MSC) and removed unions from training boards. After the elimination of the Training Commission, most of its budget

---

[23] For more details about Thatcher's ALMPs, see Finegold and Soskice (1988).

[24] See details in Chapter 5.

was transferred to local Training and Enterprise Councils (TECs). By the early 1990s, 82 TECs had taken over responsibility for the administration of Youth Training, Employment Training, the Enterprise Allowance Scheme, and other programs (Boddy 1994). The majority of the board members in TECs were required, by law, to be executives of companies. Although employers dominated their administration, neither employers' associations nor, more importantly, unions belonged to (or had formal ways to participate in) TECs. The creation of TECs also coincided with a decrease in funding for training programs by the conservative government.[25] As King explains, the government even rejected European Union funding for retraining in new technologies because it required matching funds (1997: 397). TECs were created as 'new kinds of "enterprise organisation" built around principles of performance, value for money and return on investment' (Boddy 1994: 367). However, they did not have any power to penalize inadequate training. It was hoped that the involvement of local employers in TECs would result in increases in training by their companies but this proved to be too optimistic (King 1995).

The problem was that TECs were equipped with resources that they had to 'spend in the market with various training providers in such a way as to show a maximum number of trainee places for a given expenditure' (Crouch 1995: 300). Every incentive in the system, therefore, promoted cheap training, cheap providers, and low skills. As argued by Finegold, TECs 'perpetuate the low-skill equilibrium; they can best satisfy their targets by providing narrow, employer-specific training, concentrating on low-cost, low-capital intensive courses (e.g. hairdressing over engineering), and focusing on those low-skilled occupations, such as retailing, where high turnover rates make it easier to place people in jobs' (1992: 242). King notes that there were two additional negative consequences of TECs on training: first, 'instead of linking state-based and firm-based training, TECs actually resulted in a lower level of co-ordination between the two types of training;' and second, 'they produced a further diminution in state participation in training' (1997: 404).

The final aspect of ALMP under conservative rule was the initiation of workfare. In 1988, the third Thatcher government made it a priority to couple training requirements with social benefits. The conservatives

---

[25] The decreases in funding would continue under John Major's leadership. In 1994, the money going into training (including company incentives) decreased to £1.6 billion (from £2 billion in 1992 and 1993) and in 1995 the funding was reduced by a further 19 percent (King 1997: 398 and n. 69).

implemented legislation that made unemployed people under 21 years of age face the choice of either enrolling in training programs or losing their benefits. Reminiscent of previous conservative initiatives, this measure contributed to transforming training 'into a means of supplying firms with temporary, low-cost labor' (King and Wood 1999: 388). Training, King and Wood continue, was now 'used as a threat of further insecurity rather than as an incentive to invest in employable skills' (1999: 388). In 1996, the training requirement was extended to all unemployed people who wanted to qualify for benefits. John Major's 1996 Job Seeker's Allowance program also added more restrictions to benefits and tightened the eligibility rules.[26] At the same time, Major did little to provide new financing or create new jobs for those whose benefits were being reduced (Cressey 1999: 176).

6.3.3. *New Labour's Active Labor Market Policy*

The ascendancy of Tony Blair can be identified with a change in employment promotion strategies in the Labour Party. It could be argued that the reorientation of Labour's training policies started earlier. Already in the mid-1980s, after the early defeats to Thatcher, there had been plans for a national training organization funded by a levy on all but the smallest firms. The Labour Party took vocational training and 'upskilling' seriously at that time.[27] In the 1990s, however, the party retreated somewhat and looked more toward policies promoting generic skills. Plans for a training levy were scrapped in 1996 in preparation for the 1997 elections. The new emphasis on active measures coincided with a distancing between New Labour and the unions. In the 1993 Labour Party Congress, union block voting was reduced to 70 percent (33 percent for leadership decisions) and a prior ballot of union members was instated.[28] Then in 1995, the union share in conference votes was further reduced to 50 percent. The decrease in union block voting was accompanied by a decrease in the Labour Party's economic dependence on unions. In recent years the union share of Party financing has decreased from the 90 percent averaged until the early 1980s to around 50 percent. It is

[26] As Ainley has noted, since the introduction of the Job Seeker's Allowance, the unemployed officially ceased to exist in the UK, having being redefined as job seekers (1999: 99).

[27] For the connection between Labour's employment strategies of the 1980s and those of the 1990s, see King and Wickham-Jones (1998).

[28] Previously union leaders could vote in place of their members (without needing to engage in a prior vote and being able to unify whatever diversity existed among the members). See Fielding (1995).

clear that the emergence of New Labour required a separation from the unions. The modernization of the Party envisioned by Blair was based on a closer relationship with business and a more arm's length one with unions (Taylor 2001; Ludlam, Bodah, and Coates 2002).[29] In fact, a strong association with the unions came to be perceived as an electoral handicap and a cause for the lack of support in previous elections (King 2002).

The new attitude toward employment promotion was highlighted in the 1997 manifesto as one of the points in the 'Contract with the People.' It stated the Labour Party's intention to get 250,000 young unemployed people into work (Labour Party 1997). Labour's approach to ALMPs was encapsulated in the Welfare to Work program (popularly known as the New Deal). In 1997, Blair established a windfall tax on profits of privatized utilities. It was estimated to provide £4.8 billion (over two years) which would be allocated to the New Deal (Burchardt and Hills 1999: 44). The New Deal initiative was aimed at young people, single parents, sick and disabled people, and the long-term unemployed. It included job subsidies for employers (£60 a week for participants in training programs), the establishment of 'taster' employment (short placement spells), and the provision of counseling and advice (Cressey 1999: 177). There was a commitment from New Labour to guarantee work for all 18–24-year-olds unemployed for six months or more (Grover and Stewart 1999). After being unemployed for six months, young people are required to enter a 'Gateway' period. During the Gateway period, intense job assistance is provided. If a job is not obtained, four New Deal options are open: training, subsidized work in the private sector, voluntary sector work, or work with the new Environmental Taskforce (getting benefits is not an option).[30] The Department for Education and Employment provided £58 million to start Employment Zones to attack long-term unemployment, committed to a £150 million investment in individual learning accounts and an initial £15 million to start a University for Industry (Coates 2000: 132).[31]

---

[29] Crouch argues that New Labour is not exceptional in its attempt to collaborate with the upscale groups; they are unique, however, in doing so 'with virtually no pressures from other social interests within their party to balance their influence' (1999b: 81).

[30] Van Reenen (2003) calculates that unemployed young men were 20 percent more likely to get a job as a result of the New Deal.

[31] In spite of the significance of these numbers, it must be pointed out that New Labour's training policies are fundamentally voluntaristic, with no return to a training levy or to any form of employer compulsion to train.

The Labour government also developed a number of additional policies that complement the New Deal. Blair has emphasized 'Lifelong Learning' (a process characterized by training and 'upskilling' throughout the professional careers of workers) as the goal for employment policy. In agreement with new priorities emerging at the European Union level, the focus of labor market policy has become the employability of workers (turning labor into a skilled and competitive resource). New initiatives addressing these objectives include the University for Industry (a national program to provide advice and training to workers at any stage in their professional careers), the 'Investors in People' program and plans for skills development under Objective 4 of the European Structural Funds (for details, see Cressey 2002). The Labour government also reformed the system of in-work benefits for families with children in ways directed to reduce the disincentives to work, especially in low pay activities. The most important of these 'make work pay' measures has been the Working Families Tax Credit. This initiative is considerably more generous than the Family Credit program preceding it and guarantees any family with a full-time worker £214 per week.[32]

The previous paragraphs suggest that New Labour is committed to ALMPs in a way that was not evident from the analysis of Figure 6.3. It is important to point out, however, the nature of ALMP has been transformed under Blair. There has been a certain discomfort about the link between ALMPs and social benefits (what critics have called the coercive side of Blair's training programs). The elimination of a benefits option for young people, for example, represents a continuation of conservative policies.[33] The emphasis on conditionality for social benefits is a complicated one. In defining modern social democracy in Europe, Vandenbroucke points out that '(a)ctive labor market policies presuppose a *correct* balance between incentives, opportunities and obligations' (1999: 38, my italics). It is, however, this correct balance that is difficult to find. In many people's minds, New Labour's policies matching job-searching and social benefits (just like those promoted by its conservative predecessors) are punitive. Ainley has argued that the New Labour approach

---

[32] There is an additional subsidy to cover child-care expenses, and adjustments to the bottom end of the tax and national insurance schedules (Glyn and Wood 2001: 53).

[33] It is also a rejection of what the Labour Party had stood for as late as 1992. In January 1988, the National Executive Committee of the Labour Party endorsed *The Charter Against Workfare*, which contained the following statement about active measures: 'people should join the scheme because they want to, not because they fear they will lose all or part of their benefits if they don't. Compulsion is a recipe for lower standards, resentment and discrimination' (quoted by King and Wickham-Jones 1999: 257).

to employability implies (in a very non-Leftist way) that if anyone is unemployed, 'they would only have themselves to blame through not having made themselves employable enough!' (1999: 100). The danger for New Labour is that initiatives like the New Deal end up 'alienating the traditional supporters of the Party while not producing the necessary wherewithal to keep new supporters happy' (Cressey 1999: 190).

7

Partisanship, Institutions, and Social Policy

The final policy addressed in this book's analysis is a very significant one. Social expenditure is a substantial part of the budget in most industrialized democracies. It is a vital concern for policymakers and, therefore, it has been the subject of much scholarly attention. My insider–outsider model challenges the generally accepted association between social democracy and the welfare state. As was the case with ALMPs, Left governments are not expected to promote social policy unless insiders become vulnerable to the effects of unemployment. The evidence I have presented thus far has supported this claim.

In this chapter I will also explore the effects of corporatism on the relationship between governments and social policy. In Chapter 5, I looked at partisan effects on employment protection. In Chapter 6, I emphasized the influence of employment protection on active measures. Now we turn our attention to how corporatism and, again, employment protection affect social policy in the three countries considered.

My analysis has shown that, in a noncorporatist country such as Spain, the policies of the PSOE governments have lacked a clear social dimension. PLMPs were considered secondary to other political objectives (like inflation reduction or labor market flexibilization). In a way that was impossible to do through the first half of this book's quantitative analyses, the detailed study of the Spanish case also reveals that social benefits can be manipulated to exclude outsiders and favor insiders. The PSOE limited the availability of social policies to outsiders and facilitated access for insiders who were temporarily unemployed. As for the PP government, their approach to social policy has been remarkably similar to the social democrats.

In the Netherlands, corporatism has promoted much higher levels of social policy, but, as in Spain, the influence of government partisanship is not obvious. Also as in Spain, my analysis shows that Dutch governments (regardless of partisan origin) attempted to limit social policy to temporarily unemployed insiders. Very early on, the size of the welfare state in the Netherlands became a problem for the promotion of other economic goals (like inflation control or a balanced budget). Beginning in the late 1980s, corporatist arrangements facilitated the realization that social policy (particularly sickness and disability benefits) has become a problem. Paradoxically, this appreciation promoted the exclusion of the social partners from some parts of the welfare state (since they were perceived as part of the problem).

The UK case shows that before the 1980s, both parties had engaged in expansive welfare measures. The electoral victory of Margaret Thatcher signaled the beginning of a period in which governments of both parties would limit social policy. I show that, unsurprisingly, the Conservative governments of Thatcher and Major pursued policies directed to the retrenchment of the welfare state. More unexpectedly for the traditional approach to partisanship (but supportive of an insider–outsider interpretation), New Labour has not substantially modified the conservative approach to social benefits (and it has in fact coincided in transforming welfare into workfare).

7.1. Social Policy in Spain

A number of analysts have argued that the PSOE considered social policy the ultimate goal of their administration and economic policy as simply a way to obtain social objectives (see e.g. Maravall 1995; Boix 1998*b*). It is true that the sacrifices required of workers by the González governments (like wage moderation or the consequences of a restrictive monetary policy) were often justified in terms of future social gains (Maravall 1995: 243–6). But the picture that emerges from the following analysis is quite different. The policies of the PSOE governments lacked a clear social dimension and PLMPs were promoted only as far as the consideration of many other priorities (like inflation control, budget limitations, or European integration requirements) permitted.

This can be appreciated in a preliminary way by looking at the aggregate levels of social policy in Spain. Figure 7.1 presents two measures. The first, total public social expenditure, is the same used in the analysis in

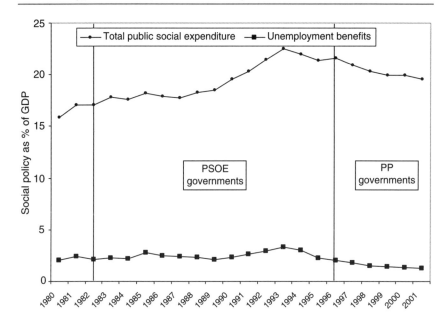

Figure 7.1. Social policy in Spain, 1980–2001

Chapter 4. It includes social benefits for old age, survivors, incapacity, health, family support, ALMP, unemployment, and housing. This is, admittedly, a very encompassing measure of social policy. Figure 7.1 also provides the levels of one component of total public social expenditure of importance to my analysis: unemployment benefits. Unemployment benefits are defined as public cash expenditures to compensate for unemployment (Armingeon et al. 2005).

Figure 7.1 shows that the levels of social policy in Spain have been consistently low since 1980. When examining the existing cross-national diversity in social policy in Chapter 4, I placed countries in three general groups: those with high, intermediate, and low levels of social policies. Spain was placed within the group of countries characterized by low levels of total public social spending (others were Australia, Canada, Japan, and the USA). All these countries dedicate less than 20 percent of GDP to social policy. Although social policy in Spain exceeded 20 percent from 1991 to 1998, the average for this period is only 19 percent (well below those in France, Belgium, Germany, Italy, and, of course, the Scandinavian countries).

It is difficult to see a strong relationship between government partisanship and social policy when we look at Figure 7.1. It is true that from

1982 to 1993, the PSOE governments in power promoted an increase in public social expenditure. The progress in total social policy was mirrored very closely by that of unemployment benefits. When PSOE came to power, social expenditure was 17 percent of GDP and unemployment benefits 2.1 percent. By 1993, social expenditure had become 22 percent of GDP and unemployment benefits 3.3 percent. However, total social expenditure and unemployment benefits dropped in the last four years of PSOE rule. Moreover, conservative government in Spain since 1996 has not been associated with a drastic reduction in either of these social measures. The analysis I develop below explores the relationship between partisan government and social policy in more detail.

7.1.1. PSOE's Social Policy in the 1980s and 1990s

Before the 1980s, Spain had low levels of social policy. During the dictatorship, the conservative nature of economic policy was mostly a consequence of Franco's overwhelming goal of regime continuation, his disinterest and ignorance about economic affairs, and a philosophical homogeneity of policymaking elites characterized by 'National Catholicism' and authoritarian, antisocialist and anti-regional nationalism (Gunther 1980).

The beginning of the democratic period in Spain signaled an increase in the social dimension of the state. The UCD governments promoted a significant increase in general government outlays, from 24.7 percent of GDP in 1975 to 37.5 percent in 1982, and in social security transfers in particular, from 10.3 to 15.5 percent.[1] To do this they had to reform the taxation system and reject the Francoist practice of balanced budgets (much of this spending had to be financed by an increase in public debt).[2] The bases for the current fiscal system in Spain were created by the UCD between 1977 and 1982. In 1977, Fernández Ordoñez (Economy Minister under Prime Minister Adolfo Suárez) coordinated a fiscal reform that culminated in the approval of the *Ley de Medidas Fiscales Urgentes*. This law created the *Impuesto sobre la Renta de las Personas Físicas* (IRPF, income tax) and the fiscal system that had prevailed during the Francoist period (characterized by regressiveness, low tax revenues, and generalized fraud) was transformed to some extent.[3]

It is important to emphasize that the levels of social protection accomplished by the end of this period were still very limited and that the main

---

[1] See OECD, *Historical Statistics* for details.   [2] See Gunther (1996).
[3] For details, see Comín (1988).

priority of the UCD governments was to secure support for democracy. The UCD leadership believed that taxes could not be drastically raised (so the upper and middle classes would not become disenchanted) but that social spending (directed to those worst hit by the oil crises of the 1970s) had to expand (see Gunther 1996). The Moncloa Pacts were part of this arrangement. Rudimentary social policies (extremely weak in many aspects) were provided in exchange for the demobilization of groups demanding more significant improvements in the welfare state, higher salaries, and an end to labor market flexibilization (Adelantado, Nogvera, and Rambla 1998: 203).

The victory of the PSOE in the 1982 elections did not change the fundamental characteristics of social policy in Spain. This was the case despite the fact that the first González administration did have to contend with some of the problems that had limited the policies of the UCD governments. Gunther argues that, unlike their predecessors, the PSOE was not subject to 'constraints on government policy options resulting from overwhelming concerns with the political demands of the transition' or to 'the extreme insecurity characteristic of a faction-ridden governing party lacking a parliamentary majority at a time of worldwide economic recession' (1996: 31). As Bermeo and Garcia-Durán point out, the PSOE electoral campaign had been built around

the vague but appealing promise of *cambio*, or 'change', but the exact nature of the change in the area of economic policy was not clarified until after the election was won. After entering office, the socialists announced that liberalization of the economy would be accelerated, that they could not create 800,000 new jobs [which they had explicitly promised during their campaign], and that their priorities would be to close the inflation differential with the European Community.

(Bermeo and Garcia-Durán 1994: 107)

These strategies generally coincided with the recommendations made by the IMF in 1981. De Velasco, the Secretary of Commerce from 1982 to 1986, remembers that when the PSOE started to govern in 1982, there were three main factors influencing policy planning: the economic crisis that Spain had been suffering since 1980; the failure of the French experience of nationalizations and expansive policies; and the belief that any failure to promote price stability would cause the IMF to intervene (1996: 20). Because of these considerations, the implementation of a successful deflationary policy became the most important objective for the PSOE government. In spite of the dire state of the economy, the González government rejected policies to stimulate demand and emphasized price stability through a combination of wage moderation and restrictive monetary policy instead (Boix 1998a: 109). Cutting public spending was an important part of this strategy. In fact, Bermeo and García-Durán argue that the socialists' 'most important fiscal reform was the attempt to cut state spending through an austerity budget announced in April 1983' (1994: 108). The dramatic increase in unemployment that followed was, according to Pérez, 'a price that was regarded by the government's economic team as a necessary step in rectifying the wage and public spending dynamic that had taken place during the transition' (1999: 671).

At this time, then, the PSOE leadership considered social policy secondary to other political objectives (like inflation reduction or labor market flexibilization). The social democratic governments modified some of the characteristics of unemployment benefits, but in a way that made them more clearly assistance-based while not changing the fundamental fact that the majority of the unemployed continued not to receive any benefits (see Recio and Roca 1998: 153). There are two kinds of unemployment benefits in Spain, one that is fundamentally earnings-related and one that is assistance-based. Earnings-related benefits are designed to compensate for lost salaries while assistance benefits are considered minimum subsistence aid (García Perea and Martín 1996). Earnings-related benefits are related both in terms of value and duration to the amount of time and the previous salary of the unemployed worker. Assistance benefits, on the other hand, are only provided to individuals with 'family responsibilities' and their value and duration depend on the nature of these responsibilities.

Starting in 1984, the characteristics of the unemployed and the nature of the PSOE's social policies combined to increase the number of assistance benefit recipients while decreasing their level of protection (Ayala 1994; Adelantado, Noguera, and Rambla 1998). In fact, from 1982 to 1990, in spite of the fluctuations in the rate of unemployment, social security transfers remained stable at a level considerably lower that the European average (around 15.7 percent of GDP). As numerous authors have pointed out, the paradoxical result of social democratic government during this period was the decrease in the intensity of assistance-based social protection (see e.g. Adelantado, Naguera, and Rambla 1998; Rodríguez Cabrero 1998). This tendency was not limited to unemployment benefits but was also confirmed by the PSOE's pension policies. In 1985, the socialists approved the Pension Law (Ley 26/1985). It significantly reduced pension spending by requiring a longer period of previous work and by making the principle of proportionality between what was earned and received as a pension stricter. As was the case with unemployment benefits, the result of the socialists' policies was a decrease in the levels of protection provided by pensions.

The first socialist administration (from 1982 to 1985) was characterized by quite a restrictive fiscal policy. At the same time the government was involved in a process of industrial restructuring that, on top of the payment on public debt, represented an important drain on public resources. Tax revenues were increased as a result of a general tax hike (concentrated in indirect taxes) and attempts to marginally reduce fraud (González Calvet 1998). The initial years following the socialists' second electoral victory (1986 and 1987) were also characterized by fiscal discipline and budgetary consolidation. The income tax was increased and strict controls over spending were enforced, mainly over social policies and debt payment (González-Páramo and López Casasnovas 1996). The PSOE government continued to make controlling inflation its most important policy goal. This was accomplished by tightening monetary policy once more and by further attempts to reduce the public deficit (see Solchaga 1988). The González government did not simply accept the European recommendations in favor of strict monetary policy but defended them enthusiastically (Recio and Roca 1998). After the peseta devaluations of 1982, the other instrument used by the PSOE government to control inflation was a high nominal exchange rate in relation to other European currencies. According to Secretary of Commerce de Velasco, this strategy was based on the PSOE policymakers' belief that high exchange rates would promote 'competitive disinflation' (1996: 22). They hoped that higher costs for Spanish companies would push them to adapt and become more competitive.

The consequences of the socialists' monetary policies were, however, ambiguous. The PSOE government succeeded in its acknowledged main goal: the reduction of inflation. From 1978 to 1983 the inflation rate in Spain had hovered around a 16 percent average while during the last PSOE term (from 1993 to 1996) the average was closer to 4.5 percent. On the other hand, the costs paid in terms of unemployment had been phenomenal and the success of 'competitive disinflation' questionable. In fact, a number of observers have argued that the monetary policies promoted by the socialists had quite the opposite effect than was intended. Pérez (1997) and Recio and Roca (1998) relate the problems of the industrial sector to the exchange appreciation strategy implemented by the socialists. The appreciation of the peseta and the oligopolistic nature of the financial sector promoted, in Pérez's view, 'an intense shift of financial resources away from sectors that were exposed to competition and therefore could not pass on costs to consumers in favor of sectors that were less exposed to competition (services, construction, utilities, and real estate) and hence able to pass on cost increases' (1999: 675).

The negative effects of monetary policy on industrial employment were compounded by PSOE's industrial policy initiatives. The restructuring undertaken by the PSOE government resulted in a significant decline in the number of workers in the industrial sector. Moreover, these workers were not systematically redirected to other activities (see Maravall 1987; Bueno Campos 1996; Castañer 1998). In most cases the reduction in the labor force was accomplished through early retirements (at times with an intermediary step supported by unemployment benefits) and the number of workers finding employment in other areas was minimal (Pastor 1992). The significant limitations of PSOE's ALMPs, explained in Chapter 6, no doubt contributed to this lack of success in the reallocation of industrial workers. In addition, PSOE industrial policies did not address the causes for the poor competitiveness in the sector (rigidities limiting competition, lack of innovation, etc.) but simply tried to mitigate their consequences (Castañer 1998).

Starting in 1988 and as a consequence of the success of the general strike in December, public spending was expanded. Pensions were part of this rise but so were investments related to both the Barcelona Olympic Games and Seville's World Exposition in 1992. This increase in public spending, as numerous observers have noted, was contradictory with the tight monetary policy implemented by the government, which was effective at controlling inflation but quite costly in terms of employment (see e.g. González Calvet 1998). It was once more supported by public deficits, although their levels became among the highest in the OECD in the 1987 to 1992 period.

The end of the economic upswing in 1991, the increasing popularity of a neoliberal economic model, and the requirements (especially in terms of public spending) of European integration reinforced the PSOE's lack of attention toward social policy (González Calvet 1998; Rodríguez Cabrero 1998). Regarding unemployment policies, in particular, the PSOE leadership's conviction that the levels of benefits were too generous and that they contributed to the high unemployment rate added to these factors. Further reductions in social spending were undertaken. Laws were passed in 1992 (*Real Decreto Ley* 1/1992, also known as the 'decretazo', which was later substituted by *Ley* 22/1992) raising the minimum period of previous work required to be eligible for unemployment benefits and lowering unemployment benefits (Dolado and Bentolila 1992: 13). Laws in 1993 and 1994 (*Ley* 21/1993 and *Real Decreto-Ley* 120/1994) and the budget for 1994 reduced unemployment benefits, increased the level of prerequisites to receive them, excluded some kinds of workers (like apprentices or those holding part-time jobs), and strengthened measures against unemployment benefit fraud (Alarcón Caracuel 1995).

Regarding pensions, in 1994 the PSOE compensated a reduction in the amount of employer contributions with an increase in the value-added tax in what was interpreted by many as a blatantly regressive measure (Adelantado, Noguera, and Rambla 1998: 209). The importance of pensioners as potential voters and the uncertainty about pensions and their possible use as an electoral weapon, however, promoted the signing of the Toledo Pact in 1995. The Pact was signed by the main political parties to guarantee the future of the pension system and therefore eliminate it as an electoral issue.

The consequences of these policies were stark for insider–outsider differences. Unemployment benefits under the socialist government were very low both in terms of levels and in terms of people covered. As Recio and Roca have argued, it is indeed striking that spending on unemployment benefits was the same proportion of GDP in 1995 as it had been in 1982, considering that unemployment had increased from 16.4 to 22.3 percent of the active population (1998: 153). Meanwhile, the proportion of those receiving some sort of benefit out of the total number of unemployed remained among the lowest in the OECD. Reflecting the increase in beneficiaries and the decrease in levels explained above, this proportion increased from 32 percent in 1985 to a not very impressive 43 percent in 1990 (López López and Melguizo Sánchez 1991: 107–8). As a consequence of the decreasing importance of social policies, in the 1990s the number of those covered by unemployment benefits declined even further.

The nature of the policies promoted by the González administrations deserves closer attention. Assistance-based benefits were provided to an increasing number of recipients but two important caveats are in order. First, although more people received benefits, their level of protection was decreased so that the resources dedicated to these policies were not expanded. Secondly, assistance-based unemployment benefits were only provided to individuals with family responsibilities, which meant that most young single workers and many females received no benefits (Symes 1995: 136). This of course meant that most outsiders were automatically precluded from receiving any unemployment benefits.

Regarding earnings-related unemployment benefits, two facts deserve particular notice. First, although comparing the Spanish unemployment benefit system with those in other OECD countries is not straightforward (e.g. given the diversity of requirements), many observers would agree that earnings-related benefits are strongly related to past earnings (see e.g. Blanco 1996). Both value and duration of benefits are dependent on past work experience. The other significant characteristic of earnings-related benefits in Spain concerns the relationship between requirements and levels. Spanish earnings-related benefits were among the most difficult to obtain. This is because the period of previous employment established as a legal requirement is among the longest in Europe. Once the very strict prerequisites have been satisfied, however, the levels of earnings-related unemployment benefits are in fact well above the EU average in spite of Spanish high unemployment rates (García Perea and Martín 1996: 89).[4]

The final characteristic of unemployment benefits in Spain concerns the difference in replacement rates associated to the length of unemployment. Replacement rates are defined as the proportion of previous earnings that unemployed individuals receive as benefits. The difference between the benefits received by the short-term and the long-term unemployed in Spain is very large. As López López and Melguizo Sánchez point out, the replacement rates provided for the short-term unemployed are among the highest in Europe while those for the long-term unemployed are among the lowest (1991: 113). High short-term replacement rates represent a considerable amount of protection for a particular kind of worker—the employed insider who is temporarily unemployed.

Putting together these elements, a picture emerges that reflects serious efforts by the PSOE to limit the availability of social policies for outsiders. Assistance-based benefits were provided only to those with family responsibilities and not, therefore, to many outsiders. The characteristics of earnings-related benefits were also strongly anti-outsider because they were very difficult to obtain (they required, in effect, the potential recipient to have been an established insider) but once they were obtained they were generous, in particular for those insiders who were unemployed only temporarily.

---

[4] The levels would be even higher if redundancy payments (among the highest in the OECD) were included in the calculation.

7.1.2. Conservative Government and Social Policy

The electoral victory of the conservative party in 1996 did not result in any drastic changes in the orientation of social policy. The PP government's consideration of social policy was affected by two fundamental factors. First, like the PSOE governments it replaced, the PP's strategies were subject to the limitations in terms of spending imposed by the Maastricht objectives and European Union convergence. But, perhaps more importantly, the PP had won the elections by a minimal margin and it understood that the policies of its minority government needed the support of a large proportion of the electorate. The development of policies which would not decrease social spending was an obvious choice. Particularly since, as explained in Chapter 5, the PP had decided to attack insider employment protection.

The PP government promoted a dialogue with unions and employers. The cooperative attitude toward unions, initially mediated through Javier Arenas (Minister of Work and Social Affairs), was a significant change from the antagonistic relationship that had characterized the relationship between unions and the PSOE governments (particularly in their last few years). In terms of policy, the PP generally maintained social spending levels (as shown in Figure 7.1). According to figures provided by the INEM, the coverage of unemployment benefits remained remarkably stable from 1996 to 2001. The total number of those receiving benefits declined slightly (both for earnings-related and assistance-based benefits) but the number of unemployed people had also decreased. The average earnings-related benefits received by the unemployed did not experience a decrease in that period either. As for pensions, in 1996 the government reached an agreement with the unions in which it committed to extend the Toledo Pact until 2001 (Adelantado, Noguera, and Rambla 1998). The continuity of the protection system for agricultural workers was also assured. The PP increased levels of social protection for the precariously employed by including in the *Acuerdo Interconfederal para la Estabilidad del Empleo* measures for the social protection of part-time workers.

Although not included in the period of my analysis, I must point out that the strategy of the PP toward social policy changed after their more comfortable electoral victory in 2000. With a majority in Parliament, the PP tried to impose more drastic reforms on unemployment benefits. The main objective of these reforms was to reduce the number of unemployed people receiving benefits and to introduce stricter workfare conditions in the system. The reforms were implemented in 2002 (see *El País*, May 24, 2002).

7.2. Social Policy in the Netherlands

The relationship between government partisanship and levels of social policy in the Netherlands is presented in Figure 7.2. As in the Spanish case, the figure contains two measures: total public social expenditure and unemployment benefits. Figure 7.2 also provides a timeline reflecting the partisan nature of the government in power.

The levels of total public social expenditure in Figure 7.2 are significantly higher than those in Spain. When comparing social policy across OECD countries in Chapter 4, I included the Netherlands in the group characterized by high levels (which also included Belgium, Denmark, Finland, France, Germany, and Sweden). The social expenditure average in the Netherlands is 26 percent of GDP during the period under analysis. There is an initial increase (from 1980 to 1983) that takes public social expenditure from 27 percent to almost 30 percent of GDP. After a gentle decrease back to 27 percent in 1986, there is a period of stability until 1989 and then an increase until 1993, which takes them to 29 percent. The rest

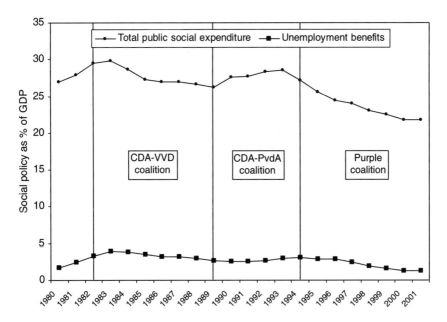

Figure 7.2. Social policy in the Netherlands, 1980–2001

of the series reflects a steady decline in the resources dedicated to social expenditure, reaching a low 22 percent of GDP in 2001. Unemployment benefits have followed a very similar path since 1980. The levels are much lower (the average for the period is 2.7 percent) but they mirror the developments of other social policies. The only exception is the period from 1990 to 1993, when unemployment benefits remain stable but total public social expenditure experiences an increase.

As in the Spanish case, the figure does not suggest a strong relationship between government partisanship and social policy. The CDA-VVD coalition governing from 1982 to 1989 promoted a decrease in total social expenditure (from around 30 percent to 26 percent) and in unemployment benefits (from 3.3 percent to 2.7 percent). But the same CDA Prime Minister (Ruud Lubbers), then in a coalition with the Labor Party, slightly increased total social expenditure and unemployment benefits from 1990 to 1994. It is true that the purple coalitions led by Wim Kok starting in 1994 governed over an unambiguous decrease in total social expenditure and unemployment benefits (from 27 percent to 22 percent and from 3 percent to 1.3 percent respectively). But no clear picture about the influence of partisanship emerges from Figure 7.2. The analysis below will shed some light on this.

7.2.1. *Social Policy in the 1970s and 1980s*

As late as the 1950s, the Netherlands did not possess a substantial welfare state. Between 1955 and 1975, however, the growth of social provisions was so high that the Dutch welfare system was transformed into one of the most comprehensive in Europe. Welfare provisions in the Netherlands developed around three main areas: universal insurance, worker insurance, and social benefits. Universal insurance was financed through general taxation and it guaranteed nonworking individuals a minimum income (Aarts and De Jong 1996*a*). This included a flat rate public pension (created in 1956), widow and orphan support, and health cost funds. The second area, worker insurance, provided benefits to wage earners in the case of illness, accident, or unemployment. These benefits were financed by contributions from workers and employers and were managed by unions and employers' associations. Since 1964, unemployment benefits equaled 80 percent of last earned wage for 26 weeks, and 75 percent for an additional two-year period. Also starting in 1964, disability benefits (again managed by unions and employers' associations) were 80 percent of last earned wage (Visser and Hemerijck 1997). The third area of the welfare state, social provisions, covered individuals with no income or other benefits (a worker who, for example, could not find work and was no longer eligible to receive unemployment benefits). These social benefits were 75 percent of the statutory minimum wage.

At this time, a generous welfare state was understood as a trade-off necessary to secure wage moderation and cooperation from labor. Social spending, however, became unmanageable by the late 1970s. The number of people receiving income support was 1.6 million in 1970 and, not counting the 300,000 people on sick leave, it had doubled by 1985 (Visser and Hemerijck 1997). Social security premiums that had only been 5 percent of national income in 1953 reached 15 percent in 1970 and 24 percent in 1983. Since this was not enough to finance the welfare system, governments increased public borrowing (OECD 1984). In the 1970s, moreover, the situation was worsened by the linkage between social benefits and private wage increases promoted by the Den Uyl government. This indexation of social benefits increased social spending and the public deficit problem. The government had no control over the growth of social benefits and neither unions nor employers faced strong incentives to exercise restraint.

Although the Labor Party won seven seats in the 1977 elections, it did not manage to reach an agreement with the Christian democrats to form a government. Instead Van Agt (CDA) took office by forming a coalition with the VVD. The new government's stated objectives were the reduction of inflation and unemployment, and controlling public expenditure and the deficit. Limiting the size of the public sector was attempted mainly by decreasing public wages and social security but without much success (Gladdish 1991). The budget deficit continued to grow. During the Den Uyl and Van Agt governments, public sector expenditures grew from 45 percent of GDP in 1970–1 to about 62 percent in 1981–2 (Wolinetz 1989: 89). This spectacular increase in public expenditures had to be financed with higher levels of public debt. The public deficit had been only 1.9 percent of GDP in 1970 but reached 3.6 percent in 1975 (the middle of Den Uyl's administration) and was 5 percent in 1980 (almost the end of Van Agt's first government). Government debt was 21 percent of GDP in 1973, it had only increased to 22 percent by the end of Den Uyl's government (1977) but it ballooned to 34 percent by the end of Van Agt's first term in office.

The formation of a center-right coalition led by Ruud Lubbers in 1982 signaled a new emphasis on fiscal responsibility. In contrast to previous governments whose main goal had been full employment, Lubbers took office with the reduction of the public deficit and the liberalization of parts of the economy as his main objectives (see e.g. Wolinetz 1989). Lubbers's fiscal strategy could be described as a deficit reduction time path—the government set a schedule for the reduction of deficit financing as a percentage of GDP (De Greef, Hilbers, and Hoodguin 1998). The first Lubbers government reduced public sector salaries (by 3 percent in 1984) and spent much of its energy in successfully reinstating wage restraint (as explained in more detail in Chapter 5).

As Gladdish has argued, 'the Lubbers cabinet made a resolute effort to take a grip on fiscal policy' (1991: 63). Public deficits did fall from 7.5 percent of GDP in 1982 to 5.9 percent in 1986. But this was one of the few successes. Any effective measure of fiscal austerity in the Netherlands needed to address income transfers. The mushrooming of the Dutch public sector was fundamentally related to the rapid growth of income transfers supporting to social insurance programs (Andeweg and Irwin 1993: 202). As was the case with wage moderation, the conservative government tried to break the deadlock that had dominated the social policies of the 1970s. The unions, however, were forcefully opposed to any limitations on the welfare state. Lubbers's first cabinet was not successful at reducing income transfers, so public debt continued to grow. Consolidated central government debt increased from 39 percent of GDP in 1982 to 55 percent in 1986.

Before the 1986 elections, the Christian Democrats had announced that, if enough seats were obtained in the Second Chamber of Parliament, they would again form a government with the Liberal Party. The CDA then ran a campaign on the economic accomplishments (mainly the reduction of the public deficit) of the Lubbers government (Irwin and van Holsteyn 1989: 119). By making the economic policies of the previous governments their strongest campaign message, the CDA was taking a risk. After all, when in 1986 the public had been asked whether unemployment or the reduction of the deficit should be the first priority of the government, 70 percent had chosen unemployment (Irwin and van Holsteyn 1989: 120). It was a calculated risk because, although many voters did not feel satisfied with Lubbers's government and believed that government policy had affected them negatively, a substantial portion of the electorate felt that the center-right coalition had improved the economic situation and, more importantly, that they were more likely to promote future economic well-being.[5]

[5] See Irwin and van Holsteyn (1989) for details.

After the 1986 elections, the CDA-VVD coalition remained in office and reinstated its fiscal objectives. A reduction of the budget deficit was still at the top of the list but the second Lubbers government was committed to not increasing taxes or social security premiums (Gladdish 1991). To accomplish this goal, Lubbers had no option but to expand attempts to reduce the size of the welfare state. In 1987, several measures to reduce unemployment benefits were promoted: extended benefits were now to be financed by worker and employee contributions instead of government funds; benefits were lowered from 80 to 70 percent of last earned wages; and more restrictive eligibility rules were implemented (potential beneficiaries needed to have worked at least twenty-six weeks during the previous twelve months). However, the results of the reform were minimal. The reduction in social benefit levels had been partially undone by collective bargaining. Social security outlays did fall but, as Aarts and De Jong (1996b) point out, this was probably more related to the economic recovery experienced during the late 1980s. Furthermore, although the minimum wage had declined in relation to average earnings (and earnings-related benefits had been reduced), in 1988 there were 300,000 more social benefit recipients than in 1983 (Gladdish 1991: 155).

Lubbers had complemented his efforts to reduce social policy by promoting very small increases in public salaries and a reduction in health care expenditures. In spite of all these measures (plus the fact that taxes had in fact been raised)[6] the public deficit did not improve. After increasing to 6.8 percent of GDP in 1987 it fell to about the 1986 level in 1988 and 1989. Consolidated central debt also continued its apparently unstoppable increase and reached 60 percent in 1989.

7.2.2. Social Policy in the 1990s

The CDA-VVD coalition that governed from 1982 to 1989 publicly and regularly stated that fiscal austerity was its primary goal. This attitude was influenced by the importance of the Liberal Party in the coalition and was particularly the case from 1982 to 1986 (when both electoral support for and cabinet participation of the VVD was almost as high as that of the CDA). Regarding fiscal policy, the Liberals 'imparted something of a Thatcherite spin, while the CDA continued to have an eye to its widely spread clientele' (Gladdish 1991: 156). By the end of the 1980s,

---

[6] Gladdish calculates that taxes had been raised by the equivalent of 1.6 percent of GDP in the 1987 budget (1991: 155).

however, all parties were in agreement that a reduction of the deficit was drastically needed. Even the social democrats were now proponents of fiscal austerity. When the PvdA joined the CDA in a governing coalition after the 1989 elections, both parties had agreed to decrease the level of the deficit to 4.75 percent of net national income by 1991 and to 4.25 percent by 1992. Wim Kok, PvdA leader and Minister of Finance at that time, was 'trying hard to shed his party's free-spending image by holding the line' (Andeweg and Irwin 1993: 210).[7]

By the end of the 1980s, therefore, a new policy consensus was emerging linking the low levels of labor force participation in the Netherlands to the welfare state crisis. A report by the Scientific Council for Government Policy, a government advisory board composed of experts, was instrumental in promoting the view that participation rates had to increase if the social system was to survive (Visser and Hemerijck 1997). The focus on participation was also affected by the presence of the PvdA in government since 1989. The Labor Party believed that the first and second Lubbers governments had pushed the reduction of social benefits as far as it would go. If a further decrease in social expenditures was to be accomplished it would have to be through the reduction of social security recipients (Hemerijck, Unger, and Visser 2000).[8] Given the Dutch social system, this would mean reducing the number of those receiving disability benefits.

OECD countries display a high degree of variation regarding the way in which they facilitate labor market exit. In the Netherlands, in the words of Visser and Hemerijck, 'generous and lenient' sickness and disability benefits had become the main subsidized exit form for older workers in the 1980s (1997: 138).[9] They illustrate this point by explaining that in

---

[7] This impression is confirmed by Hillebrand and Irwin, who observe that 'Kok seemed to be emphasizing the importance of holding this office [the Ministry of Finance] in order to help counteract the popular image of the Labor Party as "spendthrifty", unable to keep inflation down, and unable to provide for a sound economy' (1999: 127).

[8] The willingness of the PvdA to consider the reduction of the welfare state was no doubt influenced by their desire to get back in office and their new pragmatism. But it was also the result of a trade-off that they offered to insiders. In return for maintaining their employment protection, they were proposing to sacrifice some social benefits (something that would basically increase the activity rates of older insiders).

[9] Although it received much less attention than sickness and disability benefits, early retirement schemes were being used in the 1980s by older workers as an alternative way to exit the labor market (Aarts and De Jong 1996a). Early retirement indemnification is generally 90 percent of last earned wages, and pension rights are not lost (Andeweg and Irwin 1993; Gorter and Poot 1999). In 1980, 9 percent of male transfer recipients between 60 and 64 years of age received early retirement payments while 78 percent received disability benefits. By 1989, the proportion of early retirees had climbed to 41 percent while those on disability benefits were 46 percent (Aarts and De Jong 1996a: 29).

1987 there were 262 people on disability benefits per 10,000 wage earners between the ages of 55 and 64 in Germany. In the Netherlands, this number was 980. A number of factors accounted for the high number of disability recipients. There was, first of all, a very broad definition of disability. Diminished labor market opportunities (including not being able to find jobs that were 'appropriate' in comparison to the previous one) constituted disability. Additionally, the implementation of disability benefits was closely tied to other social benefits and in the hands of unions and employers' associations. This connection to other social benefits would have made disability benefits difficult to reduce even if employers and unions had faced strong incentives to decrease them. But this was clearly not the case. Disability was much more attractive to workers facing dismissals than unemployment benefits. Disability benefits tended to continue until retirement kicked in, were increased by collective agreements and did not require any job searching (Visser and Hemerijck 1997). For employers, they were also an attractive option to redundancies since, as mentioned in Chapter 5, dismissals entail a long and complicated administrative process. Paying for sickness leave and then allowing workers to get on disability benefits was often more convenient than keeping workers on the payroll or trying to fire them (Aarts and De Jong 1996a). Van den Bosch and Petersen in fact calculate that 40 percent of private disability insurance beneficiaries in 1980 represented hidden unemployment.[10]

In 1990, the fact that the economic growth experienced in the Netherlands had resulted in some job growth but not in an increase in activity rates together with the inability of the Lubbers governments to significantly decrease social expenditures made reform of social benefits necessary. In the summer of 1991, the CDA-PvdA governing coalition announced a welfare policy package that would restructure the sickness and disability benefit system. The reaction from the unions was immediate. In September, the unions organized a demonstration in The Hague in which more than one million people participated. The PvdA was considerably affected by the union's opposition to the plan. Visser and Hemerijck report that the PvdA's chairwoman had to resign and that the party lost as many as a third of its members (1997: 117). Wim Kok, then the Finance Minister of the Lubbers government, almost had to step down.

---

[10] Quoted in Aarts and De Jong (1996b: 54).

Policies to reform the social system however continued. Two key pieces of legislation were enacted following the protests: the Conditional Linking Act in 1992 and the Act on the Reduction of the Number of Disablement Claimants in 1993. The Conditional Linking Act brought back the linkage between average wage developments and social benefit increases. But it did so with an important difference: it made increases in social benefits dependent on activity rates. In essence, the Act created an Inactive/Active ratio (measuring the number of benefit recipients as a percentage of employment) and determined that the linkage between average wages and social benefits would only be maintained if the ratio did not fall below a particular value (Hemerijck, Unger, and Visser 2000). The Act on the Reduction of the Number of Disablement Claimants, on the other hand, introduced various financial incentives to discourage employers from using sickness leave and disability schemes. The first part of the Act provided a bonus for employers who hire disabled workers for a minimum of a year. The second part introduced new eligibility criteria and related benefit levels. The Act made the level of social benefits contingent upon residual earning power rather than last-earned wages and reduced the time during which new entrants into the system would receive full benefits. Benefits for those in disability under the age of 50 were also reduced (Aarts and De Jong 1996b; Hemerijck and Van Kersbergen 1997). Finally, a new definition of disability was provided that only counted those not having access to 'normal' (rather than 'appropriate') jobs as disabled (Visser and Hemerijck 1997).

The initiatives to reform the welfare system did not stop there. In 1992, the Second Chamber of Parliament started a Committee of Inquiry about the social benefit system. It was chaired by Flip Buurmeijer of the PvdA. 'When the committee published its findings in 1993, it publicly confirmed what was now common knowledge, namely that the social partners had made "very liberal use", if not misuse, of the disability scheme' (Visser and Hemerijck 1997: 144). The committee's critique of social benefit implementation received wide publicity. The report pointed out that the social policy agency had no organizational incentives to get people out of welfare and that employers and unions had in essence abused the system. The Buurmeijer committee recommended two major changes: to put a governmental agency (independent of the influence of the social partners) in charge of the implementation of social security legislation and to abolish the tripartite social policy agency. In addition, the CDA-PvdA government introduced legislation to limit the use of sickness benefits in 1994. The Sickness Act charged individual employers, instead of government funds, for the first two weeks (for enterprises with fewer than sixteen employees) or six weeks (for all other enterprises) of sickness benefits (Aarts and De Jong 1996a).

The consequences of these measures on the public deficit were mixed. The reduction in social spending (even if not as effective as desired) did help. Although its evolution was quite uneven during the CDA-PvdA administration, the public deficit fell from 5.5 percent of GDP in 1989 to 4.1 percent in 1994. Government debt proved more resilient. It continued to grow until 1993 but showed signs of a decline in 1994. In this context of contested social policy change with no clear budgetary pay off, a new election was called; the results were dramatic.

As Hemerijck, Unger, and Visser point out, the Lubbers-Kok coalition was effectively voted out of power, having lost 32 of its 103 seats in Parliament (2000: 223). No single Dutch coalition had ever lost as much support in one election. The PvdA lost a quarter of their vote share as it went from 32 percent in the 1989 elections to 24 percent. This represented a loss of twelve seats. For the CDA, the election results were even worse. Their share of the vote declined from 35 to 22 percent, losing twenty seats in the Second Chamber. The Liberal Party and D66 gained most of these votes. The VVD increased its share of the vote from 15 to 20 percent and D66 from 8 to 16 percent. Ironically, the PvdA became the largest party in parliament (given the greater losses for the CDA). Wim Kok formed a governing coalition with VVD and D66 that, mixing Labor's red and the conservative blue, was known as the purple coalition.

The results of the 1994 elections showed that, as Visser and Hemerijck put it, the 'Lubbers-Kok coalition had paid a high price for its bold politics of welfare retrenchment' (1997: 146). The new purple coalition, however, continued (if not accelerated) the reforms. Regarding fiscal policy, the first purple cabinet did not differ substantially from the previous CDA-PvdA coalition. The use of a deficit reduction time path by the Lubbers-led governments had resulted in pro-cyclical fiscal policy. In 1994, a switch was made from a deficit target to an expenditure target to promote more stable fiscal policy (Bakker and Halikias 1999).

The 1992 Conditional Linking Act had made the CDA-PvdA coalition freeze legal minimum wages and social benefits in 1993 because the Inactivity/Activity ratio was too high (Visser and Hemerijck 1997). In 1994 and 1995, the first purple coalition did the same. In addition, the new Minister of Social Affairs and Employment, Ad Melkert from the PvdA, and his State Secretary for Social Security, Robin Linschoten from the VVD, produced a number of new initiatives. First, in 1995 they introduced the Unemployment Insurance Act. This Act made earnings-related benefits more difficult to get. An applicant needed to have worked for at least twenty-six weeks out of the previous thirty-nine-week period (previously the period was twelve months) and at least four years out of the previous five-year period (previously it was three years) to receive unemployment benefits (Hoogerwerf 1999). The activation requirements for social benefits were also increased, following a general progression from welfare to workfare. Unemployment benefits were made contingent on showing that the unemployed person was willing to accept job offers and to participate in training (Salverda 2000). Then in 1996, the purple coalition introduced the Social Assistance Act reorganizing (and reducing) social provisions for people with no other source of income. The Act set up benefit standards of three basic kinds: single recipients were entitled to 50 percent of the net minimum wage, single parents to 70 percent, and married couples to 100 percent. The Act also made these benefits conditional on activation requirements (Visser and Hemerijck 1997).

The first purple coalition also produced legislation to make employers finance sickness benefits for as much as twelve months and promoted the 'marketization' of the social security system in an attempt to improve incentives and increase efficiency (Hemerijck and Van Kersbergen 1997). In 1997, the purple coalition's emphasis on activation received the backing of the Scientific Council for Government Policy. The Council published a report on social policy entitled 'From Sharing to Earning'. The report concluded that it was possible for the Dutch social policy system to survive. 'What should be fundamentally changed,' it indicated, 'is the structure of implementation, to ensure that receipt of benefits invariably demands activities of labor market search from the claimant' (Van der Veen 1999: 362). The Council expressed its approval of government policies by declaring that the preoccupation for the link between benefits and job searching 'is recognizable in the present Liberal-Social Democratic government's decision to administer social security in local "Centres for Work and Income"' (Van der Veen 1999: 367).

As for the results of the purple coalition's policies, they did produce a reduction in spending. Government social security expenditure fell by more than two billion guilders and social fund expenditure by 5.8 billion guilders from 1994 to 1998 (Hoogerwerf 1999). Trade unions had some success in circumventing the new regulations by demanding supplementary benefits be included in collective agreements (Visser and Hemerijck 1997).[11] But the budget deficit did fall from 1.9 percent of GNP to 1.5 percent and the gross national debt also fell from about 61 percent of GNP to 56 percent (Hoogerwerf 1999).

Although the 1994 elections had been the elections of discontent, the further social policy cuts and fiscal austerity implemented by the purple coalition resulted in general approval in the 1998 elections. In fact, voter satisfaction with the policies of the purple coalition was higher than for any other coalition in the previous two decades. About 60 percent of voters felt that the PvdA-VVD-D66 policies had had a positive influence on the general economic situation in the country; 64 percent thought the impact on employment had been positive; and 27 percent felt that their personal financial situation had been influenced positively (Irwin and van Holsteyn 1999: 146). These positive perceptions were no doubt influenced by the economic boom experienced in the Netherlands at this time (which allowed Kok's government to lower the deficit while increasing expenditure in some areas).[12]

After the 1998 elections, the second purple coalition continued the policies that had made it electorally successful. As before, the government used an expenditure ceiling as its fiscal strategy (Bakker and Halikias 1999). Regarding social policy, Figure 7.2 indicated that spending on social policy, in general, and unemployment benefits, in particular, carried on the steady decline they had initiated during the previous government. The replacement of welfare for workfare was expanded. The criteria for eligibility and entitlement became more limiting because it required a longer work record. These changes lead van Oorschot to remark that

only about 45 percent of people currently working would have long enough work records to be entitled to the standard wage-related benefits upon unemployment. Other groups are either entitled to short-term benefits of 70 percent of the minimum wage or have to rely on means-tested social assistance. On average, the unemployed today have lower benefits for shorter periods.

(Van Oorschot 2004)

As for the budget deficit and public debt, the second purple coalition continued the decline started by the first (OECD 2000).

---

[11] This point can be extended to the reduction of disability benefits in the 1990s. In many cases it was offset by 'topping-off' in collective bargaining agreements.
[12] See Irwin (1999: 271).

7.3. Social Policy in the UK

The relationship between government partisanship and levels of social policy in the UK is presented in Figure 7.3. As in the Spanish and Dutch cases, the figure shows the levels of total public social expenditure and unemployment benefits.

Total public social expenditure in Figure 7.3 averages 21 percent of GDP for the period under analysis. This is higher than in Spain (where the average was 19 percent) but significantly lower than in the Netherlands (where it was 26 percent). This confirms the analysis in Chapter 4, where the UK was included in the OECD group characterized by intermediate levels of social policy (together with Austria, Italy, Norway, and Switzerland). The figure also shows there is an initial increase in social policy, from 18 percent of GDP in 1980 to 21 percent in 1986, and then a decrease to 19 percent in 1989. At which time, it grows again until reaching almost 24 percent in 1993. Then it experiences a slow decline until 2001, when total social expenditure is around 22 percent of GDP. Unemployment benefits have followed a very similar path. The average for the period is a very low 1 percent of GDP (much lower than in the Netherlands, 2.7 percent,

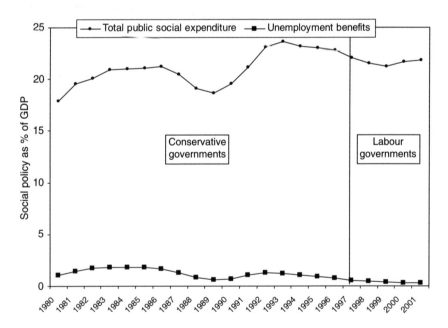

Figure 7.3. Social policy in the UK, 1980–2001

or Spain, 2.2 percent) but the levels of unemployment benefits mirror the developments of other social policies.

As in the analysis of social policy in Spain and the Netherlands, a relationship between government partisanship and social policy is not evident in Figure 7.3. Thatcher's conservative governments produced an increase and then a decrease in social policy and unemployment benefits (the developments from 1980 to 1990 described in the previous paragraph). Major, on the other hand, governed over an increase and then a leveling off of these policies, while Blair's New Labour, does not seem to have made much of a difference to social spending. The more detailed analysis below will clarify the relationship between government and social policy in the UK.

7.3.1. *Social Policy before Thatcher*

The two-tier structure of the UK's social system has its origins in the Unemployment Act of 1934. This Act established a flat-rate insurance benefit (covering risks for employees who have contributed to the system) and an income-tested assistance benefit (providing a universal social minimum).[13] The National Insurance benefit system is financed by employer and employee contributions and by the government while means-tested support is funded by general government revenues. The UK is also characterized by the lack of involvement of the social partners in the insurance benefit system (Crouch 1999*a*).

As for the influence of partisanship on social policy, it is difficult to perceive one existed before Thatcher's electoral victory in 1979. From 1950 to 1980, in fact, conservative governments are associated with higher levels of social spending than Labour. As Rhodes points out, the seventeen years of conservative government during this period were characterized by an average increase in social spending equal to 4.1 percent of GDP while the average increase was only 3.5 percent during the thirteen years of Labour government (2000: 27). These figures do not take into consideration a number of economic constraints that affected governments through this time (Labour, for example, governed over better economic circumstances). But they do reflect a certain consensus between the two parties about the general appropriateness of a relatively sizable welfare state. Admittedly, this was not the kind of extensive welfare state that had become a feature

---

[13] A third tier consisting of earnings-related benefits was created in 1966 but its abolition was one of the first things done by Mrs Thatcher after getting into office.

in other European economies. It was a social system of a limited nature, but one mostly unaffected by partisan differences.[14]

In terms of social policy, the 1970s represented a great degree of continuity from the developments that had taken place in the 1960s. The problems that the welfare system had faced in the 1960s (namely the lack of a modernization effort and the increasing financial problems inherent to the system) simply became more acute in the 1970s (Rhodes 2000). Although Chancellors of the Exchequer for both Conservative and Labour governments consistently announced their intention to reduce the use of fiscal intervention for the control of the economy, their success regarding these goals was at best limited (Westaway 1980).

Like the Thatcher government elected almost ten years later, Edward Heath had been elected in 1970 with a party program emphasizing the reduction and increased efficiency of the public sector (Westaway 1980). The 'stop-go' policies of the 1960s were publicly rejected. But Heath's fiscal measures did not fulfill his electoral goals. In 1971, public spending was reduced but tax revenues were reduced even more so the effects of these policies were expansionary. This approach was continued during the economic boom of 1972–3. The government pursued 'exceptionally expansionary fiscal and monetary policies in the Heath-Barber "dash for growth"' (Artis, Cobham, and Wickham-Jones 1992: 38). Then as economic growth slowed in late 1973, the Heath government returned to a restrictive spending policy.[15] Heath's measures did not meet with much success. The result of his policy efforts (and the increase in oil prices and imports) was a rapid increase in inflation.

Heath had also promised during the electoral campaign to reform the welfare state. The 1970 Conservative Party manifesto, however, had not been very specific about how to go about this reform. 'Our aim,' it explained, 'is to develop and improve Britain's social services to the full' (Conservative Party 1970). The manifesto hinted that 'sensible priorities' had to be established and that social policy had to be restricted to what 'we can afford'. Once in power, in any case, changes were made very difficult by increases in unemployment and inflation in the early 1970s. The 1972 Housing Finance Act reduced housing benefits and the 1973 Pensions Act limited insurance benefits and tried to expand private occupational pensions. Heath had already antagonized the unions by promoting the labor market legislation measures explained in Chapter 5

---

[14] On the topic of the limits of the UK's welfare state, see Glennerster (1998).

[15] See Westaway (1980) for details.

(the doomed 1971 Industrial Relations Act). This contributed to a hostile response to his social policy attempts.

The Labour governments of Harold Wilson (1974–6) and James Callaghan (1976–9) continued the pattern of reactive social spending set by the conservatives, but economic circumstances got worse. In 1974, tax revenues were increased (through changes in the tax rate and the VAT) to finance a hike in public spending (particularly retirement pensions, and sickness and unemployment benefits). In 1975, Wilson implemented the Social Security Act, which replaced the Beveridge flat-rate system for earnings-related contributions. The first fifteen months of Wilson's government have been generally interpreted as economically disastrous and motivated by the need to fulfill the demands of Labour's political constituencies. According to this view, the Wilson government 'was too concerned with providing "bribes" for the unions, with expanding public spending to buy votes for the second of the two 1974 elections, and with its own internal disunity' (Artis, Cobham, and Wickham-Jones 1992: 33). The expansionary orientation was reversed further in 1975 when inflation approached 20 percent. Public spending was cut and tax revenues increased. The cuts mainly affected subsidies to nationalized industries as well as food and housing subsidies (Westaway 1980).

As mentioned in previous chapters, in 1976 there was a substantial decline in sterling. At the end of September the government had to respond to the pressure on the pound by applying for an IMF standby loan. The IMF conditions mandated significant public expenditure cuts. In addition to the cuts that the Callaghan government had proposed, the IMF requested an additional decrease in public spending equal to £1 billion in the 1977–8 budget and £1.5 billion in 1978–9, as well as the sale of £0.5 billion of British Petroleum shares (Artis, Cobham, and Wickham-Jones 1992: 48). These did restore the balance of payments temporarily. In 1978, however, increasing levels of unemployment made the Labour government promote some fiscal stimulation through a decrease in personal taxation and an increase in public expenditures (especially child benefits, school meals, and labor market training).

7.3.2. Social Policy under Conservative Government

In most OECD countries, the 1980s represented a conscious effort to avoid the problems of the 1970s. As Knoester argues, the general feeling during the early 1980s was that in the previous decade policy had been too focused on a Keynesian cyclical reaction to economic problems

(1993: 108–9). This perception was no doubt influenced by the increasing acceptance of monetarism at the expense of Keynesianism in many OECD countries. In the UK, the Thatcher government represented a major break with the postwar tradition of full-employment policies and state expansion. Thatcher explicitly abandoned full employment as an objective and embraced the reduction of inflation as her most important task (see Hall 1986; Matthews and Minford 1987; King and Wood 1999). In Thatcher's economic philosophy the reduction of the role of the state was paramount. Government expenditures had increased from about 33 percent of GDP in the 1950s to about 50 percent in the 1970s but this growth was stopped by the arrival of Mrs Thatcher to power (Budge 1996).

Thatcher was elected in 1979 on a program of social system reduction. In the electoral manifesto, the Conservative Party had declared that '(a)ny future government which sets out honestly to reduce inflation and taxation will have to make substantial economies' (Conservative Party 1979). The manifesto also made clear that a Conservative government would 'look for economies' in the costs of running the social security system. The approach of the Conservative Party to social policy was best expressed by Thatcher in 1984 when she declared: 'I came to office with one deliberate intent. To change Britain from a dependent to a self-reliant society—from a give-it-to-me to a do-it-yourself nation; to a get-up-and-go instead of a sit-back-and-wait-for-it Britain' (quoted by Dellheim 1995: 184).

Social policy was transformed under Thatcher. She made the system less generous and weakened its insurance side while emphasizing its assistance side (Atkinson and Micklewright 1989:18).[16] Focusing on National Insurance unemployment benefits first, one of the earliest measures taken by the Conservative government after winning the 1979 elections was the abolition of the Earnings-Related Supplement (as part of the 1980 Social Security Act). This policy made the UK the only member of the European Community (and one of only four OECD countries) not to possess unemployment benefits linked to past earnings (Atkinson and Micklewright 1989). In 1980, unemployment benefits and supplementary benefits (later known as income support) became taxable. Unemployment benefits were also reduced through the implementation of a number of additional changes. Child additions were first reduced (in 1980 the inflation adjustment method was changed) and then abolished (in 1984). In 1986, lower rate unemployment benefits (which allowed those not having reached full

---

[16] Pierson refers to the retrenchment of unemployment benefits during Thatcher's governments as having experienced a 'death by a thousand cuts' (1994: 101).

contribution conditions to receive 75 percent or 50 percent of benefits) were also abolished. Occupational pensions were reduced in 1981 and 1988. In 1981, a person over 60 years of age receiving a pension exceeding £35 per week saw his/her unemployment benefits reduced. In 1988, the age for the reduction of unemployment benefits was lowered to fifty-five.

The other way in which the Thatcher government reduced National Insurance unemployment benefits was by promoting a more restrictive administration of benefits and by extending the disqualification period. Regarding the administration of benefits, in 1982 unemployment benefit offices took over the role of testing for the availability to work (previously done by Jobcentres). In 1984, the Department of Employment set up the Regional Benefit Investigation Teams for this purpose.[17] In 1986 and again in 1988, the questionnaires for new social benefit claimants were revised to include stricter availability-to-work conditions (Atkinson and Micklewright 1989: 43). As for the disqualification period, the 1986 Social Security Act extended the period of social benefit disqualification from six to thirteen weeks. The disqualification applied to those leaving a job without cause, losing their job because of misconduct, or refusing to take a suitable job or training program. In 1988, the period was increased to twenty-six weeks.[18] Also in 1988, the Social Security Act increased the requirements to receive unemployment benefits. Before, benefits depended on contributions in the present tax year. After the 1988 Act, benefits depended on contributions for the two years before the start of the benefit year. The Thatcher government, finally, promoted legislation to exclude full-time students from receiving unemployment or supplemental benefits during vacations (in 1986) and part-timers from getting benefits for days that they did not work (in 1987).[19]

Although the attack on insurance benefits was much harsher, the social policies of the Conservative government were also quite restrictive regarding the income-tested tier of benefits.[20] Income-tested benefits

[17] The number of Unemployment Review Officers grew from around 100 in the 1970s to 796 in 1988 (Tsebelis and Stephen 1994: 809).

[18] This legislation not only disqualified a claimant from receiving benefits. The benefit period (when it did start) was shortened to account for the disqualification.

[19] Not all measures regarding unemployment benefits implemented by the Thatcher governments were unambiguously unfavorable to the unemployed. The equal treatment provisions passed in 1983 increased the choices of unemployed couples and the redefinition of voluntary redundancy passed in 1985 guaranteed that those having experienced voluntary redundancies were not considered to have left their jobs (Atkinson and Micklewright 1989).

[20] It is true that, as most analysts point out, the social policies of the 1980s represented a change in emphasis from insurance to means-tested benefits. But this shift resulted from the fact that insurance benefits were reduced more than means-tested ones, not because means-tested benefits were improved.

were taxable starting in 1982, they were abolished for full-time students and part-time workers, and the administration of supplemental benefits became much more selective. Thatcher also eliminated housing cost additions for people under seventeen in 1983. The minimum age was then increased to twenty in 1984 and to twenty-four in 1986. More importantly, in 1988 the Thatcher government increased tapers for housing benefits. This measure reduced spending by £450 million in the 1988–9 budget and it resulted in more than five million people having their housing benefits lowered and one million having them removed altogether (Pierson 1994: 112–3). There were also increasing restrictions on the benefits school-leavers were entitled to (implemented in 1980) and those young people could claim for being boarders (in 1984–5). Mortgage interest eligible for supplemental benefits was also reduced (in 1987). In addition, in 1988, the Thatcher government eliminated the entitlement to income support (previously known as supplemental benefits) for those under the age of 18.[21] Also in that year, supplemental benefit single payments[22] were mostly substituted by Social Fund loans (the decisions of Social Fund's officials were discretionary and not subject to independent appeal).[23]

The changes in social policy in the 1980s also affected sick and maternity benefits. The system that had existed until 1982 (for sick pay) and 1986 (for maternity) was part of the Beveridge model of social security (a contributory system that provided benefits as a worker right). They were substituted by statutory sick and maternity pay to be provided directly by employers (who would then be reimbursed by the government). As Hill points out, these

two measures did not entirely abolish sickness benefit and maternity benefit; these benefits remain for that small group of people who, whilst having been recent National Insurance contributors, are not actually in employment at the point at which they become sick or entitled to maternity benefit.   (Hill 1990: 58)

The cuts in social policy had an effect on government spending, which decreased from 45.1 percent of GDP in 1980 to 42.8 percent in 1986.

[21] For a more detailed explanation of the 1988 Social Security reforms, see Dilnot and Webb (1989).

[22] Supplemental benefit single payments covered urgent needs (like budgeting problems and unforeseen crises), and maternity and funeral costs.

[23] Wilding explains the relevance of the Social Fund to the decrease in social benefits the following way: '(p)eople in desperate need can be refused help because local funds have been exhausted or because they are deemed unable to afford the repayments they would have to make' (1997: 723).

The abolition of child unemployment benefit payments represented a decrease in social spending of about £10 million a year.[24] The elimination of reduced rates of benefits for those that did not qualify for full benefits represented a decrease of about £27 million while the reduction of benefits for those with occupational pensions reduced spending by £65 million just in the 1989–90 budget. The abolition of the Earnings-Related Supplement lowered spending by more than £65 million in its first year of implementation (1979). Moreover, the extension of the unemployment benefit disqualification period from six to thirteen weeks in 1986 was estimated to reduce spending by £25 to £30 million and the increase in unemployment benefit requirement by as much as £380 million of the 1990–1 budget. Government debt (which had been around 62 percent of GDP from 1973 to 1977) was steadily reduced by Thatcher. Debt levels declined to 53.9 percent in 1983, climbed back to 60.8 percent in 1984 and then consistently decreased (58.6 percent in 1986, 49.9 percent in 1988) until they reached 39.1 percent in 1990, the lowest level in decades (OECD 2000). The size of the public sector deficit experienced an initial increase with Thatcher (caused by the spending increases associated with the early 1980s recession). The deficit grew from 1.4 percent of GDP in 1980 to 4 percent in 1984, but then it was steadily reduced until it became a surplus in 1988 (0.6 percent) and 1989 (0.9 percent) (OECD 2000).

John Major's governments (from 1990 to 1997) did not fundamentally change the Thatcherite approach to social benefits. There are three policy initiatives that deserve attention: Earnings Top-up, Parents Plus, and Job Seeker's Allowance. Earnings Top-up (ETU) was an extension for childless couples and single people of the family credit scheme that had been introduced in 1986. Its goal was to make low–paying employment more attractive to employers by subsidizing wage levels (Grover and Stewart 1999: 82–3). ETU was started in 1994 because of the Major government's belief that benefits represented disincentives to work for potential low-wage employees. Companies, therefore, needed the subsidies to hire the low-wage workers they needed. As explained by a senior civil servant: 'the only way you will increase demand [at the bottom of the labor market] is by reducing the cost of labor to the employer' (quoted by Grover and Stewart 1999: 87). Parents Plus was a program started in 1996 to promote the employment of single mothers. The government argued that no pressure was put on single mothers and that the program simply determined that case workers would ask single mothers why they did not

---

[24] The figures here are from Atkinson and Micklewright (1989: 21–4).

want to work and help them find appropriate employment. As Grover and Stewart argue, however,

(i)n the context of savage ministerial and media condemnation of lone moth-erhood (...) such disclaimers about coercion were feeble, for pressure already exists upon lone mothers to leave benefit dependency through the stigma of being labeled as feckless scroungers, responsible for breeding irresponsible and delinquent children. (Grover and Stewart 1999: 80)

The Job Seeker's Allowance program, implemented in 1996, transformed welfare into workfare. This program introduced training and job-seeking conditions to the receipt of benefits. The program did not allow benefits recipients and applicants to refuse jobs on the grounds of hours, wages, or conditions of employment (Grover and Stewart 1999: 81). Benefit claimants also could not establish a minimum wage below which they would not work (otherwise they were declared unwilling).

Wilding argues that the 'significance of the years of Conservative gov-ernment is that the impact of eighteen years of individually small nicks and chips in funding is cumulative, significant and irreversible' (1997: 720). The outcome of the conservative governments of the 1980s and 1990s was, according to Rhodes, 'a welfare state much more clearly con-nected, indeed subjugated to, the needs of an economy increasingly polar-ized in terms of employment opportunities, entitlements and incomes' (2000: 21). The considerable increase in inequality promoted by the con-servative governments (see e.g. Rueda and Pontusson 2000) also affected the amount of resources directed to social policies. As Rhodes points out, '(f)or a party that dislikes the impoverished (Lord Harris, a founder of the Thatcherite Institute of Economic Affairs, wrote a book in 1971 called *Down with the Poor*) the Conservatives did an excellent job in producing more of them—and boosting the welfare bill, which it also hates, in the process' (2000: 54).

7.3.3. *Social Policy under New Labour*

To make itself more electorally attractive, New Labour embraced many of the priorities of the previous conservative governments and abandoned most of the policy orientations that had defined social democracy in the UK's past. Some critics have argued that 'Labour has moved so far to make itself electable that it has abandoned any recognisable social democratic terrain at all' (Gamble and Wright 1999: 4; see also McIlroy 1998; Grover and Stewart 1999). Crouch notes that New Labour seems to share the view

that '(s)ocial welfare is a residual expression of compassion for the deserv-
ing poor, not a universal citizen right' (1999b: 69). As far as public expenditure was concerned, the Labour Party was committed to the 'golden
rule' of public spending (only borrowing to invest and not to finance
current spending) if it came to power. Blair, moreover, promised to stick
to the public spending plans of the previous conservative government for
the first two years of his potential administration (Labour Party 1997).[25]
In the words used in the manifesto, 'New Labour will be wise spenders,
not big spenders' and 'because efficiency and value for money are central, ministers will be required to save before they spend' (Labour Party
1997).

Labour's transformation regarding social policy has been unmistakably
reflected in its party manifestos. In 1992, Neil Kinnock started Labour's
election manifesto by declaring that 'the standards of community provision must be high and access to that provision must be wide' (Labour
Party 1992). The manifesto also promised to increase child benefits, open
up the national insurance system to new groups (especially low-paid and
part-time workers), increase income support for parents, reform means-
tested benefits, abolish the Social Fund, restore housing benefits for those
under 18, and restore benefits for 16 and 17 year olds (nothing less, therefore, than reversing most social policies implemented by conservative
governments since 1979). By the time of the 1997 election manifesto,
however, New Labour had completely transformed its social policy priorities. The emphasis was on 'how to encourage more flexible working
hours and practices to suit employees and employers alike,' keeping the
union legislation of the 1980s, not increasing taxes, and low inflation
(Labour Party 1997). Out of the ten commitments that formed Tony
Blair's 'contract with the people' in the 1997 manifesto, only one refers
to the social policies analyzed in this section and emphasized in the 1992
manifesto. It is the commitment to 'get 250,000 young unemployed off
benefit and into work' (Labour Party 1997). The emphasis has shifted from
transforming a weak system of social protection to getting people out of
the system and cracking down on benefit fraud (like previous conservative
administrations).

Mainly because of the improvement in the budgetary situation (influenced by good economic circumstances and the windfall tax on profits
for privatized utilities), Labour increased some social benefits. This was

[25] Most analysts believe that these plans were too restrictive to have been respected by the
Conservative Party had it won the elections.

the case with the minimum income for unemployed workers who find a job, the increase in child benefits and a minimum income guarantee for pensioners (Rhodes 2000: 60). The working families tax credit has been presented as an example of New Labour's social side. It also represented an example of Blair's compromise to integrate tax and benefits. But it was a policy with redistributive effects that are less clear than the old family credit (a social benefit distributed through the welfare system).[26]

When looking at levels of social protection, in fact, the social orientation of the Blair government is not that easy to distinguish from the preceding conservative governments.[27] In the first Queen's Speech debate, Blair declared, in terms very similar to previous conservative administrations, that '(w)e have reached the limit of the public's willingness simply to fund an unreformed welfare system through ever higher taxes and spending' (quoted by Powell 1999: 11). In 1997, the Labour government passed legislation (that had been designed by the previous conservative government) to cut benefits for single parents.[28] New Labour has directed more resources to education and health but it decreased those to social security (Burchardt and Hills 1999: 44).

Moreover, like the Conservatives, New Labour has defined social policy in conditional terms (see King and Wickham-Jones 1999).[29] Although the Blair government has increased the tax credits and support provisions of those in employment (this is part of the 'make work pay' initiative), the strict benefit regime established by the Tories is also one of the areas where there is a great deal of continuity (Hewitt 1999: 156). Blair has attached strong job searching and training conditions to social benefits throughout his administration. The New Deal means that young people do not have the option to receive benefits for more than 6 months. It is subsidized work in the private sector, voluntary work in the public sector, training, or nothing. New Labour has not only accepted the conditionality started

[26] The working families tax credit can arguably be considered more universal than the old benefit but there are some caveats. The credit only applies to working families (unlike a more universal benefit) and, in effect, discriminates against people who are out of work (Hewitt 1999: 166). Since the credits are often paid to the senior male member of the family, there are also questions about the gender implications of the system.

[27] As Rhodes puts it, while John Major's government can be described as Thatcherism with a gray face, Blair's government has been Thatcherism with a human face (2000: 62).

[28] This was called by critics a 'Tory measure' and the 'Peter Lilley memorial Bill', Peter Lilley being the Conservative Secretary of State for Social Security from 1990 to 1997 (Powell 1999: 12).

[29] As argued by Powell, '(t)he Third Way of citizenship moves from "dutiless rights" towards "conditional welfare" ' (1999: 19).

by previous conservative governments, it has embraced it. According to Jessop,

Blair vetoed proposals from the Labour Party to scrap the Jobseeker's Allowance and advocated workfare in series of 'tough love' speeches on rights and responsibilities. (...) It is hardly surprising, then, that the Jobseeker's Allowance remains the cornerstone of labor market policy in New Labour's welfare-to-work policies.

(Jessop 2003: 12)

Workfare is also promoted by another of New Labour's policy initiatives, Employment Zones. For Jones and Gray, 'there appears to be a shift within Employment Zones from innovation-based local partnerships, practising progressive and sustainable welfare reform through experimentation, to a workfarist local regime of labor market discipline and regulation' (Jones and Gray 2001: 5; see also Haughton et al. 2000).

New Labour also followed in the footsteps of its conservative predecessors in reducing the public sector. As Gray and Jenkins point out, New Labour 'represents a continuation, if not an intensification, of tight public spending discipline' (1998: 121). Government total outlays had been about 44 percent of GDP from 1993 to 1996 and were lowered to 40.9 percent in 1997, 40 percent in 1998, and about 39.3 percent in 1999 and 2000 (OECD 2000). Total current transfers, which had averaged more than 19 percent of GDP from 1993 to 1996, declined to about 17.8 percent in 1998 and 1999 (European Commission 2000). Current transfers to households also decreased in 1998 and 1999 to about 16.5 percent of GDP from the 17.4 percent of GDP that had been the average during the 1993–6 period (European Commission 2000). These decreases have undoubtedly been influenced by the low levels of unemployment (and therefore unemployment benefits) of recent times.[30] But they also reflect the fiscal austerity of Blair's government. Because of increases in output and tax revenues, the government succeeded in producing a public sector surplus equal to 1.1 percent of GDP in 1999, compared to the 6.3 percent deficits averaged by the Major governments from 1992 to 1996 (OECD 2000). Government debt was also lowered from the 58.5 percent of GDP level reached in 1996 to 56.2 percent in 1998 and to 53 percent in 1999.

[30] Standardized unemployment rates decreased from 10.5 percent in 1993 to 6.1 percent in 1999.

8

Insiders, Outsiders, Partisanship, and Policy: Concluding Remarks

The ideas in this book originally emerged as the response to two related issues: the increasing similarity between the Left and the Right, and the coincidence of successful social democratic governments with high levels of unemployment. Assumptions about the strategies of leftist parties have not changed substantially since the golden age of social democracy. My analysis has questioned these assumptions and provided a fuller understanding of the limitations and opportunities faced by social democrats since the 1970s. I will conclude by providing a summary of the book's main findings and some remarks about the future of social democracy.

8.1. Insiders, Outsiders, Preferences, Partisanship, and Policy

This book's analysis is based on the propositions that labor is divided into insiders and outsiders and that the interests of insiders and outsiders are fundamentally different. Insiders care about their own employment protection much more than about labor market policies aimed at promoting the interests of outsiders. Outsiders, on the other hand, care about labor market policy much more than about the employment protection of insiders. Social democratic parties have strong incentives to consider insiders their core constituency and their main policy objective is, therefore, the continuation or increase of insider job security. Furthermore, social democratic governments have few incentives to promote labor market policy. This means that government partisanship affects only pro-insider policy, since social democratic and conservative governments have opposing goals regarding employment protection but not regarding labor market policy (neither has incentives to pursue it).

There are, however, circumstances that make it easier for governments to promote policies that benefit outsiders. In the presence of insider–outsider conflict, social democratic governments will promote insider policies regardless of the consequences for outsiders. But there are factors that can make the interests of insiders more similar to those of outsiders and thus reduce insider–outsider differences and weaken their influence on social democratic governments. I have emphasized the effects of two factors: employment protection and corporatism. Employment protection insulates insiders from unemployment and makes their policy interests different from those of outsiders. As employment protection decreases, the distinction between insiders and outsiders weakens and so does its influence on social democracy. Corporatism has more ambiguous effects. On the one hand, corporatist arrangements represent protection and privilege for insiders. On the other, they prevent free riding and particularistic interests.

This insider–outsider model challenges some of the most influential interpretations of the political economy of industrial democracies. It disputes the traditional partisanship approach and its association of social democracy with the interests of labor as a whole; it contradicts the influential 'varieties of capitalism' approach and its emphasis on high skilled insiders in coordinated market economies; it calls into question the conventional wisdom regarding the influence of partisanship on active policies; and it contradicts the 'political class struggle' or 'power resources' approach to the relationship between parties and social policy.

For the insider–outsider partisanship model to make sense, it must be the case that insiders support employment protection more strongly than outsiders and that outsiders support labor market policies more than insiders. The analysis of survey data in Chapter 3 shows this to be true. Insider status is a significant determinant of employment protection (while outsider status is not). Outsiders, on the other hand, have strong preferences about labor market policy, while insiders do not. The analysis also showed that when employment protection levels decline, insiders do become more likely to share the preferences of outsiders. Finally, corporatism emerged as a factor that affected insider–outsider differences. The results suggest that corporatism insulates insiders from unemployment and makes their preferences more different from those of outsiders (rather than facilitating the consideration of outsider interests by insiders).

Once the preferences of insiders and outsiders were understood, I explored the question of whether social democratic parties respond to the interests of their core constituencies when they get to power. Chapter 4's analysis demonstrated that, as my model predicted, social democratic government promotes higher levels of employment protection and it does not impact the levels of active or passive labor market policy. When insiders do not share the goals of outsiders, social democratic governments do not promote pro-outsider policies. This is confirmed in the analysis of the mediating influence of employment protection. My analysis shows that when employment protection is high (and insiders are strongly insulated from unemployment), Left government is in fact associated with lower (rather than higher) levels of ALMP. Yet when insiders enjoy little employment protection, they do become more interested in social policy (like outsiders) and Left government is associated with higher levels of PLMP. My analysis challenges widely accepted Olsonian views regarding the effects of corporatism. The results show that the effects of corporatism are in fact very similar to those of employment protection. Social democratic governments in countries characterized by high levels of corporatism are associated with lower (rather than higher) levels of ALMPs. Higher levels of PLMPs, on the other hand, are associated with social democratic government only in countries where insiders are not protected by high levels of corporatism.

8.2. Employment Protection and Labor Market Policy in Spain, the Netherlands, and the UK

The quantitative analyses that I present in the first half of the book are powerful evidence supporting the insider–outsider partisanship model. The detailed comparisons of three country cases in the second half of the book, moreover, allow us to examine political developments as they evolved since 1970 and to trace the causal processes affecting employment protection and labor market policy.

In Chapter 5, I showed that the evolution of employment protection in Spain, the Netherlands, and the UK support my insider–outsider arguments. Spain is an ideal case to explore the effects of fourteen uninterrupted years of social democratic government on employment protection. The PSOE governments from 1982 to 1996 were decidedly pro-insider. Facing increasing economic challenges (unemployment, inflation, etc.), the PSOE responded by staunchly maintaining the high protection of insiders and by facilitating the entry into the labor market of outsiders. The social democratic emphasis on facilitating entry into and exit from precarious employment was particularly evident in the 1984 legislation and the 1994 labor market reforms. My analysis also shows that unions were an even stronger defender of insiders in Spain. Their goals were not only the defense of insider employment protection, but also the increase of insider wages. The unions' focus on wages placed them on a collision course with the PSOE government, more interested in trading high insider employment protection for wage moderation to combat inflation. The Spanish analysis also confirmed my hypotheses about the strategies of conservative parties. The electoral victory of the PP in 1996 was immediately followed by legislation reducing the protection of insiders.

The Netherlands was shown to be very similar to Spain in Chapter 5's analysis. The Netherlands is an interesting test for insider–outsider hypotheses because it experienced great variation in governing coalitions and displayed the existence of corporatist arrangements (an ideology of social partnership, centralized interest groups, informal harmonization of objectives, and coordination of wage formation). The Dutch Labor Party defended the interests of insiders by making high employment protection for standard employment its primary objective. As in the case of Spain, unions attempted to defend insider employment protection and to increase insider wages but the promotion of both goals became difficult by the early 1980s. In the Netherlands, however, conservative coalitions were not as effective in reducing employment protection levels as their counterparts in Spain and the UK. This was largely the result of their strategic objectives. In a way that reflects the limitations (but also the opportunities) present in a corporatist environment, conservative governments focused instead on promoting insider wage moderation (in a much more successful way than in Spain). The reduction of public spending was also a very important goal, and this required a restructuring of the Dutch welfare state. The retrenchment of the welfare state (coupled with the promotion of wage moderation) was controversial enough to inhibit any reduction in employment protection. As in Spain, the protection of insiders was accompanied by the creation of a large pool of outsiders. In Spain this was accomplished mostly through the promotion of fixed-term employment, in the Netherlands through part-time employment.

The analysis of employment protection in the UK epitomizes the dramatic consequences of unrestricted conservative government. The eighteen years of uninterrupted conservative government starting in 1979 witnessed a striking attack on insider protection in the UK. Thatcher and Major engaged in an unrelenting assault on insider dismissal costs, unions, and favorable bargaining conditions. Chapter 5 illustrated the

Conservative Party's commitment to lower dismissal costs, limit the scope of wage bargaining, and reduce the power of unions to protect insiders with a myriad examples. The return of Labour to power reflected, to some extent, a change in insider–outsider dynamics. Just as implied by my partisanship model, Blair's government promoted policies that have attempted (however timidly) to increase the protection of insiders (the 1998 Employment Rights Act and the 1999 Employment Relations Act are good examples). But it is also clear that the previous drastic reduction of insiderness affected Labour's strategies. The Thatcherite policies of the 1980s and 1990s decreased the protection of insiders to the extent that Labour was, paradoxically, free from some of the traditional demands of its core constituency. In the past, protected insiders backed by powerful unions needed to be satisfied by substantial concessions. After Thatcherism, this was no longer the case. Finally, unlike in Spain and the Netherlands, there has been no attempt to promote wage moderation in the UK since the end of the 1970s. According to my model this is understandable. In Spain and the Netherlands, wage moderation was offered by insiders as a concession to governments so that employment protection levels could be maintained. In the UK, Conservative governments had already decided to attack insider employment protection in 1979. Insiders had no incentives to promote wage moderation.

ALMP is a supply-side policy that can be used by partisan governments to promote employment, growth, and equality in an environment characterized by increasing levels of internationalization (see Garrett and Lange 1991; Boix 1998a). In spite of their relatively small presence in national budgets, ALMP levels have become one of the clearest exponents of a government's political choices. In this book, I argue that social democratic governments are not willing to promote labor market policy unless it is accompanied by a decline in insider protection. Chapter 6's analysis of the Spanish case confirmed this claim. Insider employment protection remained high throughout the period of PSOE rule and outsiders became a large proportion of the labor market, effectively buffering insiders from unemployment threats. In fact, the promotion of precarious employment was understood by the PSOE leadership as the main weapon to combat unemployment. This was shown first by the assessment of ALMP levels since 1982 and then by the more detailed analysis of the role of the INEM and the evolution of vocational training. Given the high levels of protection and the development of a secondary outsider labor market, the lack of interest in ALMPs from insiders, unions, and the PSOE is in line with my model. The conservative governments (starting in 1996) represented something of a change. Employment protection was reduced, and the demand for ALMP increased. The PP governments did not increase active measures in a significant way (training and public employment services remained very weak) but they did reduce the preponderance of temporary employment in the Spanish labor market.

Chapter 6 also showed that developments in the Netherlands were remarkably similar to those in Spain. Although the levels of ALMPs were higher through the period under analysis, they were not influenced by partisanship in a clear way. ALMPs remained 'underdeveloped and institutionally fragile' in the Netherlands (Hemerijck 1995; Visser and Hemerijck 1997: 174). Although they have experienced an increase in the 1980s and 1990s, the public funds dedicated to ALMPs were, as Kurzer points out, 'a small drop in a huge bucket' (1997: 114). When the Dutch system was successful at controlling unemployment (both before the 1970s and more recently), the general perception was that there was no need for active measures. When there was a problem, in the 1970s and the 1980s, the attention of policymakers was concentrated on passive social programs. In the Netherlands, just like in Spain, insider employment protection does not decline and outsiders emerge as a significant buffer for insiders. This muted both the vulnerability of insiders to unemployment and the influence of insider–outsider differences on social democractic governments. Also as in Spain, insiders (and therefore social democrats in government) had little incentive to promote active measures and little concern for deficient public employment services and training.

The analysis of the UK case portrayed a clear temporal division. During the 1970s and 1980s and most of the 1990s, government partisanship did not affect a general disinterest in ALMP. The general approach towards ALMP by both parties consisted of programs that emphasized 'the punitive experience of receiving public assistance while simultaneously failing to equip participants for effective labor-market entry' (King 1995: xii–xiii).[1] It is in fact difficult to see how ALMPs could have received more attention. Employers did not want them, unions had few incentives to pay much attention to them, and Conservative and Labour governments had no reason to favor them. For the Thatcher and Major governments, the development of effective training and public employment services was not a high priority. The conservative emphasis on low government spending and reduction of the role of the state (as well as the decrease in insider protection and union power) was not compatible with a high

---

[1] King uses this description for both the UK and the US.

217

ALMP orientation. As argued by Crouch, conservative governments since 1979 preferred, and indeed generated, 'a flexible, casualized labor force able to turn its hand to a rapidly changing variety of relatively low skilled tasks' (1995: 304). The UK analysis demonstrated how high levels of insider protection made the Labour Party indifferent to ALMPs until the 1990s. The decrease in insider protection promoted by the conservative governments of Thatcher and Major facilitated a new interest in ALMPs by insiders and the emergence of Blair's Third Way. Although the nature of ALMPs has changed (having acquired conditionality requirements not envisioned by traditional social democracy), New Labour has been characterized by an emphasis on active measures. The analysis of the UK case in Chapter 6 also illustrated the effects of the institutional connection between unions and social democratic parties. ALMPs were easier to ignore when the influence of unions over the Labour Party was strong. As this institutional link grew weaker, the Labour Party became more interested in outsiders. Just as it is difficult to imagine the Labour government's 'Social Contract' from 1974 to 1979 without the influence of unions, it is difficult to imagine New Labour without the weakening of union power within the party.

Finally, Chapter 7 addressed social policy as an outcome affected by insider–outsider differences. As the defining component of the welfare state, social expenditure is a substantial part of the budget in most industrialized democracies. The insider–outsider model challenges the generally accepted association between social democracy and the welfare state. As was the case with ALMPs, Left governments were not expected to promote social policy unless insiders become vulnerable to the effects of unemployment. The effects of corporatism, however, are more ambiguous. In a noncorporatist country like Spain, the policies of the PSOE governments lacked a clear social dimension. PLMPs were considered secondary to other political objectives (like insider protection, inflation reduction, and labor market flexibilization). The Spanish case also revealed that social benefits can be manipulated to exclude outsiders and favor insiders. The PSOE limited the availability of social policies to outsiders and facilitated access for insiders who were temporarily unemployed. As for the PP government, their approach to social policy has been remarkably similar to the social democrats.

In the Netherlands corporatism promoted much higher levels of social policy, but, as in Spain, the influence of government partisanship was not obvious. By the early 1980s, the welfare state in the Netherlands had become too inefficient not to affect other economic objectives like inflation control or fiscal austerity (this was particularly the case with sickness and disability benefits). It is difficult to distinguish any partisan effects on the retrenchment of the Dutch welfare state. The Lubbers governments of the 1980s were as eager to reorganize the social system and reduce benefits as the Kok governments of the 1990s. And it was the PvdA-led governments of the late 1990s that were most successful in reducing the welfare state. Also as in Spain, my analysis showed that Dutch governments (regardless of partisan origin) attempted to limit social policy to temporarily unemployed insiders. Social benefits in the Netherlands emerged as protection for insiders. The Dutch welfare state, argue Burgoon and Baxandall, typified 'Christian Democracy's passive stratification of status and gender, premised upon a fulltime, male breadwinner' (2004: 465).[2] The strong reaction of unions against the reduction of social benefits must also be understood as a reflection of the implications of social policy for insiders. Although they had come to accept wage moderation, unions strongly opposed welfare retrenchment. The unions wanted to continue a social security system 'designed to help a shrinking category of workers who do not need assistance (workers with full time and secure jobs), while a growing number of labor market participants are not entitled to enter or benefit from the system' (de Neubourg 1990: 137).[3]

The UK analysis in Chapter 7 showed that before the 1980s, both parties had engaged in relatively expansive welfare measures. Although Heath did get to power in 1970 with the intention of reducing the welfare state, his policies were in essence not that different from those promoted by both parties in the 1960s and by Wilson and Callaghan after 1974. There was a consensus in both parties about the general appropriateness of a relatively sizable welfare state. This understanding of the social system was fundamentally transformed by Thatcher's electoral victory. I have shown that, unsurprisingly, the conservative governments of the 1980s and 1990s engaged in sustained efforts to reduce the size and role of the welfare state in the UK. This was the case (to a lesser or greater extent) regarding all social polices analyzed. Thatcher and Major reduced insurance and incomes-tested benefits. They also started the transformation of social policy from welfare to workfare (the most

---

[2] Visser and Hemerijck quote Will Albeda (Minister of Social Affairs from 1977 to 1981) who declared that the emphasis placed on the breadwinner principle in the Dutch social system is based on the belief that married women should stay at home (1997: 127).

[3] Unions were very successful, in any case, protecting insiders from the harshest consequences of retrenchment measures. This was done through the 'topping-off' of social benefits through collective agreements but also through the limitations in retrenchment legislation.

important measure being John Major's Job Seeker's Allowance program). More unexpectedly for the traditional approach to partisanship (but supportive of an insider–outsider interpretation), New Labour has not substantially modified the conservative approach to social benefits. I showed that Blair's social initiatives, although in some cases dedicating more resources to passive labor market measures, have not transformed the basis of the conservative welfare state. In fact, New Labour has continued and extended the transformation of social benefits into an element of the conditional workfare system. Although the decrease in insider protection promoted by the previous conservative governments facilitated a new interest in ALMPs by insiders and New Labour, Blair's governments have not needed to increase the resources dedicated to PLMPs to the same degree.

8.3. The Future of Social Democracy?

Insider–outsider politics have become an important part of any adequate account of social democracy since the 1970s. It is unambiguous that recent social democratic governments have had a tendency to fail in the promotion of some of the policies that could have been expected from them. The strategies prevalent in the golden age of social democracy have been abandoned and the provision of equality and security to the most vulnerable sectors of the labor market does not seem to be as important a goal any longer. The arguments in this book find that in the presence of insider–outsider conflicts, there exists a strong temptation for social democratic governments to promote less than egalitarian policies.

The insider–outsider model opens the door to a debate about the success of social democracy's emphasis on the interests of insiders. Given some recent electoral setbacks in industrialized democracies, it is unclear that insider strategies are unquestionably beneficial to social democratic parties. Perhaps more importantly, there is also the question of what outsiders can do when ignored by social democratic governments. Outsiders have become a significant part of the political economy of industrialized nations. The emergence of outsiders, moreover, is the result of political factors and, in turn, has political consequences. My findings shed some light on two issues. First, a number of scholars have explored the reasons behind the decline in partisanship observed at the individual level in recent years (see e.g. Dalton 2002). My analysis suggests that insider–outsider differences help explain why some people do not feel represented by mainstream political options. It is reasonable to assume that outsiders would be increasingly less likely to identify with parties that do not defend their interests. In fact, they may withdraw from the political system altogether when it is perceived as one fundamentally unconcerned about their needs.

Second, starting in the 1970s, most Western democracies have experienced the emergence of powerful anti-system parties (especially extreme right ones). The losers in the labor market arena (outsiders who are not the focus of traditional left or right parties) have reasons to turn to anti-system options. The existence of insider–outsider differences in advanced capitalist societies underlines the challenges that the most marginal parts of the labor market face when organizing and the ambivalent stance of left parties toward a part of the electorate that should be among their core constituencies (Przeworski 1985; Kitschelt 1995; Pontusson 1995). Outsiders have become a substantial part of the labor markets in industrialized democracies, but they remain under-represented. Conventional analyses give the role of mobilizing the underprivileged to social democratic parties. However, as shown in the previous chapters, social democratic parties choose to advance the interests of one sector of the labor force, insiders, and deliberately to neglect the concerns of outsiders. Today, outsiders in many European countries would be willing to pay the costs of higher levels of labor market policy but their priorities are not shared by other groups. Some political parties can gain from the increasing importance of insider–outsider differences. Those in nonstandard employment have few incentives to support a system that provides such limited benefits. Historically the appeal of anti-system parties to the marginal has become significant at critical moments in polity's developments (Bermeo 2003; Capoccia 2005). This view of the potential political consequences of outsider exclusion is compatible with what other authors have observed (e.g. Betz 1994; Kitschelt 1995). In some cases, the increasing marginalization of outsider interests has already resulted in an increase in the support to extreme right parties.[4]

Social democratic governments face strong incentives to promote the interests of insiders. Insiders are the core constituency of social democratic parties and their interests are paramount. Rather than the inevitability of unsolidaristic social democracy, the main message of this book is that

---

[4] See Esping-Andersen (1999) for a general analysis, Kolinsky (1992) for the German case, Hainsworth (1992) for the French case, and Husbands (1992a, 1992b) for the Dutch and Belgian cases.

inclusive policies can be promoted by social democratic governments in the right circumstances. To understand the challenges facing social democracy, it is essential to first analyze the incentives that promote these noninclusive strategies. This has been the main goal of my analysis. This book emphasizes some of the considerable difficulties confronting social democratic policymakers who are interested in equality. The acknowledgment of these difficulties may be the first step in finding truly solidaristic solutions.

References

Aarts, Leo and Philip De Jong (1996a). 'The Dutch Disability Program and How it Grew', in Leo Aarts, Richard Burkhauser, and Philip de Jong (eds.), *Curing the Dutch Disease*. Brookfield, VT: Avebury Ashgate.

——— (1996b). 'Evaluating the 1987 and 1993 Social Welfare Reforms', in Leo Aarts, Richard Burkhauser, and Philip de Jong (eds.), *Curing the Dutch Disease*. Brookfield, VT: Avebury Ashgate.

Abellán, Consuelo, Florentino Felgueroso, and Joaquín Lorences (1997). 'La Negociación Colectiva en España: Una Reforma Pendiente', *Papeles de Economía Española*, 72: 250–60.

Addison, John and Jean-Luc Grosso (1998). 'Job Security and Employment: A Comparative Analysis', in John Addison and Paul Welfens (eds.), *Labor Markets and Social Security*. New York: Springer.

—— and Paulino Teixeira (1999). 'Is Portugal Really So Arteriosclerotic? Results from a Cross-Country Analysis of Labour Adjustment', Unpublished manuscript.

—— and Stanley Siebert (1993). 'The UK Labour Market Institutions, Law and Performance', in Joop Hartog and Jules Theeuwes (eds.), *Labour Market Contracts and Institutions*. London: North Holland.

Adelantado, José, José Antonio Noguera, and Xavier Rambla (1998). 'Las Políticas de Protección Social: Sistema de Pensiones y Prestaciones por Desempleo', in Ricard Gomà and Joan Subirats (eds.), *Políticas Públicas en España*. Barcelona: Ariel.

Ainley, Patrick (1999). 'New Labour and the End of the Welfare State?', in Gerald Taylor (ed.), *The Impact of New Labour*. New York: St. Martin's Press.

—— and Mark Corney (1990). *Training for the Future: The Rise and Fall of the Manpower Services Commission*. London: Cassell.

Alarcón Caracuel, Manuel (1995). 'La Reforma del Desempleo', in CCOO, *El Estado del Bienestar*. Barcelona: Columna.

Alba Ramírez, Alfonso (1996). 'En Busca del Primer Empleo: El Precio de la Experiencia', *Economistas*, 70: 14–22.

Alesina, Alberto (1989). 'Inflation, Unemployment and Politics in Industrial Democracies'. *Economic Policy*, 8: 55–98.

—— Nouriel Roubini, and Gerald Cohen (1997). *Political Cycles and the Macroeconomy*. Cambridge, MA: MIT Press.

References

Alt, James (1985). 'Political Parties, World Demand, and Unemployment', *American Political Science Review*, 79: 1016–40.

Alujas Ruiz, Joan Antoni (2002). *Políticas Activas de Mercado de Trabajo en España (1985–2000)*. Ph.D. Thesis, Universidad de Barcelona.

Alvarez Aledo, Carlos (1997). 'Negociación Colectiva y Contratación Temporal en 1997', in UGT, *Anuario de Negociación Colectiva*. Madrid: UGT.

Alvarez, Michael, Geoffrey Garrett, and Peter Lange (1991). 'Government Partisanship, Labor Organization, and Macro-Economic Performance', *American Political Science Review*, 85: 539–56.

Amenta, Edwin (1991). 'Making the Most of a Case Study: Theories of the Welfare State and the American Experience', in Charles C. Ragin (ed.), *Issues and Alternatives in Comparative Social Research*. Leiden: E. J. Brill.

Anderson, Christopher and Jonas Pontusson (2007). 'Workers, Worries, and Welfare States: Social Protection and Job Insecurity in 15 OECD Countries', *European Journal of Political Research* (forthcoming).

—— and Yuliya Tverdova (2003). 'Corruption, Political Allegiances, and Attitudes Toward Government in Contemporary Democracies', *American Journal of Political Science*, 47(1): 91–109.

Andeweg, Rudy and Galen Irwin (1993). *Dutch Government and Politics*. New York: St. Martin's Press.

Aragón Medina, Jorge and Eduardo Gutiérrez Benito (1996). 'La Negociación Colectiva y la Formación de los Salarios en España', *Cuadernos de Relaciones Laborales*, 9: 77–99.

—— and Fernando Rocha Sánchez (2003). 'La Dimensión Territorial de las Políticas de Fomento del Empleo en España', *Documento de Trabajo de la Fundación 1° de Mayo*, 3/2003.

Armingeon, Klaus, Philipp Leimgruber, Michelle Beyeler, and Sarah Menegale (2005). *Comparative Political Data Set 1960–2002*. Institute of Political Science, University of Berne.

Artis, Michael, Cobham David, and Mark Wickham-Jones (1992). 'Social Democracy in Hard Times', *Twentieth Century British History*, 3(1): 32–58.

Asplund, Rita and Inga Persson (2000). 'Low Pay—A Special Affliction of Women', in Gregory, Mary, Wiemer Salverda, and Stephen Bazen (eds.), *Labour Market Inequalities*. Oxford: Oxford University Press.

Atkinson, Tony and John Micklewright (1989). 'Turning the Screws: Benefits for the Unemployed 1979–88', in Andrew Dilnot and Ian Walker (eds.), *The Economics of Social Security*. New York: Oxford University Press.

Ayala, L. (1994). 'Social Needs, Inequality and the Welfare State in Spain: Trends and Prospects', *Journal of European Social Policy*, 4: 159–79.

Baker, Dean, Andrew Glyn, David Howell, and John Schmitt (2004). 'Unemployment and Labor Market Institutions: The Failure of the Empirical Case for Deregulation', Report to the International Labour Organization and available as Working Paper 2004-04, Schwartz Center for Economic Policy Analysis.

Bakker, Bas and Ioannis Halikias (1999). 'Policy Reforms and Employment Creation', in Maxwell Watson et al. (eds.), *The Netherlands: Transforming a Market Economy*. Washington, DC.: International Monetary Fund.

Bannerjee, Anindya, Juan Dolado, John Galbraith, and David Hendry (1993). *Integration, Error Correction, and the Econometric Analysis of Non-Stationary Data*. Oxford: Oxford University Press.

Batstone, Eric (1989). 'The Frontier of Control', in Duncan Gallie (ed.), *Employment in Britain*. New York: Basil Blackwell.

Beck, Nathaniel (2001). 'Time-Series–Cross-Section Data: What Have We Learned in the Past Few Years?', *Annual Review of Political Science*, 4: 271–93.

—— and Jonathan Katz (1995). 'What to Do (and Not to Do) with Time-Series Cross-Section Data', *American Political Science Review*, 89: 634–47.

——–— (1996). 'Nuisance vs. Substance', in John Freeman (ed.), *Political Analysis: Volume 6*. Ann Arbor, MI: University of Michigan Press.

Bellairs, Charles (1985). *Conservative Social and Industrial Reform: A Record of Conservative Legislation Between 1979 and 1984*. London: Conservative Political Centre.

Bentolila, Samuel and Giuseppe Bertola (1990). 'Firing Costs and Labour Demand: How Bad is Eurosclerosis?', *Review of Economic Studies*, 57: 381–402.

Berger, Suzanne and Michael Piore (1980). *Dualism and Discontinuity in Industrial Societies*. New York: Cambridge University Press.

Beramendi, Pablo and David Rueda (2007). 'Social Democracy Constrained: Indirect Taxation in Industrialized Democracies', forthcoming, *British Journal of Political Science*.

Bermeo, Nancy (2003). *Ordinary People in Extraordinary Times*. Princeton, NJ: Princeton, University Press.

—— and José García-Durán (1994). 'Spain: Dual Transition Implemented by Two Parties', in Stephan Haggard and Steven B. Webb (eds.), *Voting for Reform: Democracy, Political Liberalization, and Economic Adjustment*. New York: Oxford University Press.

Bertola, Giuseppe (1990). 'Job Security, Employment and Wages', *European Economic Review*, 34: 851–86.

—— (1992). 'Labor Turnover Costs and Average Labor Demand', *Journal of Labor Economics*, 10: 389–411.

Betz, Hans-Georg (1994). *Radical Right-Wing Populism in Western Europe*. New York: St. Martin's Press.

Blanchard, Olivier et al. (1986). 'Employment and Growth in Europe: A Two Handed Approach', in Olivier Blanchard et al. (eds.), *Restoring Europe's Prosperity*. Cambridge, MA: MIT Press.

—— and Lawrence Summers (1986). 'Hysteresis and the European Unemployment Problem', in *NBER Macroeconomic Annual*. Cambridge, MA: MIT Press.

—— and Justin Wolfers (2000). 'The Role of Shocks and Institutions in the Rise of European Unemployment: the Aggregate Evidence', *The Economic Journal*, 110: C1–C33.

Blanco, Juan Manuel (1996). 'El Seguro de Desempleo en España y en Europa', *Economistas*, 70: 70–9.

Boddy, Martin (1994). 'Evaluating Local Labour Market Policy: The Case of TECs', in Randall Smith and Jane Raistrick (eds.), *Policy and Change*. Bristol, UK: SAUS Publications.

Boeri, Tito, Axel Börsch-Supan, and Guido Tabellini (2001). 'Would You Like to Shrink the Welfare State? A Survey of European Citizens', *Economic Policy*, 32: 7–50.

Boix, Carles (1998a). *Political Parties, Growth and Equality*. New York: Cambridge University Press.

——(1998b). 'El Gobierno de la Economía: Naturaleza y Determinantes de la Política Económica en España', in Ricard Gomà and Joan Subirats (eds.), *Políticas Públicas en España*. Barcelona: Ariel.

Bonoli, Giuliano (2005). 'The Politics of the New Social Policies: Providing Coverage against New Social Risks in Mature Welfare States', *Policy & Politics*, 33(3): 431–49.

Booth, Alison (1997). 'An Analysis of Firing Costs and their Implications for Unemployment Policy', in Dennis Snower and Guillermo de la Dehesa (eds.), *Unemployment Policy: Government Options for the Labour Market*. New York: Cambridge University Press.

Bosworth, Derek and Robert Wilson (1980). 'The Labour Market', in Peter Maunder (ed.), *The British Economy in the 1970s*. London: Heinemann Educational Books.

Bradshaw, York and Michael Wallace (1991). 'Informing Generality and explaining Uniqueness: The Place of Case Studies in Comparative Research', in Charles Ragin (ed.), *Issues and Alternatives in Comparative Social Research*. Leiden: E. J. Brill.

Braumoeller, Bear (2004). 'Hypothesis Testing and Multiplicative Interaction Terms', *International Organization*, 58: 807–20.

Braun, Anne Romanis (1986). *Wage Determination and Incomes Policy in Open Economies*. Washington, DC.: International Monetary Fund.

Brown, William (1994). 'Incomes Policy in Britain: Lessons from Experience', in Ronal Dore, Robert Boyer, and Zoë Mars (eds.), *The Return to Incomes Policy*. London: Pinter Publishers.

——Simon Deakin, and Paul Ryan (1997). 'The Effects of British Industrial Relations Legislation 1979–97', *National Institute Economic Review*, 161: 69–83.

Budge, Ian (1996). 'Great Britain and Ireland: Variations on Dominant Party Government', in Josep Colomer (ed.), *Political Institutions in Europe*. New York: Routledge.

Bueno Campos, Eduardo (1996). *Dirección Estratégica de la Empresa*. Madrid: Pirámide.

Burchardt, Tania and John Hills (1999). 'Public Expenditure and the Public/Private Mix', in Martin Powell (ed.), *New Labour, New Welfare State?* Bristol, UK: The Policy Press.

Burgoon, Brian and Phineas Baxandall (2004). 'Three Worlds of Working Time', *Politics & Society*, 32: 439–73.

Cachón Rodríguez, Lorenzo (1997). 'Dispositivos para la Inserción de los Jóvenes en el Mercado de Trabajo en España (1975–1994)', *Cuadernos de Relaciones Laborales*, 11: 81–116.

Cachón, Lorenzo and Juan Ignacio Palacio (1999). 'Política de empleo en España desde el Ingreso en la UE', in Miguélez, Faustino and Carlos Prieto (eds.), *Las Relaciones de Empleo en España*. Madrid: Siglo XXI.

Calero, Jorge and Oriol Escardíbul (2005). 'Financiación y Desigualdades en el Sistema Educativo y de Formación Profesional en España', in Vicenç Navarro (ed.), *La Situación Social en España*. Madrid: Biblioteca Nueva.

Calmfors, Lars (1993). 'Lessons from the Macroeconomic Experience of Sweden', *European Journal of Political Economy*, 9 (March): 25–72.

——(1994). 'Active Labour Market Policy and Unemployment: A Framework for the Analysis of Crucial Design Features', *OECD Working Papers*. Paris: OECD.

—— and John Driffill (1988). 'Bargaining Structure, Corporatism, and Macroeconomic Performance', *Economic Policy*, 6: 13–61.

—— and Harald Lang (1995). 'Macroeconomic Effects of Active Labour Market Programmes in a Union Wage-Setting Model', *The Economic Journal*, 105 (May): 601–18.

Cameron, David R. (1978). 'The Expansion of the Public Economy: A Comparative Analysis', *American Political Science Review*, 72 (4): 1243–61.

——(1984). 'Social Democracy, Corporatism, Labour Quiescence, and the Representation of Economic Interest in Advanced Capitalist Societies', in John Goldthorpe (ed.), *Order and Conflict in Contemporary Capitalism*. Oxford: Oxford University Press.

Capoccia, Giovanni (2005). *Defending Democracy*. Baltimore, MD: Johns Hopkins University Press.

Casas, María Emilia and Manuel Carlos Palomeque (1994). 'La Ruptura del Monopolio Público de Colocación', *Relaciones Laborales*, 1: 236–53.

Castañer, Xavier (1998). 'La Política Industrial. Ajustes, Nuevas Políticas Horizontales y Privatización: 1975–1996', in Ricard Gomà and Joan Subirats (eds.), *Políticas Públicas en España*. Barcelona: Ariel.

CES (1997). *Economía, Trabajo y Sociedad: Memoria Sobre la Situación Socioeconómica y Laboral*. Madrid: Consejo Económico y Social.

Chater, Robin, Andrew Dean, and Robert Elliott (1981). 'Introduction', in Robin Chater, Andrew Dean, and Robert Elliott (eds.), *Incomes Policy*. Oxford: Clarendon Press.

Chozas, Juan (2000). 'Las Políticas Activas de Fomento del Empleo en España', in *La evaluación de las políticas de ocupación*. Madrid: Ministerio de Trabajo y Asuntos Sociales.

References

Coates, David (2000). 'New Labour's Industrial and Employment Policy', in David Coates and Peter Lawler (eds.), *New Labour in Power*. Manchester, UK: Manchester University Press.

Comín, Francisco (1988). 'Reforma Tributaria y Política Fiscal', in José Luis García Delgado (ed.), *España: Economía*. Madrid: Espasa-Calpe.

Conservative Party (1970). *A Better Tomorrow*. London: Conservative Party.

——(1979). *Conservative Manifesto, 1979*. London: Conservative Party.

Cressey, Peter (1999). 'New Labour and Employment, Training and Employee Relations', in Martin Powell (ed.), *New Labour, New Welfare State?* Bristol, UK: The Policy Press.

——(2002). 'The New Labour Government and Employment, Training and Employee Relations', Paper presented at the conference on 'New Labour in Europe: Promoting Success or Decline?' Brussels, April 5–6.

Crouch, Colin (1994). 'Incomes Policies, Institutions and Markets: An Overview of Recent Developments', in Ronald Dore, Robert Boyer, and Zoë Mars (eds.), *The Return to Incomes Policy*. London: Pinter Publishers.

——(1995). 'Organized Interests as Resources or as Constraint: Rival Logics of Vocational Training Policy', in Colin Crouch and Franz Traxler (eds.), *Organized Industrial Relations in Europe*. Brookfield, VT: Avebury Ashgate.

——(1999*a*). 'Employment, Industrial Relations and Social Policy', *Social Policy and Administration*, 33: 437–57.

——(1999*b*). 'The Parabola of Working-Class Politics', in Andrew Gamble and Tony Wright (eds.), *The New Social Democracy*. Malden, MA: Blackwell Publishers.

Cruz-Castro, Laura and Gavan Conlon (2001). 'Initial Training Policies and Transferability of Skills in Britain and Spain', Working Paper 2001/162. Madrid: Juan March Institute.

Cusack, Thomas (1997). 'Partisan Politics and Public Finance', *Public Choice*, 91: 375–95.

——and Pablo Beramendi (2006). 'Taxing Work', *European Journal of Political Research*, 45: 43–75.

Dalton, Russell (2002). *Citizen Politics*. New York: Chatham House Publishers.

Daly, Mary (2000). 'A Fine Balance: Women's Labor Market Participation in International Comparison', in Fritz Scharpf and Vivien Schmidt (eds.), *Welfare and Work in the Open Economy: Volume II*. New York: Oxford University Press.

Dawkins, Peter (1980). 'Incomes Policy', in Peter Maunder (ed.), *The British Economy in the 1970s*. London: Heinemann Educational Books.

De Beer, Paul (1999). 'The Dutch "Polder Model:" A Miracle in the Mud?', Lecture for the Jahrestagung 1999 der Sektion Sozialpolitik in der Deutschen Gesellschaft für Soziologie. Frankfurt am Main.

De Greef, Irene, Paul Hilbers, and Lex Hoogduin (1998). 'Moderate Monetarism: A Brief Survey of Dutch Monetary Policy in the Post-War Period', De Nederlandsche Bank Staff Reports. Amsterdam: De Nederlandsche Bank.

De Koning, Jaap (2004). 'The Reform of the Dutch Public Employment Service', Paper presented at the TLM meeting on active labor market policies. Rotterdam, SEOR.

De Neubourg, Chris (1990). *Unemployment and Labour Market Flexibility: The Netherlands*. Geneva: International Labour Office.

De Velasco, Luis (1996). *Políticas del PSOE 1982–1995*. Barcelona: Icaria.

Deakins, Eric (1988). *What Future for Labour?* London: Hilary Shipman.

Del Rey Guanter, Salvador et al. (1998). *La Negociación Colectiva Tras La Reforma Laboral de 1994: Perspectivas a la Luz de los Acuerdos Colectivos de 1997*. Madrid: Consejo Económico y Social.

Dellheim, Charles (1995). *The Disenchanted Isle*. New York: Norton and Company.

Dercksen, Willem and Jaap de Koning (1995). 'The New Public Employment Services in the Netherlands (1991–1994)', WZB Discussion Paper, Berlin.

Dilnot, Andrew and Steven Webb (1989). 'The 1988 Social Security Reform', in Andrew Dilnot and Ian Walker (eds.), *The Economics of Social Security*. New York: Oxford University Press.

Doeringer, Peter and Michael Piore (1971). *Internal Labor Markets and Manpower Analysis*. Lexington, MA: Heath.

Dolado, Juan José and Samuel Bentolila (1992). 'Who Are the Insiders? Wage Setting in Spanish Manufacturing Firms', Working Paper no 9229. Madrid: Banco de España.

Dore, Ronald (1994). 'Incomes Policy: Why Now?', in Ronald Dore, Robert Boyer, and Zoë Mars (eds.), *The Return to Incomes Policy*. London: Pinter Publishers.

Dorey, Peter (1999). 'The Blairite Betrayal: New Labour and the Trade Unions', in Gerald Taylor (ed.), *The Impact of New Labour*. New York: St. Martin's Press.

Duréndez Sáenz, Ignacio (1997). *La Regulación del Salario en España (1931–1996)*. Madrid: CES.

Ebbinghaus, Bernhard and Jelle Visser (1996). *The Development of Trade Unions in Western Europe*. Frankfurt: Campus Verlag.

—————(2000). *Trade Unions in Western Europe since 1945*. New York: Grove's Dictionaries.

Eckstein, Harry (1975). 'Case Study and Theory in Political Science', in Nelson W. Polsby and Fred I. Greenstein (eds.), *Handbook of Political Science*. Reading, MA: Addison-Wesley.

Edwards, Paul, Mark Hall, Richard Hyman, Paul Marginson, Keith Sisson, Jeremy Waddington, and David Winchester (1992). 'Great Britain: Still Muddling Through', in Anthony Ferner and Richard Hyman (eds.), *Industrial Relations in the New Europe*. Cambridge, MA: Blackwell.

Engbersen, Godfried, Kees Schuyt, Jaap Timmer, and Frans Van Waarden (1993). *Cultures of Unemployment*. Boulder, CO: Westview Press.

Esping-Andersen, Gøsta (1985). *Politics against Markets*. Princeton, NJ: Princeton University Press.

Esping-Andersen, Gøsta (1990). *The Three Worlds of Welfare Capitalism*. Princeton, NJ: Princeton University Press.

—— (1996). 'After the Golden Age?', in Gøsta Esping- Andersen (ed.), *Welfare States in Transition*. Thousand Oaks, CA: Sage.

—— (1999). 'Politics Without Class: Postindustrial Cleavages in Europe and America', in Herbert Kitschelt, Peter Lange, Gary Marks, and John Stephens (eds.), *Continuity and Change in Contemporary Capitalism*. New York: Cambridge University Press.

Estevez-Abe, Margarita, Torben Iversen, and David Soskice (2001). 'Social Protection and the Formation of Skills', in Peter Hall and David Soskice (eds.), *Varieties of Capitalism*. New York: Oxford University Press.

Estivill, Jordi and Josep M. de la Hoz (1990). 'Transition and Crisis: The Complexity of Spanish Labor Relations', in Guido Baglioni and Colin Crouch (eds.), *European Industrial Relations: The Challenge of Flexibility*. London: Sage.

European Commission (2000). *European Economy*. Luxembourg: The Directorate General.

—— (2006). *AMECO Database*. Luxembourg: The Directorate General.

Ferreiro Aparicio, Jesus (2003). 'Políticas de Rentas y Reformas Laborales en España', *Revista del Ministerio de Trabajo y Asuntos Sociales*, 46: 15–40.

Fielding, Steven (1995). *Labour: Decline and Renewal*. Manchester, UK: Baseline.

Finegold, David (1992). 'TECs and Education', Report for the National Training Task Force.

—— and David Soskice (1988). 'The Failure of Training in Britain: Analysis and Prescription', *Oxford Review of Economic Policy*, 4(3): 21–53.

Finn, Dan (1987). *Training without Jobs*. Hampshire: Macmillan Education.

—— (1988). 'Training and Unemployment Schemes for the Long-Term Unemployed', *Work, Employment and Society*, 2(4): 521–34.

Freeman, Richard, Joop Hartog, and Coen Teulings (1996). 'Pulling the Plug', OSA Working Paper W144. The Hague: OSA Publications.

Führer, Ilse Marie (1996). *Los Sindicatos en España*. Madrid: CES.

Gabel, Matthew and John Huber (2000). 'Putting Parties in Their Place', *American Journal of Political Science*, 44: 94–103.

Gamble, Andrew and Tony Wright (1999). 'The New Social Democracy', in Andrew Gamble and Tony Wright (eds.), *The New Social Democracy*. Malden, MA: Blackwell Publishers.

García Perea, Pilar and María Jesús Martín (1996). 'Situación Actual de las Prestaciones por Desempleo en España', *Papeles de Economía Española*, 69: 86–92.

Garrett, Geoffrey (1998). *Partisan Politics in the Global Economy*. New York: Cambridge University Press.

—— and Peter Lange (1991). 'Political Responses to Interdependence: What's "Left" for the Left?', *International Organization*, 45(4): 539–64.

Garrido Medina, Luis (1996). 'Paro Juvenil o Desigualdad', *Revista Española de Investigaciones Sociológicas*, 75: 235–67.

Giddens, Anthony (1998). *The Third Way*. London: Polity Press.

Gill, Ken (1981). 'Incomes Policy: The Trade Union View', in Robin Chater, Andrew Dean, and Robert Elliott (eds.), *Incomes Policy*. Oxford: Clarendon Press.

Gladdish, Ken (1991). *Governing from the Center*. DeKalb, IL: Northern Illinois University Press.

Glennerster, Howard (1998). 'Welfare with the Lid On', in Howard Glennerster and John Hills (eds.), *The State of Welfare: The Economics of Social Spending*. New York: Oxford University Press.

Glyn, Andrew and Stewart Wood (2001). 'Economic Policy Under New Labour', *Political Quarterly*, 72: 50–66.

Glynn, Dermot (1981). 'Incomes Policy: An Employer's View', in Robin Chater, Andrew Dean, and Robert Elliott (eds.), *Incomes Policy*. Oxford: Clarendon Press.

Golden, Miriam (1993). 'The Dynamics of Trade Unionism and National Economic Performance', *American Political Science Review*, 87: 439–54.

——Peter Lange, and Michael Wallerstein (2006). 'Union Centralization among Advanced Industrial Societies: An Empirical Study', Dataset available at http://www.shelley.polisci.ucla.edu/.

González Calvet, Josep (1998). 'La Política Fiscal: Expansion con Escasos Impactos Redistributivos', in Ricard Gomà and Joan Subirats (eds.), *Políticas Públicas en España*. Barcelona: Ariel.

——(2002). 'Employment Policies in Spain: From Flexibilisation to the European Employment Strategy', in Caroline de la Porte and Philippe Pochet (eds.), *Building Social Europe through the Open-Method of Co-ordination*. New York: Peter Lang.

González-Páramo, José Manuel and Guillem López Casasnovas (1996). 'El Gasto Público: Problemas Actuales y Perspectivas', *Papeles de Economía Española*, 69: 2–36.

Gordon, David (1972). *Theories of Poverty and Underemployment: Orthodox, Radical, and Dual Labor Market Perspectives*. Lexington, MA: Heath.

Gorter, Cees and Jacques Poot (1999). 'The Impact of Labour Market Deregulation', Tinbergen Institute. Research Paper 99–001/3. Amsterdam: Tinbergen Institute.

Goul Andersen, Jørgen and Jan Bendix Jensen (2002). 'Employment and Unemployment in Europe', in Jørgen Goul Andersen et al. (eds.), *Unemployment and Unemployment Policies in Europe*. Bristol, UK: The Policy Press.

Gray, Andrew and Bill Jenkins (1998). 'New Labour, New Government? Change and Continuity in Public Administration and Government 1997', *Parliamentary Affairs*, 51(2): 111–30.

Gregory, Mary, Wiemer Salverda, and Stephen Bazen (eds.) (2000). *Labour Market Inequalities*. Oxford: Oxford University Press.

Grover, Chris and John Stewart (1999). 'Market Workfare', *Journal of Social Policy*, 28(1): 73–96.

Gunther, Richard (1980). *Public Policy in a No-Party State: Spanish Planning and Budgeting in the Twilight of the Franquist Era*. Berkeley, CA: University of California Press.

Gunther, Richard (1996). 'Spanish Public Policy: From Dictatorship to Democracy', Working Paper 1996/84. Madrid: Juan March Institute.

Hainsworth, Paul (1992). 'The Extreme Right in Postwar France: The Emergence and Success of the National Front', in Paul Hainsworth (ed.), *The Extreme Right in Europe and the USA*. New York: St. Martin's Press.

Hall, Peter (1986). *Governing the Economy*. New York: Oxford University Press.

—— (1994). 'Central Bank Independence and Coordinated Wage Bargaining: Their Interaction in Germany and Europe', *German Politics and Society*, 31: 1–23.

—— and David Soskice (2001). *Varieties of Capitalism: The Institutional Foundations of Comparative Advantage*. New York: Oxford University Press.

—— and Robert Franzese (1998). 'Mixed Signals: Central Bank Independence, Coordinated Wage Bargaining, and European Monetary Union', *International Organization*, 52: 505–35.

—— and Rosemary Taylor (1996). 'Political Science and the Three New Institutionalisms', *Political Studies*, 44: 936–57.

Hamann, Kerstin (1999). 'Union Strategies to Adjustment: The Spanish Case', Paper presented at the Sixth Biannual International Conference of the European Community Studies Association, Pittsburgh.

Hartog, Joop, Edwin Leuven, and Coen Teulings (1999). 'Wages and the Bargaining Regime in a Corporatist Setting', Tinbergen Institute Discussion Paper. Amsterdam: Tinbergen Institute.

Haughton, Graham, Martin Jones, Jamie Peck, Adam Tickell, and Aidan White (2000). 'Labour Market Policy as Flexible Welfare: Prototype Employment Zones and the New Workfarism', *Regional Studies*, 34: 669–80.

Hemerijck, Anton (1995). 'Corporatist Immobility in the Netherlands', in Colin Crouch and Franz Traxler (eds.), *Organized Industrial Relations in Europe*. Brookfield, VT: Avebury Ashgate.

—— and Kees van Kersbergen (1997). 'A Miraculous Model? Explaining the New Politics of the Welfare State in the Netherlands', *Acta Politica*, 1997/3: 258–80.

—— and Mark Vail (2004). 'The Forgotten Center: The State as Dynamic Actor in Corporatist Political Economies', Working Paper, Institute of European Studies, University of California, Berkeley.

—— Brigitte Unger, and Jelle Visser (2000). 'How Small Countries Negotiate Change', in Fritz Scharpf and Vivien Schmidt (eds.), *Welfare and Work in the Open Economy: Volume II*. New York: Oxford University Press.

—— Marc Van der Meer, and Jelle Visser (2000). 'Innovation Through Coordination: Two Decades of Social Pacts in the Netherlands', in Giuseppe Fajertag and Philippe Pochet (eds.), *Social Pacts in Europe*. Brussels: European Trade Union Institute.

Hewitt, Martin (1999). 'New Labour and Social Security', in Martin Powell (ed.), *New Labour, New Welfare State?* Bristol, UK: The Policy Press.

Hibbs, Douglas (1977). 'Political Parties and Macroeconomic Theory', *American Political Science Review*, 71: 1467–87.

—— (1987). *The Political Economy of Industrial Democracies*. Cambridge, MA: Harvard University Press.

Hicks, Alexander and Lane Kenworthy (1998). 'Cooperation and Political Economic Performance in Affluent Democratic Capitalism', *American Journal of Sociology*, 103:1631–72.

Hill, Michael (1990). *Social Security Policy in Britain*. Brookfield, VT: Edward Elgar.

Hillebrand, Ron and Galen Irwin (1999). 'Changing Strategies: The Dilemma of the Dutch Labour Party', in Wolfgang Müller and Kaare Strøm (eds.), *Policy, Office, or Votes?* New York: Cambridge University Press.

Holmlund, Bertil (1991). *Unemployment Persistence and Insider-Outsider Forces in Wage Determination*. Stockholm: FIEF.

—— and Johnny Zetterberg (1991). 'Insider Effect in Wage Determination', *European Economic Review*, 35: 1009–35.

Hoogerwerf, Andries (1999). 'Policy Successes and Failures of the First Purple Cabinet', *Acta Politica*, 1999/2–3: 158–78.

Hosmer, David and Stanley Lemeshow (2000). *Applied Logistic Regression*. New York: John Wiley.

Hsiao, Cheng (1986). *Analysis of Panel Data*. New York: Cambridge University Press.

Huber, Evelyne and John Stephens (2001). *Development and Crisis of the Welfare State*. Chicago, IL: University of Chicago Press.

Huber, John and Bingham Powell (1994). 'Congruence Between Citizens and Policymakers in Two Visions of Liberal Democracy', *World Politics*, 46: 291–326.

Husbands, Christopher (1992*a*). 'Belgium: Flemish Legions on the March', in Paul Hainsworth (ed.), *The Extreme Right in Europe and the USA*. New York: St. Martin's Press.

—— (1992*b*). 'The Netherlands: Irritants on the Body Politic', in Paul Hainsworth (ed.), *The Extreme Right in Europe and the USA*. New York: St. Martin's Press.

Irwin, Galen (1999). 'The Dutch Parliamentary Election of 1998', *Electoral Studies*, 18: 271–300.

—— and Joop van Holsteyn (1989). 'Towards a More Open Model of Competition', in Hans Daalder and Galen Irwin (eds.), *Politics in the Netherlands*. Totowa, NJ: Frank Cass.

—— —— (1999). 'Parties and Politicians in the Parliamentary Election of 1998', *Acta Politica*, 1999/2–3: 130–57.

Iversen, Torben (1996). 'Power, Flexibility and the Breakdown of Centralized Wage Bargaining', *Comparative Politics*, 28: 399–436.

—— (1998). 'Wage Bargaining, Central Bank Independence, and the Real Effects of Money', *International Organization*, 52(3): 469–504.

—— and David Soskice (2001). 'An Asset Theory of Social Preferences', *American Political Science Review*, 95: 875–93.

—— and Thomas Cusack (2000). 'The Causes of Welfare State Expansion: Deindustrialization or Globalization?', *World Politics* 52: 313–49.

References

Jackman, Richard, Christopher Pissarides, and Savvas Savouri (1990). 'Unemployment Policies', *Economic Policy*, October: 449–90.

Janoski, Thomas (1990). *The Political Economy of Unemployment: Active Labor Market Policy in West Germany and the United States*. Berkeley, CA: University of California.

—— (1994). 'Direct State Intervention in the Labor Market: The Explanation of Active Labor Market Policy from 1950 to 1988 in Social Democratic, Conservative and Liberal Regimes', in Thomas Janoski and Alexander M. Hicks (eds.), *The Comparative Political Economy of the Welfare State*. New York: Cambridge University Press.

Jessop, Bob (2003). 'From Thatcherism to New Labour: Neo-Liberalism, Workfarism, and Labour Market Regulation', unpublished manuscript. Department of Sociology, Lancaster University.

Jick, Todd (1979). 'Mixing Qualitative and Quantitative Methods: Triangulation in Action', *Administrative Science Quarterly*, 24 (4): 602–11.

Jimeno, Juan (1993). 'La Reforma del Instituto Nacional de Empleo como Mecanismo de Intermediación en el Mercado de Trabajo', *Boletín del Círculo de Empresarios*, 57: 235–51.

—— (1996). 'La Persistencia del Paro: Economía y Factores Institucionales'. Working Paper 96–01. Madrid: Federación de Estudios de Economía Aplicada (FEDEA).

—— and Luis Toharia (1994). *Unemployment and Labour Market Flexibility: Spain*. Geneva: International Labour Office.

Jones, Erik (1998). 'Is 'Competitive' Corporatism an Adequate Response to Globalization?', Unpublished Paper. Department of Politics, University of Nottingham.

Jones, Martin and Anne Gray (2001). 'Social Capital, or Local Workfarism? Reflections on Employment Zones', *Local Economy*, 16: 2–10.

Juliá, Santos (1988). *La Desavenencia: Partidos, Sindicatos y Huelga General*. Madrid: El País/Aguilar.

Katzenstein, Peter (1985). *Small States in World Markets*. Ithaca, NY: Cornell University Press.

Keech, William (1995). *Economic Politics*. New York: Cambridge University Press.

Keele, Luke (2007). 'Social Capital and the Dynamics of Trust in Government' *American Journal of Political Science*, forthcoming.

Kenworthy, Lane (2001). 'Wage-Setting Measures: A Survey and Assessment', *World Politics*, 54: 57–98.

—— (2003). 'Quantitative Indicators of Corporatism', *International Journal of Sociology*, 33: 10–44.

King, Anthony (2002). 'Tony Blair's First Term', in Anthony King (ed.), *Britain at the Polls, 2001*. New York: Chatham House.

King, Desmond (1995). *Actively Seeking Work? The Politics of Unemployment and Welfare Policy in the United States and Great Britain*. Chicago, IL: University of Chicago Press.

—— (1997). 'Employers, Training Policy, and the Tenacity of Voluntarism in Britain', *Twentieth Century British History*, 8(3): 383–411.

—— and David Rueda (2006). 'Cheap Labor: The New Politics of "Bread and Roses" in Industrial Democracies?', Paper presented at the International Conference of Europeanists, Chicago.

—— and Mark Wickham-Jones (1998). 'Training Without the State? New Labour and Labour Markets', *Policy and Politics*, 26: 439–55.

—— —— (1999). 'Bridging the Atlantic: The Democratic (Party) Origins of Welfare to Work', in Martin Powell (ed.), *New Labour, New Welfare State?* Bristol, UK: The Policy Press.

—— and Stewart Wood (1999). 'The Political Economy of Neoliberalism', in Herbert Kitschelt, Peter Lange, Gary Marks, and John Stephens (eds.), *Continuity and Change in Contemporary Capitalism*. New York: Cambridge University Press.

King, Gary, Robert Keohane, and Sidney Verba (1994). *Designing Social Inquiry: Scientific Inference in Qualitative Research*. Princeton, NJ: Princeton University Press.

Kitschelt, Herbert (1994). *The Transformation of European Social Democracy*. New York: Cambridge University Press.

—— (1995). *The Radical Right in Western Europe*. Ann Arbor: University of Michigan Press.

—— (1999). 'European Social Democracy Between Political Economy and Electoral Competition', in Herbert Kitschelt, Peter Lange, Gary Marks, and John Stephens (eds.), *Continuity and Change in Contemporary Capitalism*. New York: Cambridge University Press.

Kittel, Bernhard (2000). 'Trade Union Bargaining Horizons in Comparative Perspective: The Effects of Encompassing Organization, Unemployment and the Monetary Regime on Wage-Pushfulness', *European Journal of Industrial Relations*, 6 (2): 181–202.

Knoester, Anthonie (1993). 'The Inverted Haavelmo Effect and the Effects of Fiscal Policies in the United States, the United Kingdom, Germany and the Netherlands', in Anthonie Knoester (ed.), *Taxation in the United States and Europe*. New York: St. Martin's Press.

Kolinsky, Eva (1992). 'A Future for Right Extremism in Germany?', in Paul Hainsworth (ed.), *The Extreme Right in Europe and the USA*. New York: St. Martin's Press.

Korpi, Walter (1978). *The Working Class in Welfare Capitalism*. London: Routledge and Kegan Paul.

—— (1983). *The Democratic Class Struggle*. London: Routledge and Kegan Paul.

Kunkel, Christoph and Jonas Pontusson (1998). 'Corporatism vs. Social Democracy', *West European Politics*, 21: 1–31.

Kurzer, Paulette (1993). *Business and Banking: Political Change and Economic Integration in Western Europe*. Ithaca, NY: Cornell University Press.

References

Kurzer, Paulette (1997). 'Placed in Europe: The Low Countries and Germany in the European Union', in Peter Katzenstein (ed.), *Tamed Power: Germany in Europe.* Ithaca, NY: Cornell University Press.

Labour Party (1992). *It's Time to Get Britain Working Again.* London: Labour Party.

—— (1997). *New Labour because Britain Deserves Better.* London: Labour Party.

Laver, Michael and Norman Schofield (1990). *Multiparty Government.* New York: Oxford University Press.

Layard, Richard (1979). 'Have Jobcentres Increased Unemployment?', *The Guardian*, November 5.

Lazear, Edward (1990). 'Job Security Provisions and Employment', *The Quarterly Journal of Economics*, 105(3): 699–726.

Lehmbruch, Gerhard (1979). 'Consociational Democracy, Class Conflict and the New Democracy', in Philippe Schmitter and Gerhard Lehmbruch (eds.), *Trends Towards Corporatist Intermediation.* Beverly Hills, CA: Sage.

Lijphart, Arend (1971). 'Comparative Politics and the Comparative Method', *American Political Science Review*, 65(3): 682–93.

Lindbeck, Assar (1993). *Unemployment and Macroeconomics.* Cambridge, MA: MIT Press.

—— and Dennis Snower (1988). *The Insider-Outsider Theory of Employment and Unemployment.* Cambridge, MA: MIT Press.

—— —— (1990). 'Demand- and Supply-side Policies and Unemployment: Policy Implications of the Insider-Outsider Approach', in Bertil Holmlund and Karl-Gustaf Löfgren (eds.), *Unemployment and Wage Determination in Europe.* Oxford: Basil Blackwell.

Lindert, Peter (2004). *Growing Public.* New York: Cambridge University Press.

Longstreth, Frank (1979). 'The City, Industry and the State', in Colin Crouch (ed.), *State and Economy in Contemporary Capitalism.* London: Croom Helm.

López López, María Teresa and Angel Melguizo Sánchez (1991). 'El Gasto Publico en Prestaciones por Desempleo', *Papeles de Economía Española*, 48: 106–16.

Lovering, John (1994). 'A Perfunctory Sort of Post-Fordism: Economic restructuring and Labour Market Segmentation in Britain in the 1980s', in Randall Smith and Jane Raistrick (eds.), *Policy and Change.* Bristol, UK: SAUS Publications.

Ludlam, Steve, Matthew Bodah, and David Coates (2002). 'Trajectories of Solidarity: Changing Union-Party Linkages in the UK and the US', *British Journal of Politics and International Relations*, 4: 222–44.

—— and Andrew Taylor (2003). 'The Political Representation of the Labour Interest in Britain', *British Journal of Industrial Relations* 41: 727–49.

Luebbert, Gregory (1986). *Comparative Democracy.* New York: Columbia University Press.

Maier, Friederike (1994). 'Institutional Regimes of Part-Time Working', in Günther Schmid (ed.), *Labor Market Institutions in Europe: A Socioeconomic Evaluation of Performance.* New York: M. E. Sharpe.

Malo, Miguel and Fernando Muñoz-Bullón (2002). 'Temporary Help Agencies and the Labour Market Biography', Fundacion de Estudios de Economía Aplicada (FEDEA), Estudios Sobre la Economía Española.

Maravall, Fernando (1987). *Economía y Política Industrial en España*. Madrid: Pirámide.

Maravall, José María (1995). *Los Resultados de la Democracia*. Madrid: Alianza Editorial.

Mares, Isabela (2006). *Taxation, Wage Bargaining, and Unemployment*. New York: Cambridge University Press.

Martín, Carlos (2004). 'El Empleo en España: Su Evolución de 1996 a 2003 y los Efectos de las Reformas Laborales', *Cuadernos de Información Sindical*, 52.

Martin, Cathie Jo and Duane Swank (2004). 'Does the Organization of Capital Matter?', *American Political Science Review*, 98: 593–611.

Martín, F. A. and J. Santos (1994). 'Proyecto del Gobierno Sobre Reforma del Mercado de Trabajo', *Sociología del Trabajo*, 20: 117–49.

Martin, John (1998). 'What Works Among Active Labour Market Policies: Evidence From OECD Countries' Experiences', *OECD Labour Market and Social Policy Occasional Papers*, No. 35. Paris: OECD.

Martínez Lucio, Miguel (1991). 'Employer Identity and the Politics of the Labour Market in Spain', *West European Politics*, 14: 41–55.

Matthews, Kent and Patrick Minford (1987). 'Mrs. Thatcher's Economic Policies 1979–87', *Economic Policy*, 5: 57–101.

Mayhew, Ken (1981). 'The Institutional Context of Incomes Policy', in Robin Chater, Andrew Dean, and Robert Elliott (eds.), *Incomes Policy*. Oxford: Clarendon Press.

McIlroy, John (1998). 'The Enduring Alliance? Trade Unions and the Making of New Labour, 1994–1997', *British Journal of Industrial Relations*, 36(4): 537–64.

Meijer, Kees (1991). 'Reforms in Vocational Education and Training in Italy, Spain and Portugal', *European Journal of Education*, 26: 13–27.

Metcalf, David (1994). 'Transformation of British Industrial Relations?', in Ray Barrell (ed.), *The UK Labour Market*. New York: Cambridge University Press.

Milner, Simon and David Metcalf (1994). 'Spanish Pay Setting Institutions and Performance Outcomes', Working Paper 9420. Madrid: Bank of Spain.

Ministerio de Trabajo y Asuntos Sociales (1998). *Guía Laboral 1998 y de Asuntos Sociales*. Madrid: Ministerio de Trabajo y Asuntos Sociales.

Minkin, Lewis (1992). *The Contentious Alliance: Trade Unions and the Labor Party*. New York: Columbia University Press.

Moene, Karl Ove and Michael Wallerstein (1999). 'Social Democratic Labor Market Institutions', in Herbert Kitschelt, Peter Lange, Gary Marks, and John Stephens (eds.), *Continuity and Change in Contemporary Capitalism*. New York: Cambridge University Press.

——— (2003). 'Earnings Inequality and Welfare Spending', *World Politics*, 55: 485–516.

Morán, Agustín (1996). 'Auge y Crisis de los Grandes Acuerdos Sociales de los 80. De la Clase Obrera al Mercado de Trabajo', *Cuadernos de Relaciones Laborales*, 9: 13–52.

Moreno, Agustín (1989). *De los Pactos de la Moncloa al AES*. Madrid: Confederación Sindical de CCOO.

Moses, Jonathan (1994). 'Abdication from National Policy Autonomy: What's Left to Leave?', *Politics and Society*, 22: 125–48.

Mosley, Hugh (1994). 'Employment Protection and Labor Force Adjustment in EC Countries', in Günther Schmid (ed.), *Labor Market Institutions in Europe: A Socioeconomic Evaluation of Performance*. New York: M. E. Sharpe.

—— and Thomas Kruppe (1996). 'Employment Stabilisation through Short-time Work', in Günther Schmid, Jacqueline O'Reilly, and Klaus Schömann (eds.), *International Handbook of Labour Market Policy and Evaluation*. Cheltenham, UK: Edward Elgar Publishing.

Mughan, Anthony and Dean Lacy (2002). 'Economic Performance, Job Insecurity, and Electoral Choice', *British Journal of Political Science*, 32(4): 513–33.

Müller, Wolfgang and Kaare Strøm (eds.) (2000). *Coalition Government in Western Europe*. New York: Oxford University Press.

Nickell, Stephen and Luca Nunziata (2000). 'Employment Patterns in OECD Countries', Centre for Economic Performance Discussion Paper 0448. London: LSE.

—— and Sushil Wadhwani (1990). 'Insider Forces and Wage Determination', *Economic Journal*, 100: 496–509.

Nordhaus, William (1975). 'The Political Business Cycle', *Review of Economic Studies*, 42: 169–90.

Norris, Paul (1999). 'New Labour and the Rejection of Stakeholder Capitalism', in Gerald Taylor (ed.), *The Impact of New Labour*. New York: St. Martin's Press.

Notermans, Ton (2000). *Money, Markets and the State: Social Democratic Economic Policies since 1918*. New York: Cambridge University Press.

OECD (1984). *Economic Survey of the Netherlands*. Paris: OECD.

—— (1993). *Employment Outlook*. Paris: OECD.

—— (1994). *The OECD Jobs Study*. Paris: OECD.

—— (1996). *Economic Survey of the Netherlands*. Paris: OECD.

—— (1997). *Employment Outlook*. Paris: OECD.

—— (1998). *Employment Outlook*. Paris: OECD.

—— (1999). *Employment Outlook*. Paris: OECD.

—— (2000). *Economic Outlook*. Paris: OECD

—— (2004). *Social Expenditure Database*. Paris: OECD

Olson, Mancur (1982). *The Rise and Decline of Nations: Economic Growth, Stagflation and Social Rigidities*. New Haven: Yale University Press.

Palacio, Juan Ignacio (1991). 'La Política de Empleo', in Faustino Miguélez and Carlos Prieto (eds.), *Las Relaciones Laborales en España*. Madrid: Siglo XXI.

Pastor, A (1992). 'La Política Industrial en España: Una Evaluación Global', in C. Martin (ed.), *Política Industrial, Teoría y Práctica*. Madrid: Colegio de Economistas de Madrid.

Pekkarinen, Jukka, Matti Pohjola, and Bob Rowthorn (1992). 'Social Corporatism and Economic Performance', in Jukka Pekkarinen, Matti Pohjola, and Bob Rowthorn (eds.), *Social Corporatism: A Superior Economic System?* Oxford: Oxford University Press.

Peña Pinto, Marcos (1994). 'Reforma del Mercado de Trabajo', *Cuadernos Laborales*, 28: 52–3.

Pérez, Sofía (1997). *Banking on Privilege: The Politics of Spanish Financial Reform*. Ithaca, NY: Cornell University Press.

——(1999). 'From Labor to Finance: Understanding the Failure of Socialist Economic Policies in Spain', *Comparative Political Studies*, 32(6): 659–89.

Pérez-Díaz, Victor (1999). 'The 'Soft Side' of Employment Policy: The Spanish Experience', in Paul Heywood (ed.), 'Politics and Policy in Democratic Spain', Portland, OR: Frank Cass.

Pierson, Paul (1994). *Dismantling the Welfare State?* New York: Cambridge University Press.

Piore, Michael (1969). 'On-the-Job Training in the Dual Labor Market', in Arnold R. Weber, Frank Cassell, and Woodrow L. Ginsberg (eds.), *Public-Private Manpower Policies*. Madison: Industrial Relations Research Association, University of Wisconsin.

Pohjola, Matti (1992). 'Corporatism and Wage Bargaining', in Jukka Pekkarinen, Matti Pohjola, and Bob Rowthorn (eds.), *Social Corporatism: A Superior Economic System?* Oxford: Oxford University Press.

Piven, Frances Fox (1992). 'The Decline of Labor Parties', in Frances Fox Piven, (ed.), *Labor Parties in Postindustrial Societies*. New York: Oxford University Press.

Pontusson, Jonas (1992). *The Limits of Social Democracy*. Ithaca, NY: Cornell University Press.

——(1995). 'Explaining the Decline of European Social Democracy', *World Politics*, 47: 495–533.

Powell, Bingham (1982). *Contemporary Democracies*. Cambridge: Harvard University Press.

——(2000). *Elections as Instruments of Democracy*. New Haven, CT: Yale University Press.

Powell, Martin (1999). 'Introduction', in Martin Powell (ed.), *New Labour, New Welfare State?* Bristol, UK: The Policy Press.

Prasad, Eswar, Kenneth Rogoff, Shang-Jin Wei, and M. Ayhan Kose (2003). *Effects of Financial Globalization on Developing Countries: Some Empirical Evidence*. International Monetary Fund Occasional Paper 220. Washington, DC.: International Monetary Fund.

References

Prezworski, Adam (1985). *Capitalism and Social Democracy*. Cambridge: Cambridge University Press.

—— and John Sprague (1986). *Paper Stones: A History of Electoral Socialism*. Chicago, IL: University of Chicago Press.

Rabe-Hesketh, Sophia and Anders Skrondal (2005). *Multilevel and Longitudinal Modeling using Stata*. College Station, TX: Stata Press.

—— —— and Andrew Pickles (2005). 'Maximum Likelihood Estimation of Limited and Discrete Dependent Variable Models with Nested Random Effects', *Journal of Econometrics*, 128(2): 301–323.

Recio, Albert (1998). 'La Política Laboral: Acuerdo y Conflicto en un Contexto de Reforma Continua', in Ricard Gomà and Joan Subirats (eds.), *Políticas Públicas en España*. Barcelona: Ariel.

—— and Jordi Roca (1998). 'The Spanish Socialists in Power: Thirteen Years of Economic Policy', *Oxford Review of Economic Policy*, 14(1): 139–158.

Reif, Karlheinz and Anna Melich (1993). *Euro-Barometer 40.0: Poverty and Social Exclusion* [computer file]. Brussels: INRA [producer]. Ann Arbor: Inter-University Consortium for Political and Social Research [distributor].

—— and Eric Marlier (1996). *Eurobarometer 44.3OVR: Employment, Unemployment and Gender Equality* [computer file]. Brussels: INRA [producer]. Ann Arbor: Inter-University Consortium for Political and Social Research [distributor].

Rhodes, Martin (1997). 'Spain', in Hugh Compston (ed.), *The New Politics of Unemployment*. New York: Routledge.

—— (2000). 'Restructuring the British Welfare State', in Fritz Scharpf and Vivien Schmidt (eds.), *Welfare and Work in the Open Economy: Volume II*. New York: Oxford University Press.

Richards, Andrew and Javier García de Polavieja (1997). 'Trade Unions, Unemployment and Working Class Fragmentation in Spain', Working Paper 1997/112. Madrid: Juan March Institute.

Risager, Ole and Jan Rose Sørensen (1999). 'Job Security Policies and Trade Union Behaviour in an Open Economy', *Canadian Journal of Economics*, 32(1): 139–51.

Rodríguez Cabrero, Gregorio (1998). 'El Estado del Bienestar en España: Pautas Evolutivas y Reestructuración Institucional', in Ricard Gomà and Joan Subirats (eds.), *Políticas Públicas en España*. Barcelona: Ariel.

Rodríguez-Piñero, Miguel (1996). 'Público y Privado en el Mercado de Trabajo de los Noventa', *Temas Laborales*, 40: 29–51.

Rohrschneider, Robert (2002). 'The Democracy Deficit and Mass Support for an EU-wide Government', *American Journal of Political Science*, 46: 463–75.

Rowthorn, Bob (1992). 'Corporatism and Labour Market Performance', in Jukka Pekkarinen, Matti Pohjola, and Bob Rowthorn (eds.), *Social Corporatism: A Superior Economic System?* Oxford: Oxford University Press.

Royo, Sebastián (2000). *From Social Democracy to Neoliberalism*. New York: St. Martin's Press.

Rubery, Jill, Mark Smith, Colette Fagan, and Damian Grimshaw (1996). *Women and the European Employment Rate*. Brussels: European Commission.

Rueda, David (2005). 'Insider-Outsider Politics in Industrialized Democracies: The Challenge to Social Democratic Parties', *American Political Science Review*, 99: 61–74.

——(2006). 'Social Democracy and Active Labour Market Policies: Insiders, Outsiders, and the Politics of Employment Promotion', *British Journal of Political Science*, 36: 385–406.

——and Jonas Pontusson (2000). 'Wage Inequality and Varieties of Capitalism', *World Politics*, 52: 350–83.

Sáez, Felipe (1997). 'Políticas de Mercado de Trabajo en España y en Europa', *Papeles de Economía Española*, 72: 309–25.

Saint-Paul, Gilles (1997). *Dual Labor Markets*. Cambridge, MA: MIT Press.

——(1998). 'A Framework for Analysing the Political Support for Active Labor Market Policy', *Journal of Public Economics*, 67: 151–165.

——(2000). *The Political Economy of Labour Market Institutions*. New York: Oxford University Press.

Salverda, Wiemer (1999*a*). 'Youth Unemployment: A Dutch Solution?', Paper presented at the International Seminar on Strategies to Combat Youth Unemployment. European Trade Union Institute and Friedrich Ebert Foundation. Brussels.

——(1999*b*). 'Is There More to the Dutch Miracle than a Lot of Part-time Jobs?', Research Report 99C46. Graduate School, Research Institute, Systems Organization and Management. Groningen: University of Groningen.

——(2000). 'Dutch Policies to Increase Low-Skilled Employment', Unpublished paper. AIAS, University of Amsterdam.

Scharpf, Fritz (1991). *Crisis and Choice in European Social Democracy*. Ithaca, NY: Cornell Universiy Press.

——and Vivien Schmidt (eds.) (2000). *Welfare and Work in the Open Economy*. New York: Oxford University Press.

Schmidt, Manfred (1996). 'When Parties Matter', *European Journal of Political Research*, 30: 155–83.

Schwartz, Herman (1994). 'Small States in Big Trouble', *World Politics*, 46(4): 527–55.

Schwartz, Pedro (1997). 'Los Sindicatos y la Reforma Laboral', *El País*, April 19.

Segura, Julio (2004). 'Una Guía de las Reformas del Mercado de Trabajo Español en la Democracia', *Papeles de Economía Española*, 100: 102–11.

Shalev, Michael (1983). 'The Social Democratic Model and Beyond', *Comparative Social Research*, 6: 315–51.

Simpson, R. C (1981). 'Employment Act 1980', *The Modern Law Review*, 44: 188–98.

Smith, Eric (1980). 'Collective Bargaining', in Peter Maunder (ed.), *The British Economy in the 1970s*. London: Heinemann Educational Books.

Solchaga, Carlos (1988). *El Final de la Edad Dorada*. Madrid: Taurus.

Soskice, David (1990). 'Wage Determination: The Changing Role of Institutions in Advanced Industrialized Countries', *Oxford Review of Economic Policy*, 6: 36–61.

Steenbergen, Marco and Bradford Jones (2002). 'Modeling Multilevel Data Structures', *American Journal of Political Science*, 46(1): 218–37.

Steinmo, Sven, Kathleen Thelen, and Frank Longstreth (1992). *Structuring Politics: Historical Institutionalism in Comparative Analysis*. New York: Cambridge University Press.

Stephens, John (1979). *The Transition from Capitalism to Socialism*. London: Macmillan.

Strom, Kaare (1990). 'A Behavioral Theory of Competitive Political Parties', *American Journal of Political Science*, 34: 565–98.

Summers, Lawrence (1988). *Relative Wages, Efficiency Wages, and Keynesian Unemployment*. Cambridge, MA: NBER.

Swank, Duane (2002). *Global Capital, Political Institutions, and Policy Change in Developed Welfare States*. New York: Cambridge University Press.

—— and Cathie Jo Martin (2001). 'Employers and the Welfare State', *Comparative Political Studies*, 34: 889–923.

Swenson, Peter (1989). *Fair Shares: Unions, Pay, and Politics in Sweden and West Germany*. Ithaca: Cornell University Press.

Symes, Valerie (1995). *Unemployment in Europe: Problems and Policies*. London: Routledge.

Tarrow, Sidney (1995). 'Bridging the Quantitative-Qualitative Divide in Political Science', *American Political Science Review*, 89(2): 471–4.

Taylor, Robert (2001). 'Employment Relations Policy', in Anthony Seldom (ed.), *The Blair Effect*. London: Little Brown.

Teulings, Coen (1997). 'A New Theory of Corporatism and Wage Setting', *European Economic Review*, 41: 659–69.

—— and Joop Hartog (1998). *Corporatism or Competition?* New York: Cambridge University Press.

Thelen, Kathleen (2001). 'Varieties of Labor Politics in the Developed Economies'. in Peter A. Hall and David Soskice (eds.), *Varieties of Capitalism*. Oxford: Oxford University Press.

Therborn, Göran (1986). *Why Some Peoples are More Unemployed than Others*. London: Verso.

—— (1988). 'Does Corporatism Really Matter?' *Journal of Public Policy*, 7: 259–84.

—— (1992). 'Lessons from "Corporatist" Theorizations', in Jukka Pekkarinen, Matti Pohjola, and Bob Rowthorn (eds.), *Social Corporatism: A Superior Economic System?* Oxford: Oxford University Press.

Toharia, Luís (1993). 'Las Entradas y Salidas del Mercado de Trabajo: ¿Qué Hay que Liberalizar?', *Círculo de Empresarios*, 57: 117–35.

Traxler, Franz (1999). 'The State in Industrial Relations', *European Journal of Political Research*, 36: 55–85.

Tsebelis, George and Roland Stephen (1994). 'Monitoring Unemployment Benefits in Comparative Perspective', *Political Research Quarterly*, 47: 793–820.

Tufte, Edward (1978). *Political Control of the Economy*. Princeton, NJ: Princeton University Press.

Van der Veen, Robert (1999). 'Participate or Sink', *Acta Politica*, 1999/4: 351–81.

Van Oorschot, Wim (2004). 'Balancing Work and Welfare: Activation and Flexicurity policies in The Netherlands, 1980–2000', *International Journal of Social Welfare*, 13: 15–27.

Van Peijpe, Taco (1998). *Employment Protection under Strain*. Boston, MA: Kluwer.

Van Reenen, John (2003). 'Active Labor Market Policies and the British New Deal for the Young Unemployed in Context', *NBER Working Paper No. W9576*.

Vandenbroucke, Frank (1999). 'European Social Democracy: Convergence, Divisions, and Shared Questions', in Andrew Gamble and Tony Wright (eds.), *The New Social Democracy*. Malden, MA: Blackwell Publishers.

Visser, Jelle (1989). 'New Working Time Arrangements in the Netherlands', in Alan Gladstone (ed.), *Current Issues in Labour Relations*. New York: Walter de Gruyter.

—— (1990a). 'Continuity and Change in Dutch Industrial Relations', in Guido Baglioni and Colin Crouch (eds.), *European Industrial Relations*. Newbury Park, CA: Sage.

—— (1990b). *In Search of Inclusive Unionism*. Boston, MA: Kluwer.

—— (1992). 'The Netherlands', in Anthony Ferner and Richard Hyman (eds.), *Industrial Relations in Europe*. Cambridge, MA: Blackwell.

—— (1998). 'Two Cheers for Corporatism, One for the Market', *British Journal of Industrial Relations*, 36: 269–82.

—— and Anton Hemerijck (1997). *A Dutch Miracle*. Amsterdam: Amsterdam University Press.

—— and Joris Van Ruysseveldt (1996). 'From Pluralism to... Where? Industrial Relations in Great Britain', in Joris Van Ruysseveldt and Jelle Visser (eds.), *Industrial Relations in Europe*. Thousand Oaks, CA: Sage.

Weekes, Brian, John Lloyd, Linda Dickens, and Michael Mellish (1975). *Industrial Relations and the Limits of Law*. Oxford: Blackwell.

Westaway, Tony (1980). 'Stabilisation Policy and Fiscal Reform', in Peter Maunder (ed.), *The British Economy in the 1970s*. London: Heinemann Educational Books.

Western, Bruce (1997). *Between Class and Market*. Princeton, NJ: Princeton University Press.

Wilding, Paul (1997). 'The Welfare State and the Conservatives', *Political Studies*: 716–26.

Wilensky, Harold (1975). *The Welfare State and Equality: Structural and Ideological Roots of Public Expenditures*. Berkeley, CA: University of California Press.

—— (2002). *Rich Democracies Political Economy, Public Policy, and Performance*. Berkeley, CA: University of California Press.

References

Wilensky, Harold and Lowell Turner (1987). 'Democratic Corporatism and Policy Linkages', Institute of International Studies, Research Series, No. 69. Berkeley, CA: University of California.

Williams, John (1990). 'The Political Manipulation of Macroeconomic Policy', *American Political Science Review*, 84(3): 767–95.

Wolinetz, Steven (1989). 'Socio-Economic Bargaining in the Netherlands', in Hans Daalder and Galen Irwin (eds.), *Politics in the Netherlands*. Totowa, NJ: Frank Cass.

—— (1990). 'A Quarter Century of Dutch Politics', *Acta Politica*, 1990/4: 403–31.

Zorn, Christopher (2001). 'Generalized Estimating Equation Models for Correlated Data: A Review with Applications', *American Journal of Political Science*, 45(2): 470–90.

Zweig, Michael (2000). *The Working Class Majority*. Ithaca, NY: Cornell University Press.

Index

ALMPs, *see* labor market policies

Blair, Tony 143–5, 201, 209, 210, 211, 216, 220

Christian Democratic Party (CDA) 105, 108, 129–32, 159, 163, 164, 165, 190–7
Christian-National Union Confederation (CNV) 108
Confederación Española de Organizaciones Empresariales (CEOE) 107, 116, 117, 118, 123, 124
Confederación Española de Pequeña y Mediana Empresa (CEPYME) 107
Confederation of British Industry (CBI) 112
Confederation of Dutch Trade Unions (FNV) 108, 132
Conservative Party 138, 140, 142, 147, 148, 167, 170, 173, 179, 202–5, 208–10, 216, 217
conservative parties/conservative governments, *see* Christian Democratic Party; Conservative Party; Liberal Party; *Partido Popular; Unión de Centro Democrático*
Comisiones Obreras (CCOO) 106–7, 115–22, 124–6
corporatism 28–35, 82–4, 94, 98–103, 178–9, 213, 218
  effects on ALMP preferences 64–7
  effects on insider-outsider differences 56, 59–61
  effects on PLMP preferences 64–7

disability benefits in the Netherlands 179, 190, 194–5, 199

employer associations, see also *Confederación Española de Organizaciones Empresariales; Confederación Española de Pequeña y Mediana Empresa;*
Confederation of British Industry; Federation of Dutch Industry and the Dutch Federation of Christian Employers 111–12
employment protection 22–3, 70–2, 81–2, 94–8, 147–8, 169, 213, 214
  effects on insider-outsider differences 56–9
  determinants 88–91
  legislation 27–8, 69, 155
  Netherlands 126–37, 160
  preferences 40–7, 51
  social democratic governments and 68–9
  Spain 112–26, 151, 155
  UK 137–46, 168

Federation of Dutch Industry and the Dutch Federation of Christian Employers (VNO-NCW) 108
fixed-term contracts/employment:
  Netherlands 108, 134–5, 160, 161
  Spain 105, 113–15, 117–18, 121, 123, 153

González, Felipe 114, 117, 119, 120, 122, 123, 179, 182, 184, 186
government partisanship, *see* partisanship and policy

INEM 154–7, 162, 188
insiders:
  ALMP preferences 46, 53, 62
  definition 15, 22, 38–9
  employment protection:
    preferences 40–7, 51, 70,
    decline in Spain 124–6
  labor market policy preferences 40–6
  PLMP preferences 47, 55, 62
  social benefits in Spain 178–9, 187
insider-outsider partisanship model 12–17, 25, 104, 152, 212–22